Schelling's Idealism
and
Philosophy of Nature

SCHELLING'S IDEALISM AND PHILOSOPHY OF NATURE

Joseph L. Esposito

Schelling, the most profound of the Transcendentalists, in whose writings Mr. Stirling, would he know the true "secret of Hegel" should look for the root of his subject.

—Frederic Hedge

Lewisburg
Bucknell University Press
London: Associated University Presses

© 1977 by Associated University Presses, Inc.

Associated University Presses, Inc.
Cranbury, New Jersey 08512

Associated University Presses
Magdalen House
136-148 Tooley Street
London SE1 2TT, England

Library of Congress Cataloging in Publication Data
Esposito, Joseph L   1941-
Schelling's idealism and philosophy of nature.

Bibliography: p.
Includes index.
1. Schelling, Friedrich Wilhelm Joseph von,
1775-1854.   2. Philosophy of nature.   3. Idealism.
4. Philosophy, American--19th century.   I. Title.
B2899.N3E85   193   76-764
ISBN 0-8387-1904-X

PRINTED IN THE UNITED STATES OF AMERICA

TO
WILLIAM BARRETT

Contents

8

The School of *Naturphilosophie*
Schelling's Later Period: Science or Religion?

Preface

For over a century Schelling's early thought has been confined within the interpretation given it by Hegel. We have come to see him as an incomplete Hegel, lacking breadth and critical capacity, and seeing only dimly what Hegel himself could reflect with sun-clear brilliance.

However, if, instead of looking back to Schelling from Hegel, we begin with the pivotal years 1790-1796, and then trace the development of Fichtean idealism through Schelling to Hegel, it becomes clear that it was Schelling who drew up the table of contents of German Idealism, defined the problems philosophers would concern themselves with for decades, and, indeed, probably took idealism as far as it could go in the process. Then, with Schelling's works in his hand, it only remained for Hegel to give reflective comprehension to the movement, codify its methods, answer its critics, and generally landscape the territory roughly cleared out in Schelling's earlier explorations.

This is not to say that Schelling did not deserve some of the criticism he received. For the most part his works in *Naturphilosophie* are poorly organized, undeveloped, and almost totally lacking in sustained argumentation, a fact that presents a considerable difficulty for any interpreter of his work. There can be little doubt that a great deal of the mystique of Schelling in his time derived, not only from his precocity, but from his philosophic style as well. He gives the impression that he had received the Truth, and that it was simply a matter of getting as much of it before the public as possible in the shortest time. For these reasons his work has often been regarded as a fanciful conglomeration of bits and pieces of information, picked up here and there in conversations, journals, and lectures, but devoid of any guiding vision. To a certain extent Schelling's reputation as a *Wunderkind* has probably contributed to the low opinion historians have had of his work. It is tempting to ask how serious one is expected to be about the work of someone, in his teens and early twenties, who had a manner of speaking of Kant, Herder, and Spinoza as if they were his peers, or who thought he could assimilate the lifelong work of Buffon, Lichtenberg, and many others into a single system of thought.

Then there is the reputation of *Naturphilosophie* itself, whether Schelling's or anyone else's; outside of Germany it has been regarded as a paradigm of bad philosophy, serving neither philosophy nor natural science very well. It is now clear, however, that the interpretation of *Naturphilosophie* that has come down to us is the result, not as much of a Baconian attitude in the sciences of the latter part of the nineteenth century, as of the spectacular achievements of laboratory scientists, who themselves were, to an extent, nourished by the very spirit of *Naturphilosophie*, which they later disavowed. No doubt such criticism at the time was a healthy reaction in science to the "fantastical" theories that were emerging in the latter years of the movement. However, a reinterpretation of the movement is in order once more, for in recent years evidence has accumulated that suggests the continuing viability of the *Naturphilosoph* concept of nature in the form of what is now called *General System Theory*.

From this perspective Schelling looks more like a visionary ahead of his time, surprisingly modern in his attitude toward science, with his failures resulting largely from the haste with which he assembled his system, the crudity of his scientific data, and mainly from the sheer scope of the endeavor to bring all contemporary scientific knowledge before him. Because we find it easy today to accept the idea of the unity of nature, and only look back at Schelling with the wealth of recent discoveries before us, it is with difficulty that we can appreciate the struggle in the minds of eighteenth-century scientists to make sense of physical and biological phenomena. However, from the perspective of the sciences of his own time, Schelling's vitalism and organicism, his advocacy of connections between magnetism, electricity, and chemical reaction, and his belief in a "scientific geology" emerge as the needed catalyst for the transition from eighteenth- to nineteenth-century science. It is hoped that this work will contribute in a small way to the reinterpretation of the role of *Naturphilosophie*, both past and present, in the sciences.

Finally, there is the matter of philosophic idealism itself, particularly in his German variety of the last century. The present time in philosophy would be characterized by the idealists of Schelling's day as concerned only with an "external reflection" involving dogmatism and materialism. We no longer seem to regard self-consciousness and the "transcendental" standpoint as capable of posing a problem for philosophic reflection. Yet, it is in the phenomenology of self-consciousness, begun by Kant and Fichte, that German Idealism has its birthplace and soul. Contemporary philosophy would be none the worse for cultivating some of these older habits of mind.

Acknowledgments

I would like to thank the following for permission to reprint copyrighted material:

George Allen and Unwin Ltd, for permission to quote from G. W. F. Hegel, *Science of Logic,* translated by A. V. Miller, 1969. Reprinted by permission of George Allen and Unwin Ltd.

Harvard University Press, for permission to quote from the *Collected Papers of Charles Sanders Peirce,* 1960.

Macmillan London and Basingstoke, for permission to quote from the Norman Kemp Smith translation of Kant's *Critique of Pure Reason,* 1965, and from J. H. Bernard's translation of Kant's *Critique of Judgment,* 1951. By permission of Macmillan London and Basingstoke.

Prentice-Hall, Inc., for permission to quote from Peter Heath and John Lachs, Eds., Fichte: SCIENCE OF KNOWLEDGE (Wissenschaftslehre), © 1970. By permission of Prentice-Hall, Inc., Englewood Cliffs, New Jersey.

I also wish to thank Harvard University for the use of materials in the Schelling Collection and in the Houghton Library archives.

A Note on Schelling's Early Works

Schelling began writing at eighteen, and between 1793 and 1807 he had produced a considerable output of books, articles, and lecture notes. This material, the concern of this book, falls roughly into the earlier Fichtean period (1793-1796) and the later work in *Naturphilosophie*, including in the years after 1802 works that are transitional to Schelling's second philosophic life. It is this second period that has been given the most attention by historians of philosophy, and consequently has exerted the greatest influence in this century.[1] The earlier works have largely been forgotten, perhaps because it is generally believed that Schelling came to reject them himself, but more likely because *Naturphilosophie* itself was among the casualties produced by the collapse of German Idealism.

The following is a list of titles of all the major works of this period, including some shorter pieces, which constitute some six or seven volumes of the *Sämmtliche Werke*:[2]

1793
Über Mythen, historische Sagen und Philosopheme der ältesten Welt (1: 41-84).
1794
Über die Möglichkeit einer Form der Philosophie überhaupt (1: 85-112).
1795
Von Ich als Prinzip der Philosophie, oder Über das Unbedingte im menschlichen Wissen (1: 149-244).

Philosophische Briefe Über Dogmatismus und Kritizismus (1: 281-342).
1796
Neue Deduction des Naturrechts (1: 245-80).
Abhandlungen zur Erläuterung des Idealismus der Wissenschaftslehre (1: 343-452).
1797
Ideen zu einer Philosophie der Natur (2: 1-343).
1798
Von der Weltseele, einer Hypothese der höheren Physik zur Erklärung des allgemeinen Organismus (2: 345-584).
1799
Erster Entwurf eines Systems der Naturphilosophie (3: 1-268).
Einleitung zu dem Entwurf eines Systems der Naturphilosophie, oder Über den Begriff der speculative Physik und die inner Organisation eines Systems dieser Wissenschaft (3: 269-326).
1800
System des transzendentalen Idealismus (3: 327-634).
Allgemeine Deduktion des dynamischen Processes, oder der Kategorien der Physik (4: 1-78).
1801
Ueber den wahren Begriff der Naturphilosophie und die richtige Art ihre Problem aufzulösen (4: 79-103).
Darstellung meines Systems der Philosophie (4: 105-212).
1802
Bruno, oder Über das göttliche und natürliche Prinzip der Dinge: Ein Gespräch (4: 213-332).
Über das Wesen der philosophischen Kritik überhaupt, und ihr Verhältnis zum gegenwärtigen Zustand der Philosophie besondere (5: 1-17).
Über das Verhältnis der Naturphilosophie zur Philosophie überhaupt (5: 106-24).
Ferner Darstellungen aus dem System der Philosophie (4: 333-510).
Die vier edlen Metalle (4: 511-523).
Ueber das absolute Identitäts-System und sein Verhältniss zu dem neuesten (Reinholdischen) Dualismus (5: 18-77).
Philosophie der Kunst (5: 355-487).
1803
Vorlesungen über die Methode des akademischen Studiums (5: 207-352).
Über die Construction in der Philosophie (5: 125-51).
Über Dante in philosophischer Beziehung (5: 152-63).
1804
Philosophie und Religion (6: 11-70).

Immanuel Kant (6: 1-10).
Propädeutik der Philosophie (6: 71-130).
System der gesammten Philosophie und der Naturphilosophie inbesondere (6: 131-576).

   1806

Contributions to the *Jahrbüchern der Medizin als Wissenschaft* (7: 127-288).

   1807

Ueber das Verhältniss der bildenden Künste zu der Natur (7: 289-330).

Introduction

When in 1786 Schiller characterized Reason as a "torch in a dungeon," he was reflecting the attitude of a growing number of thinkers in Germany regarding what the Kantian tradition of critical philosophy had come to.[1] Critical philosophy, it was thought, had sown the seeds of its own destruction, for it had not critically established the conditions for its own possibility. For everywhere Reason probed, it encountered limitations, even if those which Reason itself had critically established. Eventually this situation became intolerable. Either the practice of critical philosophy was impossible to begin with, or else a transcendental deduction of the possibility of critical philosophy itself had to be established. Those who chose the former course turned either to the fideist tradition found in Hamann's work, and later in the work of Jacobi and his followers, or else developed the predictable forms of skepticism reflected in the writings of G. E. Schulze by returning to the largely forgotten empiricism of the French and English, which had lingered in Germany for half a century with little effect on the rationalist schools of Wolff or Kant.

The second course was chosen by those who thought it possible to meet the challenge by completing the Kantian program and putting it on a solid philosophic foundation once and for all. Among thinkers like Reinhold, Fries, and Fichte, plans were drawn up for an eventual escape from the dungeon that would maintain the prestige of Reason intact.

19

It was essentially out of the branch of this tradition begun by Fichte that the movement now known as German Idealism was born. Here no compromise with heteronomy in any form was to be allowed into philosophic argumentation. For as long as there could exist a noumenal reality beyond the ken of human intelligence, critical philosophy could never guarantee that it had achieved completion.[2] The completeness of the categories of Reason, then, could not be established beyond doubt. Consequently, a genuine transcendental deduction would emerge only once one could be certain that there was nothing remaining for Reason to transcend.

We know now that those who chose the second course chose the harder one. Rational autonomy found itself no match for the growing influence of the heteronomous outlook found in the sciences, and so, just as with the critical philosophy before it, German Idealism collapsed. Those who could live with heteronomy in philosophy in the form of a noumenal reality or an uncriticized faculty of knowing had no other chore but to proclaim this. Yet, to the Idealists, this was not a consistent response, for the question that haunted them was how it could be possible for Reason to proclaim its limitations without seeing beyond them in some way. It was perhaps this tendency, characteristic of the period, to be preoccupied with philosophic foundations that produced the frenetic pace and contentious atmosphere of philosophical activity during the period between Hamann and Hegel. Friends were won or lost over the question of where Reason stood with respect to the heteronomous. The lines of conflict always seemed clearly drawn, even when they were not: Hamann against the Wolffian metaphysicians, Jacobi against Moses Mendelssohn over the matter of Lessing's alleged Spinozism, Herder's break with Kant, Kant's subsequent rejection of Herder's *Ideen zur Philosophie des Geschichte des Menschheit*, Jacobi and Hamann's condemnation of Herder's *Gott*, Fichte and the youthful Schelling against Reinhold, Schelling against Fichte, Fichte's outburst against all opponents in his "Sun-Clear Report," Schelling against Jacobi over Spinoza once more, and finally Hegel's rejection of the whole previous tradition in the Preface to the *Phänomenologie*. Pantheism, atheism, egoism, dogmatism were some of the anti-critical positions to be avoided if one wanted to maintain the critical approach by remaining transcendentally pure.

In retrospect we can see that the development of post-Kantian idealism was marked by a continual process of seeking out what had hitherto been considered sources of heteronomy and incorporating those sources into a larger, autonomous framework. The heteronomous, then, could become an aspect or "moment" in the life of the autonomous principle. With this in mind it is easy to understand the fascination monistic philosophers like Bruno and Spinoza held for many of the idealistic thinkers of the time. The key concepts for such monistic philosophers were *synthesis* and *reciprocity*. There could be no heteronomous end-points in their metaphysical system, and, for this reason, the traditional notions of God and the thing-in-itself were among the earliest concepts to be rejected by the idealists.

In demanding that philosophy establish the conditions for its possibility, the transcendental philosophers usually assumed transcendental powers—special feelings, intimations, and intellectual intuitions. They looked upon man's apparent ability to form concepts and judgments as the surest indication that genuine transcendence of heteronomy was possible. In this respect they assumed an economy or fitness in the nature of things, for if man could have a concept of something—such as his own freedom—somehow that concept had to be real or realizable, and its conditions transcendentally established. Kant had opened the way for this optimism in the "Transcendental Dialectic" of the *Critique of Pure Reason*. And yet, ironically, in that same section he denied to Reason the power to effect the "highest unity of thought": "All our knowledge starts with the senses, proceeds from thence to understanding, and ends with reason, beyond which there is no higher faculty to be found in us for elaborating the matter of intuition and bringing it under the highest unity of thought."[3] It was this "higher faculty" the idealists sought as the actual philosophizing faculty.

The idealists also questioned how, within Kant's scheme, it could be a *synthetic* principle of Reason in general that the conditioned be conditioned ultimately by an unconditioned. Why, they asked, must there be the inevitable failure, according to Kant, in Reason's dialectical play of antinomies "whenever it endeavors to free from all conditions and apprehend in its unconditioned totality that which according to the rules of experience can never be determined save as conditioned"?[4] Such "absolute totality" was ruled out only because it could not be *empirically* understood. In fact, the *Idea* of such totality was, for Kant, a "mere creature of reason." In the fields of mathematics and ethics the application of the idea of completeness bears fruit, but "in natural science. . .there is endless conjecture, and certainty is not to be counted upon."[5]

Kant's difficulty derived from his adherence to an essentially *dogmatic* (in this case, Newtonian) metaphysics of nature in which the primacy of the heteronomous was never challenged. It was no wonder, then, that the notion of a truly autonomous rationality could not be found in such a thoroughly uncritical notion of reality. It would be the task of a *Naturphilosophie* to show that the concept of the *empirical* would have to be abandoned and along with it such other important scientific notions as induction and causality, as commonly understood.

German Idealism has been closely associated with that family of attitudes and temperaments usually characterized as *romantic*. Yet, certainly before 1803 Schelling could not be considered a romantic in the sense in which Frederick Schlegel was. The desire for a thoroughgoing rationality, which drove Fichte, Schelling, and Hegel toward a full-blown systematic philosophy, was not to be found in Coleridge, Wordsworth, Emerson, or other romantics. The genuine romantic remains suspicious of philosophical systems that leave nothing unknown; and while he joins with the idealists in their rejection of sensationalism, mechanism, and atomism, he is usually not in sympathy with the architectonic approach taken by them. The romantics, for the most part, looked upon the speculative systems of Fichte, Schelling, and Hegel as so many empty shells, which could give no adequate account of the full range of human experience. Speaking of such philosophers Schlegel remarked, "Each of these builders in the edific of endless error commences with pulling down the fabric that his immediate predecessor and all before him may have commenced, while in the space he has thus cleared from his own labors, he founds and rears the imaginary tower of *his own* knowledge and science."[6]

The romantic, like the fideist, begins with the assumption that Reason is not capable of establishing its own credentials and certainly is not capable of achieving the task the idealists had set for it. It was from this viewpoint that Schlegel had summed up the philosophical development from Kant to Hegel when he remarked, "Beginning with a strict, not to say absolute, limitation of the reason, and with an opposition to its assumptions, it also ended in its investiture with supreme authority—not to say in its deification."[7]

In reaction to idealism, the romantic philosophers argued that philosophy itself emerges out of a context of imbalance and disharmony and could never transcend these primordial limitations using speculation alone. Speaking of speculative philosophy, Schlegel observed that "this so-called pure and abstract thinking takes nothing for granted, and allows of no postulate or axiom; it acknowledges none besides, and generally has no foundation save itself. . . .Consequently, without proper end or aim, it goes on continually revolving around itself as a center, and within its own charmed circle." Instead, because "man's consciousness, in its existing state, at least, is already too much rent and distracted by division" for abstract philosophy to be possible, the only role of philosophy would be to "analyse and clearly understand the psychological fact of the discord and dissension which subsists between the several faculties of soul and spirit, and to exhibit it just as it is."[8]

Of course, while there is nothing romantic about the program of the idealists, there is about the manner in which the idealists brought idealism to its end. Here Höffding's characterization of romanticism does apply to the idealists as well: "The romantic school was in a state of constant oscillation. Romanticism oscillates between overweening self-pride (where the pure ego is made identical with the empirical ego) and the mystical surrender of the self (where the empirical self disappears in the pure infinite ego)."[9] The "pride" of Fichte's ego-centered Subjective Idealism turns into the surrender of selfhood in Schelling's Objective Idealism, to be followed by Schelling's attempt to unify the heteronomous and autonomous in his system of identity, and this to be followed by Hegel's elaboration of the equation with his dialectic of the Absolute.

The young Marx had even more perceptively noted the struggle between the autonomous and the heteronomous that was being carried on within the idealists and had concluded that this philosophy "burdened with contradictions in its innermost essence" could not succeed. Thus he concluded, "While philosophy, as will [Fichte], turns toward the apparent world, the system is reduced to an absract totality [self positing nonself], that is, it becomes one side of the world facing another. Its relation to the world is reflexive relation. Enthusiastic in its drive to realize itself, it enters into tension with everything else. The inner self-contentedness and roundness is broken down. The former inner light becomes a consuming flame turning outward [Schelling and Hegel]. The consequence, hence, is that the world's becoming philosophical is at the same time philosophy's becoming worldly, that its realization is at the same time its loss. . . ."[10]

This dialectic between the self and nonself is found with increasing complexity in the development of each of the idealistic systems of Fichte, Schelling, and Hegel. The difficulties that faced the idealists emerged almost at once in what is surely the most important first statement of their position, Fichte's *Wissenschaftslehre*. In this work, Fichte proposed to establish a "transcendental science" that would ground the previous work of the critical tradition. He began his attempt to dissolve the heteronomous by maintaining that any nonself or thing-in-itself had to be considered actually as a being *for* the self. He then presented the following principles:

The self is absolutely active, and merely active — that is our absolute presupposition.
There can be absolutely nothing in the self that constitutes an effect. . . .Hence, the not-self in question must itself be an effect of the self and of the absolute self at that.

However,

The self cannot. . . .be cause of the not-self in the same fashion, that is, by an absolute positing.

This is because,

The self cannot posit the not-self without restricting itself. For the not-self is completely opposed to the self; what the not-self is, the self is not; and thus insofar as the not-self is posited. . . .the self is not posited.

Fichte explains that if the self were to posit the not-self as infinite, this would entail the annihilation of the self, which, of course, is impossible according to the "absolute presupposition." Hence, the not-self must be posited as finite and determinate. In the act of positing the not-self, the self limits itself "by the amount of reality posited in the not-self." This is the crucial point in the dialectic, for why should the self, which posits the not-self "without a ground of any kind," *limit* itself in this way? To do so, Fichte maintains, "the self would be essentially opposed to, and in conflict with, itself; it would contain a doubly opposed principle, which is itself a self-contradictory assumption." Yet, the self does just this. Why it does so, Fichte concludes, cannot be deduced from any "higher ground of possibility"; rather, "*that* such a positing occurs can be demonstrated by nothing other than a fact of consciousness, and everyone must demonstrate it for himself by this fact; nobody can prove it to another on rational grounds."[11]

This "fact of consciousness" is nothing else than an experience of a reality separate from the self. Any "finite rational being" must recognize this awareness in himself, Fichte claims, but *why* this is so is precisely what must be established.[12]

Wishing to avoid an appeal to a heteronomous principle and thus bring about the collapse of the transcendental science, Fichte argues that *within the self* there is an activity that opposes the self's absolute, unconditioned positing of the nonself.[13] But this will not do, for the primacy of the autonomous over the heteronomous cannot be established in this manner.

Here, in Fichte's dialectic of self and nonself, can be seen Hegelianism in miniature. The self posits the nonself to oppose itself; in the same manner the Idea generates Nature in its operation on matter as its opposite. And just as the goal of the self is to bring the nonconformity of the nonself into conformity with itself, the destiny of matter as slumbering, disorganized Spirit is to bring itself toward the fullest realization of the Idea in the form of the Absolute.

Having gone this far, Fichte has no choice but to conclude that the relation of the self to the nonself is one of *striving*. The absolute self actually is "nothing *for* itself."[14] It reaches beyond itself for fulfillment; it is by nature an unhappy consciousness when it realizes that it is "itself incapable of causality."[15] We have now come full circle. Starting from the unquestionable autonomy of the absolute self, we arrive at the heteronomy of an empty self longing for fulfillment; truly this is a philosophy "burdened with contradictions," one that is "continually revolving around itself as a center."

Fichte's philosophy, which had been designed as the science to establish a transcendental ground for the possibility of a genuine critical philosophy, could not deduce *a priori* the principle of heteronomy, the most crucial task of the science. Indeed, the force of the heteronomous in Fichte's thought loomed larger and larger as his idealism went through one formulation after another, so that after 1805 his own surrender to the heteronomous was complete: "In individual human beings the Eternal Divine Idea takes up its abode as their Spiritual Nature. . . and then we say, adapting our language to common appearance, this man loves the Idea, and lives the Idea, —when in truth it is the Idea itself, which in his place and in his person, lives and loves itself. . ."[16]

In 1831, looking back over the course taken by idealism, an opponent of the movement, O. F. Gruppe, noted that all that was needed in order to be able to escape Fichte's problem was to maintain that "being is one with thinking; man himself is the measure of a world which no longer stands opposed to him as a stranger; it depends on his Spirit and is connected to it internally and of necessity."[17] This is precisely what Schelling, as the precocious student of Fichte, set out to prove. What follows is the journey he took toward reaching that goal.

Schelling's Idealism
and
Philosophy of Nature

79-2438

1

The Fichtean Period

In 1790 at the age of fifteen Schelling entered the Tübingen theological seminary where he began a rigorous study of natural science, philosophy, and religion.[1] His exposure to Herder's *Ideen* and essay on the origin of language, along with his own biblical and classical studies, led to an essay on the origin and function of myths a few years later.[2] In this essay, *Uber Mythen, historsche Sagen und Philosopheme der ältesten Welt*, Schelling reveals the influence of Herder's insight that human culture in all of its forms must be viewed from the perspective of history, including natural history. In both the *Ideen* and the essay on language Herder's approach is genetic and holistic, where even human thought has a history and follows a developmental pattern that reflects the systemic principles applicable to all of reality. For this reason, the standpoint of critical philosophy is impossible to attain. The historical conditions of thought, language, and culture undermine any philosophy that pretends to begin from an unconditioned and nonhistorical standpoint. The healthy-minded message of the Enlightenment is apparent—man himself is something capable of being studied, understood, and eventually improved upon. What must be done is to locate those circumstances which have been influential in the formation of thought and culture; in this way a groundless egoism and ethnocentrism can be overcome. The chief obstacle

31

to be overcome is the philosopher's tendency to see man as being either somehow outside of history, or, at most, as being capable of making history, while remaining, as an individual, unaffected by it. Consequently, the central task of the genetic/holistic method is to establish the existence of a historical dialectic of human reflective thought itself. Unless this is done, the critical standpoint can always feel confident that it remains outside of history.

This approach to thought, which Schelling took to early in his life, eventually became for him a Trojan horse in the house of Fichtean idealism. Only years later, in his *Philosophie der Kunst*, after the major theoretical work of *Naturphilosophie* had been completed, did he return to the theme of a philosophical examination of culture. There he would argue that in ancient myths could be found the first indications of historical and philosophical consciousness. "The Gods of every mythology," he argued, "are nothing other than the ideas of philosophy intuited as objective or real."[3] This means that poetic and mythic fantasy is really the earliest form of intellectual intuition.[4] The creation myths tell the story of how differentiation comes about out of the undifferentiated, the latter being symbolized by the images of *night*, the *void*, the *deep*, and so on. The struggles between reason and passion, the rational and irrational, then come to be seen in the exploits of Apollo, Jupiter, Minerva, Pluto, Vulcan, Pan, and the Fauns and Satyrs.[5]

In the earlier work, *Über Mythen*, Schelling argues that a study of myths should adhere to the context in which those poetic forms arose. The need to rely on an oral tradition, he notes, determined not only the quantity, but also the character of the thought that could be transmitted in such a fashion. Consequently, it is wrong to subject mythic expression to the standards made possible by a written tradition. If we were to take up the world view of cultures that existed before writing, we would be able to see how effective the explanatory role played by myths was in that world view; in such a world invoking "the name of the father" is enough.[6] Myths, like those of Prometheus and Pandora, have as their purpose not a record of past events, but the transmission of doctrines about the universe.[7] Unlike the philosophers of the written tradition, mythic philosophy is more "impassioned, rich, and alive."[8] Its use of what to the modern mind appears to be allegory is actually the result of a sensuous and organic concept of reality. It does not produce myths consciously as works of art, but rather does so innocently as the natural product of its sensuous and symbolic outlook.

However, at a certain point in history the exclusively sensuous outlook is lost and hence the character of poetic expression changes as well: "As man grows toward higher activity, he forgets the images and dreams of his youth, and seeks to make nature comprehensible to his understanding. Previously he was a friend or son of nature, now he is its lawgiver; previously he wanted to experience himself in all of nature, now he wishes to explain all of nature in himself; previously he sought his image in the mirror of nature, now he seeks the archetype of nature in his understanding which is the mirror of everything."[9] Myth gives rise to theology, while history takes the place of nature as the realm of human activity. The Christian Trinity eventually replaces the many ancient gods as a result of the increasing refinement and abstraction of philosophical ideas.[10] The belief in miracles becomes necessary as reason and nature become more estranged.[11] Yet, the transition from images to concepts is not a smooth one. The *unified* vision of reality is lost, for "the modern world has no true *epos*."[12] Instead, "the modern world is in general a world of antagonisms, whereas in the ancient world. . .on the whole the finite and infinite were united under a common veil."[13] To bring metaphysics back to its earlier unity, but now including the hard-won advances in human freedom and knowledge, would be Schelling's own task in his *Naturphilosophie* to come. Unlike Schiller, who had argued for the necessity of reintegrating the *sensuous* within modern man as the way of reestablishing the Greek harmony of self, Schelling in his own approach would be more rationalistic and abstract. At this point, however, his desire for a moral, political, and philosophical reintegration of man with culture, nature, and history remained only a dream, for he had not yet discovered Spinoza.

Very likely Schelling's criticism of the character of modern thought played a significant role in his break with Fichte. His tendency, manifested early in his writings, to see thought from a historical point of view made this break with Fichte almost inevitable. For the "absolute" positing of the self in the *Wissenschaftslehre* had to be regarded as necessarily ahistorical, inasmuch as Fichte was attempting to establish an *a priori* science of knowledge. When it came time to write the justification for a need a nature-philosophy in contrast to Fichte's own ego-philosophy, the historical method was once more put to use by Schelling. Having argued in *Uber Mythen* that ancient man, while he could be considered childlike, was certainly not irrational in what he believed, Schelling was able to maintain that in the earliest stages of man's development there was an absolute equilibrium between the forces of nature and human consciousness. Man, at that time, was one with nature. The categories with which he viewed himself were those he witnessed operating in nature itself. But then, because of man's *freedom*, this equilibrium was upset, thus marking the beginning of *philosophy*: "Speculation first begins with this separation. What nature had always united he now separates—the object from intuition, the concept from the image, and finally, when he will be his own object, himself from himself," resulting finally in a long period of "spiritual sickness."[14] Philosophy would have to supply the cure for this sickness; for if it was the "first philosopher" who, by asking the question of how representations of external objects could arise in us, upset the primordial equilibrium, then it would to be reestablished by philosophy as well. It is this very act of philosophic questioning that disrupts the unity of man and nature and creates the opposing realm of matter and spirit. Yet, in the process man's essence [*Wesen*] becomes a being-in-itself [*Sein-an-sich*] and it is in this capacity of man to experience transcendence that there now exists the possibility of reuniting the dualities that had arisen as a result of the first exercise of freedom.[15]

This account of the origin and role of philosophy puts Schelling fundamentally at odds with Fichte, and actually separates him at the outset from the tradition of critical philosophy. If nature coexists with thought, or even precedes it, then the *first* task of philosophy is not to chart the realm of the self's unconditioned, reflective experience, but to understand the nature of the original relation between the self and nature. However, it would be several years before Schelling could see his differences with Fichte this clearly. During the years 1794 and 1795, he engaged in his own quest for the unconditioned much along Fichtean lines. Only later would he write of this period: "There was a time when I believed that Herr Fichte was not understood, a time when I sought something higher and deeper in his doctrine than I could actually find there."[16]

The first of these Fichtean works is *Über die Möglichkeit einer Form der Philosophie überhaupt* (1794). Here he argues that the *idea* of philosophy demands that it would be impossible to entertain a situation in which two difference philosophies could both be true. Instead, philosophy is *Wissenschaft* and as such it must be governed by the idea of a unity of thought.[17] This means that all of the propositions [*Sätze*] must be drawn together under a single unifying principle [*Grundsatz*]. Unlike other sciences, which have their own fundamental principles determined by their content—for example, the principles of physics are governed by the subject matter of physics, moving bodies—philosophy's fundamental principle must be absolutely unconditioned, for philosophy is the science of all science [*Urwissenschaft*].[18] This means, among other things, that both the content and form of philosophy must be unconditioned; for if the content alone were unconditioned, then the form philosophy would take to study that content would have to be determined by the content itself. But then, Schelling notes, we would always wonder whether the content was being served well by the treatment given it by philosophy, and this would push philosophy beyond the previous content to more theoretical questions. Reinhold's attempt to establish a foundation for Kant's philosophy in the existence of a *psychological faculty* does not succeed in supplying a transcendental base for critical philosophy, for it remains problematic how such a faculty is made possible, and whether it can be fully understood.[19] On the other hand, any philosophy that attempts to begin with the most *formal* principle possible must express that principle in some determinate form, and then this principle can always be questioned as to its ground.[20] Establishing the unconditioned nature of philosophy, then, becomes a seemingly impossible task: "Here we find ourselves in a magic circle," Schelling concludes.[21]

But there is a way out. The basic defect of all previous pre-Fichtean attempts to establish an unconditioned basis for philosophy was that they sought to establish the principle of all other principles on either a formal or a material basis, but not on both at once. Consequently, the formal basis remained abstract and groundless, while the material basis (either a spiritual or material substance) could never be established as unconditioned due to its heteronomous nature. The answer had to lie in something that, by its very nature, combines at once a formal and material basis, namely, the absolute positing of the self by the self. This positing has the character of "absolute causality."[22] Insofar as it is a real, active self that posits, the material condition is satisfied; and insofar as the act of positing is not conditioned by any particular content, but is, instead, a pure, self-identical act, the formal condition is satisfied as well. This is the unconditioned foundation of the science of all other sciences. There can be no science that does not in some way imply its truth, and there can be no other principle that could establish the unconditioned nature of philosophy.

In this principle, according to Schelling, can be found the basis for Kant's distinction between analytic and synthetic judgments. An analytic judgment is possible only if an identity between subject and predicate is established in some way. However, such an identity could result only if the self is aware of its own self-identity, for to establish the identity of substances is not possible. From this, synthetic *a posteriori* judgments become possible insofar as an absolutely positing self can posit a nonself and, therefore, come to a knowledge of the conditioned. Finally, synthetic *a priori* judgments result from the self's reflection upon and unification of the previous two judgments, inasmuch as it can grasp the identity of identity and difference under the idea of *necessity*.

A year later Schelling presented what at first appears to be simply a more detailed elaboration and justification of the fundamental principle of philosophy in his *Von Ich als Prinzip der Philosophie, oder Über das Unbedingte im menschlichen Wissen* (1795). Unmistakably, however, the work reflects Schelling's desire to push beyond the Fichtean self, while at the same time not turning to the heteronomous and dogmatic outlook. "Knowledge without reality is no knowledge," he writes, clearly referring to the mode of knowing possible for the Fichtean self.[23] And this time when he comes to describe the fundamental principle of philosophy, he significantly characterizes it as a principle that must establish the connection between *being* and *thought*, and not simply that between the self and its activity.

The point of departure for his analysis is his contention that the positing itself of an absolutely unconditioned self must be found in the *freedom* of the self. If the self is truly unconditioned [*Unbedingt*], then it could not be a thing [Ding]; this is only possible if the ground of its being is freedom, otherwise no positing would occur. This also means that if the principle of principles is based on freedom, so must be philosophy itself, which is based on the principle that "the beginning and end of all philosophy is freedom."[24]

No doubt Fichte would have been in agreement with Schelling on this, and he probably was at the time. Yet, we can see Schelling's first steps away from Fichte's idea of the self in this seemingly uncontroversial observation. For in asking for the *condition* for the possibility of the self's positing, Schelling is leaving the phenomenological point of view of the self, and is, in effect, asking a "dogmatic" question whose ground, from Fichte's point of view, would be impossible to establish transcendentally. In claiming that "the essence of the ego is freedom," Schelling has subtly pushed his analysis beyond the Fichtean self.[25] In characterizing the primordial act of self-awareness that grounds the Fichtean ego (intellectual intuition), Schelling has, in effect, described the condition (freedom) and the capacity (nonsensuous intuition) of the Fichtean self as if they were properties of some sort of spiritual *being*, and not simply activities only grasped in the very *act* of self-consciousness. This is a subtle but important shift and might even suggest that Schelling never really understood what Fichte was attempting to do. As long as the positing of the self was considered the basis for a transcendental science, it could always be possible that the positing did not result from the self's own "absolute causality," even granting that the self could not inconsistently *think* itself to be anything but its own ground. On the level of the self's own self-certification of the ground of its positing—its own self—at least, the autonomy of the self could never be challenged. Schelling, however, appears to want a stronger guarantee. His claim, for example, that "the ego contains all being [*Sein*], all reality" is not compatible with a phenomenological approach that limits its perspective to the first person.[26] Schelling may have realized that he has ventured too far, for he goes on to remark, "we stand at the limit of all knowing beyond which all reality, thinking and conceiving vanish."[27]

The influence of Spinoza had already made itself felt in this early essay, not only in what has just been said, but in Schelling's increasing identification of the transcendental self with the Spinozistic Substance.[28] Yet Schelling is not ready to embrace Spinozism fully, and appears to be clearly aware of what is at stake here, for he continues to make, following Kant, the distinction in the course of his discussion between "empirical idealism" which, he holds, is manifested in the ideas of Berkeley and Leibniz, and the transcendental idealism of Fichte and himself.[29] Also in a Fichtean vein he claims that, because the limits of thought are wider than the limits of language, the "self-generated intuition" [*Selbsterrungenes Anschauen*] *he* refers to cannot actually be described and so must be *experienced* by the individual self.[30]

In spite of this ambivalence, Schelling nonetheless goes on to attempt a "pure" deduction of the "forms of modality," which, in his view, had yet to be accomplished.[31] With such a deduction, he claims, the "fundamental forms [*Urformen*] of being and non-being" would be transcendentally established.[32] The following is the summary of the "Table of all Forms of Modality" to be derived from the fundamental principle of the transcendental self:[33]

THESIS
Absolute being, based on the absolute positing of the ego.

ANTITHESIS
Absolute nonbeing, in opposition to, and absolutely independent of the ego, determined by absolute nonpositing.

SYNTHESIS
Conditioned being, resulting from the admittance [*Aufnahme*] in the ego of a determinate positing, i.e., of the *possibility* of the nonself.

From the latter *Synthesis* he derives the three modes of conditioned being:

Thesis: existence in time in general (objective-logical possibility).
Antithesis: existence in a determinate time (actuality).
Synthesis: existence throughout all possible determinate time (necessity).

All categories derive from the activity of the self. Time, which is "the condition of all synthesis," he regards as a structure of intellectual intuition, without further considering why it is that the self is capable of structuring its experience temporally. Either he overlooks the question of the condition for temporality itself, or else he, in some way, identifies time with the "pure being" of the self. We have some reason to doubt the latter, however, for he also observes that "for the absolute ego there are no possibility, actuality and necessity."[34] It is only the "finite ego" with its "theoretical and practical tasks" that makes use of these structures of time.[35] With this distinction between the "pure" and the "finite" self Schelling can avoid the question of time altogether. Yet, until that question had been raised and answered, any account such as he goes on to give of the dimensions of the "finite" self must remain, from the transcendental point of view, purely gratuitous.[36] The basis for the distinction between the temporal and atemporal self must have remained a problem that concerned him, for at one point he asks: "How can the transcendental causality of an empirical self be in agreement with the natural causality [*Naturcausalität*] of that self?"[37] If, as he had argued previously, unity is an essential component of a self, then the finite and absolute selves are really one self; and if so, how are these selves to be related? Indeed, of what use is the finite self to the absolute? This is a question that Schelling does not, and, as with Fichte before him, cannot answer in the present confines of his transcendental science. He simply assures us that the empirical causality of the finite self must ultimately be derived from the transcendental causality of the absolute self and conveniently leaves the question there.[38]

Schelling continued with his program to deduce philosophical categories from the Fichtean starting point in his *Neue Deduction des Naturrechts*. In this work he intends to use the results of transcendental science to establish a theory of rights on an *a priori* basis alone, a task in line with the desire of the early idealists to restructure all of the disciplines upon a transcendental foundation. Here he introduces for the first time since his earliest writings on myths the concept of *nature* and its relation to the self, and in so doing takes his most decisive step away from Fichte's version of transcendental idealism. If, as he argues, the entire world is a "moral realm" to the transcendental self, then natural laws must be moral laws and, indeed, the causality of freedom must also be manifested through physical causality. Physical causality no longer is an alien force opposed to the self, for it reflects the

demands of law and rationality that are grounded absolutely
and exclusively in the pure self. And so Schelling concludes
confidently that he has found a way to unify autonomy and
heteronomy.[39] Physical causality, regarded from the point of
view of *objects* is, of course, heteronomous — the manifestation
of an alien power to the self. But, Schelling maintains, if we
think of physical causality not as being determined by *laws* of
nature, but as a mechanism for the expression of autonomy,
then we need no longer consider it a source of heteronomy.[40] In
fact, he concludes, we already have a concept for such a
possibility — *life*: "Life is autonomy in the realm of appearance;
it is the schema of freedom insofar as it manifests itself in
nature."[41] Throughout the rest of the deduction this contention
is left uncriticized; however, it is the bridge needed to cross
from transcendental philosophy to the "knowledge of reality"
Schelling desired earlier. The Fichtean ego has for the first
time become flesh and now steps out into the world of nature
and action: "Where my *physical* power finds opposition is
nature. . . .where my *moral* power finds opposition no longer
can simply be nature. Shuddering, I remain still. Here is
man!"[42]

Also in 1795 Schelling wrote *Philosophische Briefe über
Dogmatismus und Kritizismus*, a work in which he displays
further his growing dissatisfaction with the development of the
critical tradition reflected in Fichte's thought. However, the
main thrust of the work is still decidedly anti-dogmatic, for
once again its purpose is to establish a sounder basis for
critical philosophy. Kant's *Critique of Pure Reason*, he tells
us, is merely a critique of *knowledge*, and, as such, does not
undercut dogmatism which, by its very nature, is not concerned
with a critical account of the knowing faculties. Only a "better
system" can be effective against dogmatism, he concludes, and
not simply a critical attack upon it.[43] For the *Critique* only
rejects as dogmatic those philosophies which had not first
investigated the conditions of knowledge, Schelling argues.[44]

Schelling's wish to construct a philosophical system in the
traditional sense is surely apparent here. He wishes to leave

the narrow confines of the Fichtean self, while at the same time not becoming "dogmatic." To do this he must find a way to speak of reality in a manner that does not make that reality a thing-in-itself beyond the transcendental self. And so, not wishing to overturn the truths of transcendental science, he sought to combine critical epistemology with dogmatic metaphysics. His criticism of the *Critique* already assumes a realm outside of knowledge to which an appeal can be made to legitimize a philosophical system on a transcendental basis. This basis is no longer the Fichtean absolute ego, but rather Spinoza's Substance. In this concept Schelling has found a way to unify dogmatism and criticism, and to produce a philosophy of reality within the limits of transcendental knowledge. "Why," he asks, "did Spinoza present his philosophy as a system of *ethics*?"[45] To Schelling the answer is obvious. Spinoza had understood the bankruptcy involved in pursuing a purely critical approach in philosophy. He was not interested in thinking about the capacity of thinking, but rather wanted to comprehend reality in a practical and active way. Early in 1795 in a letter to Hegel, Schelling described, even if ambiguously, his growing involvement with Spinoza's doctrine:

For us, too, the orthodox concepts of God are no more.[46] My answer is: we can go *beyond* a personal being. I have meanwhile become a Spinozist! Don't be amazed. You'll soon hear how. For Spinoza, the world (the object as opposed to the subject) was *everything*; for me this is true of the *ego*. The real difference between the critical and the dogmatic philosophy seems to me to lie in the fact that the former starts from the absolute ego (not yet conditioned by any object), while the latter starts from the absolute subject of non-ego. The latter, pushed to its ultimate consequences, leads to Spinoza's system; the former, to Kant's. Philosophy has got to start from the *unconditioned*. Once this question is decided, *everything* is decided. For me the highest principle of all philosophy is the pure, absolute ego, insofar as it is mere ego, not yet conditioned by objects but posited through *freedom*.[47]

The ego remains the starting-point, but not the *extent* of philosophy. For both dogmatism and criticism are one-sided philosophical approaches, the former insofar as it speaks of reality, but not in a transcendental manner; the latter because within its transcendental formalism there is no way to speak of reality. Yet, while Schelling appears to give more support to the critical approach, he actually is struggling with the "dogmatic" implications of the self's positing of the nonself. At some point between late 1794 and early 1795 the crucial difficulty in the Fichtean approach, mentioned earlier, of how the absolute self can posit a nonself and then come to be limited by it, must have occurred to Schelling. He raises this question, which he calls "the riddle of the world," in the following form: "How did the Absolute come out of itself and oppose a world to itself?"[48] Neither dogmatism nor criticism has answered this question, in his view, because of their one-sidedness. For the "riddle of the world" is actually a question of how the finite can proceed from the infinite. Yet, in the dogmatic or critical approaches, in order to answer this question, we must seek the answer in an "intermediate" between the finite and infinite which makes this supposed opposition possible; but by the very nature of what we are trying to explain, this is impossible.[49] *We*, as part of the Absolute, cannot explain how opposition comes to the Absolute; instead, *we must proceed from the finite and transcend it toward the infinite.* This, in Schelling's view, is precisely what Spinoza's insight had been. The finite and infinite no longer are opposed to each other as contingent and transcendent beings. The finite is but an aspect of the infinite; consequently, there are not two separate realities—finite and infinite—but only one, distinguished as process and event, *natura naturans* and *natura naturata*. This radically changes the point of departure for transcendental science, which Schelling realizes, for he remarks that in Spinoza's system the self is no longer its own realm [*Eigentum*], but belongs to an infinite reality.[50] The absolute causality of the transcendental self, then, is actually possible only because the self is part of the causality of the Absolute.

While Schelling probably read Spinoza in the original, as his references seem to indicate, he was also very likely influenced by Jacobi's account of Spinoza's doctrine in *Ueber die lehre des Spinoza in briefen an den Herrn Moses Mendelssohn* (1789). In that work, which was part of the "Spinoza Controversy" involving Jacobi and Moses Mendelssohn, and later Jacobi and Herder, Jacobi expresses his admiration for the intellectual consistency of Spinoza's system. However, because Spinoza's system did not make possible human freedom or God's personality, Jacobi concluded that if we are to grant these, we can only do so intuitively. Clearly, with respect to human freedom, at least, Schelling was in agreement with Jacobi's statement of the problem, though not necessarily with his particular solution to it, for Schelling also desired a ground in nature for the possibility of such an intuition.

The idea of the unity of nature, which is emphasized in Jacobi's work, must have been to Schelling the missing link in his attempt to establish a connection between autonomy (the Fichtean self) and heteronomy (nature).[51] Schelling's "riddle of the world" is even asked in the person of Giordano Bruno in that work: "How is it possible that one and the same being. . . could be both inner and outer, principle and cause."[52] And the answer given is that the inner and outer are merely aspects of reality, only distinguishable from a particular point of view within the total system.

Jacobi's work was doubtless of importance to Schelling, for it contains notions that were to reappear as the theoretical foundation for the latter's *Naturphilosophie*, namely, the ideas that matter is really force, that there are no isolated causal events, and that "nothing is so insignificant or small that spirit does not dwell within it."[53]

Schelling's earliest formulation of the "better system" toward which his thought had been pointing for the past three years was set forth in a work entitled *Abhandlungen zur Erläuterung des Idealismus der Wissenschaftslehre* (1796). His starting point in this essay is the question of how knowledge is possible. The traditional answer, which he associates primarily with Kant, is that knowledge is the unity of external material and internal form.[54] But what must be explained is precisely the condition for that unity. To say that the object is somehow the cause of its idea is to fail to explain how the idea comes to *represent* the object. Schelling, therefore, concludes that no such unity could be established without assuming as the basis for that unity a condition involving the "self-intuiting of a spirit."[55]

Similarly, the connection between finite objects and the infinite, unconditioned totality cannot be explained through cause and effect, for it is precisely the existence [*Dasein*] of finite things that remains unexplained in this manner. Instead, the unity of the finite and the infinite can be found only in "the being [*Sein*] of a spiritual nature."[56]

From this point on, Schelling has moved completely beyond the limitations of the Fichtean self, for he is no longer speaking of the individual self here. Instead, the character of Fichte's unconditioned positing has been transferred from the individual self, as we ordinarily understand it, to the world and nature at large. This is ultimately what Spinoza made possible for Schelling. Now the self's dual positings of itself and nonself become primordial "tendencies" within the universe itself—the active tendency to impose limitations [*Sphäre*], and the passive tendency to let them be imposed [*Grenz*].[57] Out of these tendencies Schelling suggests the following interpretation of the categories of experience:

Matter: the equilibrium of these dual spiritual tendencies.
Space: the result of the unlimiting tendency in intuition.
Time: the result of the limiting tendency in intuition.
Quality: a dimension of time.

It is through these categories that the particular finite object is constructed, for the purpose of all spiritual activity is to represent the infinite in the finite.[58] The result of this is *self-consciousness*, inasmuch as "the history of these activities is nothing other than the *history of self-consciousness*."[59]

This early attempt to bring Fichte and Spinoza within one system, however, only results in a work full of ambiguity and inconsistency. Schelling vacillates, for example, between two views of consciousness, each more or less reflecting the approaches taken by Fichte and Spinoza. He insists that absolute freedom and autonomy must be granted to the ultimate nature of reality, and yet he does not characterize the opposing primordial activities as self-conscious ones; instead, they seem to *produce* self-consciousness by their opposition.[60] Consciousness is the Archimedean point, he tells us at one time, and yet he also remarks that "the source of self-consciousness is the *will*," through which alone we become conscious of our freedom.[61] The will of the individual self, however, must have a ground beyond the self, for Schelling calls the particular will *"the absolute will under the limits of finiteness."*[62]

Until now Schelling's unsure efforts had gone largely into modifying Fichte's subjective idealism to his satisfaction. By 1797 it had become clear to him that nothing less than a complete overturning of the Fichtean starting-point was necessary. He was then ready to lay the foundation for his own *Naturphilosophie*, a philosophy that would bring unity to philosophy by establishing an underlying connection between autonomy and heteronomy, and between theoretical and practical reason.[63]

2

The Theoretical Groundwork
of the Philosophy of Nature

R. G. Collingwood has argued that philosophy always operates within the limits of the "absolute presuppositions" of the natural sciences of its day. To Schelling just the opposite is true. Natural science is the practical application of philosophical claims about the nature of reality; consequently, natural science must be studied philosophically.[1] In tracing the development of his thought from 1793 to 1797 it has become clear that the major task of *Naturphilosophie* is to solve what Schelling had called the "riddle of the world." This riddle can be reformulated in a traditional manner as the problem of the One and Many: either plurality and variety are generated out of real unity, or else unity is established out of real variety. Schelling's Spinozistic sympathies led him to accept the former case, that is, the existence of real unity from which variety must be deduced.

Unlike previous transcendental philosophy, *Naturphilosophie* begins, first of all, within the historical tradition of philosophical questioning. This means that it emerges out of the condition of philosophizing itself, namely, the separation between man and nature that makes possible the act of philosophical questioning. To Schelling philosophy begins with

the question of why there is an external world appearing as
Nature. The initial separation of natural man from nature is
explained by him as the result of an act of freedom. And for
a long period the separation is maintained because of a
"spiritual sickness" of men — their tendency to engage in "mere
reflection."[2] The conditions of knowledge are sought by these
spiritually sick philosophers in cognitive faculties, *a priori*
schemata, or *a posteriori* sensationalist psychology, but the
separation between knower and known is still not overcome.
Instead, either skepticism, fideism, or, at best, a Kantian/
Fichtean subjectivism is the result achieved. Man paradoxically
remains estranged from the world he has freely set against
himself.

Yet, a way out can be found. For, if philosophical
questioning presupposes freedom, then there must lie within
man's freedom the capacity to reestablish a sense of unity of
himself within the world. It is contradictory, Schelling maintains,
for man's free thought to result in man's thinking himself
unfree. Blame for the outcome must lie in man's tendency to
regard mechanistic thinking as the paradigm of legitimate
thinking. Man comes to see himself as an object among objects,
as an effect among causes; and then, using mechanistic thinking
to explain the very process of thinking, he can no longer find
a place for the idea of freedom in his self-identity.[3]

If, however, it can be shown that the basic assumptions
of mechanistic thinking are implausible, and that behind them
lie more fundamental assumptions with which they are in
conflict, then mechanistic thinking will be abandoned, and so,
with it, man's philosophic confusion and estrangement. The
assumptions of mechanistic thinking that Schelling selects for
criticism are: (1) that matter exists independently of thought
and spirit, (2) that only physical (efficient) causality operates
in nature, and (3) that only reductive explanations of natural
organisms are possible. His arguments against these assumptions
will constitute the theoretical foundation of his *Naturphilosophie*.
For while Schelling may have been viscerally at odds with
Fichte's manner of philosophizing at almost the very outset

of his own career, it was not until the turn from a Fichtean subjectivism had been given philosophical respectability through argumentation that a *Naturphilosophie* could be regarded as a genuine advance beyond Kant and Fichte. Here it appears that Schelling did, in fact, first formulate these arguments before he had any idea of what a completed *Naturphilosophie* would look like.

The Analysis of Matter

Schelling was not the first philosopher to argue that "spirit does not arise from matter, but rather matter arises from spirit."[4] His analysis leans heavily on Kant's discussions of the nature of matter in the *Metaphysische Anfangsgründe der Naturwissenschaft* (1786) and also in the *Critique of Pure Reason*. These two works, together with Jacobi's Spinoza work, present the key ideas that would serve as the point of departure for Schelling's own approach to the concept of matter, so that there can be no doubt of Schelling's indebtedness to Kant here, as with later arguments as well. However, Hegel was incorrect, as we shall see later, when he said that Kant's *Naturphilosophie* called for a construction of matter from powers and activities, not from atoms, "and Schelling still holds to this without getting further."[5] In fact, Schelling did go beyond Kant. By the time Hegel had formulated his own idealistic system, the character of philosophy had moved so far from the critical philosophy of Kant that he probably could no longer appreciate the significance of Schelling's elaboration of Kant's analysis of matter.

According to Kant, for natural science to be more than a mere accumulation of empirical observations, it had to have a formal structure. Natural science was *Naturwissenschaft*, and *Wissenschaft* could only mean an ordered system of principles. Knowledge derivative of these principles was then called by him *apodictic*.[6] As an example of sciences that had not yet achieved such a status, Kant singled out chemistry and psychology. The laws of chemistry were merely "laws of experience"

[*Erfahrungegesetze*], that is, they were simply empirical generalizations with no genuine lawlike character, the reason being
that the chemist filled his notebooks with descriptive accounts,
for example, of the color changes of compounds under various
temperatures, or designed taste tests to differentiate acids from
bases. His knowledge of physical events remained on the
sensory level and never contained the *a priori* laws that governed
the processes of chemical interaction. It was futile for him to
classify the compounds into *salts*, *earths*, or *calces*, as had been
done extensively prior to the end of the eighteenth century,
and still hope to achieve a universal scientific knowledge in
this fashion. What Kant was seeking in order to make chemistry
scientifically respectable were the theories of Dalton, Avagodro,
and Guy-Lussac, which were still some years off, as well as
the kind of knowledge available today concerning bond energies,
electron affinities, and the structure of sub-atomic particles.
Chemistry, at the time, then, was no more than a "systematic
art or an experimental doctrine."[7]

Kant thought that the conceptual predicament of psychology was even worse than that of chemistry. For, inasmuch
as he contended that "in every particular doctrine of nature
there is only that much science, properly speaking, as there is
the mathematics found in it," psychology could not be a science
properly speaking because mathematics was not applicable to
the phenomena of the inner sense;[8] the manifold presented to
inner observation could not be separated and recombined at
will. In the *Critique* Kant differentiates psychology or the
"doctrine of the soul" from physics, saying that "in the latter
science much that is *a priori* can be synthetically known from
the mere concept of an extended impenetrable being, but in
the former nothing whatsoever that is *a priori* can be known
synthetically from the concept of a thinking being."[9] A philosophical psychology, then, is impossible because its subject
matter is never totally isolable. Consequently, its procedure
results only in the formulation of *paralogisms*.

Kant assumes that to know something "synthetically" from
its "mere concept" is to be able to construct that concept

mathematically. It is sufficient to know if a thought is *thinkable* if we know that it involves no contradiction. This was the criterion used in the *Critique* and would serve that work inasmuch as it remained the theoretical preamble to a complete *Metaphysics of Nature*.[10] In a metaphysics of nature, however, the task would be to discover *a priori* whether a thing could have existence outside our thoughts, and to do this we would have to discover whether its thought could be *constructed*. This would mean constructed mathematically, for "all construction of a concept is mathematical."[11]

Kant also argued in the *Metaphysische Anfangsgründe* that the formal completeness of any set of first principles, which would constitute the framework for a metaphysical system of nature, was guaranteed by the completeness of the table of categories that had been established previously in the *Critique*. Hence, the nature of reality had to be analyzed exclusively in terms of the four pure concepts of the Understanding — Quantity, Quality, Relation, and Modality. Having supplied the formal structure for the *a priori* analysis of natural science in the *Critique*, Kant introduces the *material* content of this science — *motion*. He writes, "the fundamental determination of a something which should be an object of the external sense, must be motion, for through this alone can this sense be affected."[12] Even though Kant considered motion to be the concept to be analyzed, "matter as such" remained the object of his investigation. For it is in the mode of material objects that nature manifests itself to the Understanding, but it is primarily as movable that matter is to be analyzed *a priori*.

Applying the concept of motion to the four categories, we get the four ways it is to be analyzed: (1) as a pure quantum of movement, disregarding what is moved, (2) qualitatively as the motion resulting from various kinds of forces, (3) as the relation of forces to each other, and (4) as motion and rest in the ways they appear to our external sense. The sciences dealing with these four topics are, respectively, *Phoronomy*, *Dynamics*, *Mechanics*, and *Phenomenology*.

In the *Critique* matter was not the "inner" or indeterminate

"X" that made things-in-themselves precisely *things* apart from us. Instead, Kant termed this "X" the *transcendental object*, while matter itself was merely another *concept* of the Understanding: "Neither the *transcendental object* which underlies outer appearances nor that which underlies inner intuition is in itself either matter or a thinking being, but a ground (to us unknown) of the appearances which supply to us the empirical concept of the former as well as of the latter mode of existence."[13]

However, in the *Metaphysische Anfangsgründe* Kant comes very close to speaking of matter as *that which* guarantees to any concept that it actually possesses all the features to be synthetically derived from it. In short, one gets the impression that it is *matter* that makes the analysis of an *external* object justifiable as an analysis of motion.[14] Using the scheme based on the categories, Kant's first definition of matter is: *matter is the movable in space*.[15] In other words, the concepts of matter and motion are not equivalent. Matter is analyzable in terms of motion, but as *that which moves* [*das Bewegliches*] in space, and also "as something movable" [*als etwas Bewegliches*].[16]

The fundamental principle of dynamics, Kant maintains, is matter as the movable insofar as it fills space. A space is full if it resists all other movable objects from moving into that space. Matter does not fill a space by virtue of merely existing, but rather through a specific force. In this way matter can be regarded as the ability or *power* of a body to change the course of, or inhibit the motion of, other bodies, rather than as a substance filling space by virtue of its solidity or impenetrability. In the latter case only the law of noncontradiction guarantees that two material objects cannot occupy one space at the same time, and, as previously noted, Kant rejected logical contradiction as the sole arbiter for determining questions of fact.

Kant also rejected impenetrability as the most essential characterization of matter, calling it a *qualitas occulta*.[17] Instead, he postulated forces that would make possible the dynamic interaction between bodies. The force involved in a body's resisting intrusion by another was its *repulsive force*. It was this force that made possible an understanding of material objects as impenetrable. However, it is not enough to think of objects in space as possessing only repulsive force, for from this it would follow that all objects must be infinitely far apart from one another. An *attractive force* is needed to counter-balance the repulsive force. Kant considers this force necessary in order to establish the very "possibility of matter"; otherwise, without it there could only be empty space.[18] On the other hand, a repulsive force is no less necessary for the possibility of matter, for without it the whole universe would collapse into a mathematical point of infinite density. From such an argument it was evident to Kant that the possibility of matter as it manifests itself in sense-perception depended on these two basic forces [*Grundkrafte*].

The ideas developed in the *Metaphysische Anfangsgründe* on matter are anticipated in a general fashion in the *Critique* also, particularly in the "Amphiboly of Concepts of Reflection," and in the "Paralogisms." Kant's main contention in the *Critique* is that in any analysis of matter we can never achieve so deep an insight into its essence that we can neglect the role "relation" plays in our concept of it. In other words, it is impossible that matter have a truly "inner" being, for what is solely "inner" is without relation to anything different from itself. Such a belief in the absolutely inner nature of matter Kant calls a "whim" [*Grille*].[19] If it were possible, he admits, that the Understanding could break loose from the contingencies of the Sensibility and abstract from all conditions of intuition, then it would conceive of matter as an absolutely necessary inner being. But this is impossible, for Kant discounted an intuition based solely on the use of pure categories without the schemata of the Sensibility employed as well; and therefore he concluded that "all we know in matter is merely relation."[20] Even if we were suddenly given a gift of intellectual insight, it would be of no use to us, he argues, because the concepts of the Understanding could be valid only in relation to the Sensibility that gives them "positive meaning" in relation to their objects. He does not demonstrate that some other kind of intuition is not possible, but simply remarks that "our kind of intuition does not extend to all things" and that "its objective validity is limited."[21]

In this respect Kant notes that Leibniz, for example, had sought to determine the "inner" essence of matter. But the only inner being he could turn to was a thinking substance, and so, for Leibniz, matter had to be comprised of simple subjects with the power of "representation."[22] While this alternative was plainly unacceptable to Kant, it would find more sympathy with Schelling when the latter came to ponder the meaning of Kant's analysis.

What Kant's analysis meant to Schelling can be summarized in a remark of Coleridge from his *Biographia Literaria* (1815): "For since impenetrability is intelligible only as a mode of resistance, its admission places the essence of matter in an act or power which it possesses in common with spirit, and body and spirit are therefore no longer absolutely heterogeneous, but may, without any absurdity, be supposed to be different modes or degrees in perfection of a common substratum."[23] In Schelling's view Kant had not gone far enough in drawing out the implications of the dynamic conception of matter. In his *Abhandlungen zur Erläuterung des Idealismus der Wissenschaftslehre*, Schelling, like Kant, had characterized matter as an equilibrium of opposing forces. Where he departs from Kant, however, is over the interpretation of what the analysis of matter actually reveals to us. In the preface to the *Metaphysische Anfangsgründe* Kant had distinguished *natural science* from *natural history*. The former was supposed to treat its subject matter in a purely *a priori* fashion, while the latter would involve the description and classification of natural phenomena. Ultimately, in Kant's view, natural history would have to be based on the *a priori* principles of natural science, which themselves would be derived from metaphysics. And this metaphysics of nature itself would be grounded in the "Analytic of Principles" found in the *Critique*. It is at this point that Schelling sees a contradiction between Kant's stated intentions in the *Metaphysische Anfangsgründe* and his method set out in the *Critique*. How, in fact, could Kant guarantee that his "Metaphysics of Nature" would be "incomparably richer in content" than the *Critique* if the *Critique* were to rule out the possibility of a genuine metaphysics?[24] If noumenal reality is inaccessible to the Understanding, on what grounds could the *a priori* analysis, which would comprise the "doctrine of the body" and the "doctrine of the soul," be considered an actual foundation for natural phenomena, as is maintained by Kant? In Schelling's view, within the limitations set forth in the *Critique*, there can be no guarantee that a link between metaphysics and natural science had been established. However, if the *Critique* itself were rejected, it would become clear that Kant's distinction between an *a priori* analysis of matter (as a concept) and an analysis of transcendental objects as things-in-themselves was completely unnecessary. Once it had been shown, as, to Schelling's way of thinking, Kant had already shown, that "matter is matter only insofar as it is an object of intention or action," then nothing actually remained of the noumenal object apart from spiritual activity.[25] Kant was correct in denying to matter, *as traditionally understood*, an inner reality; what he also should have realized was that there is *no* concept of matter apart from our idea of spirit and activity. Only those beings which "give themselves their own realm" can be said to possess an inner reality, but this is possible only for an intuiting, self-conscious being.[26] What we call *matter* is really "spirit intuiting its activities in equilibrium."[27] The attractive and repulsive forces of which Kant spoke are for Schelling really dimensions of spiritual reality itself, and are just as inconceivable as existing outside the realm of spirit as is matter itself.[28]

Against Kant, Schelling argued that there can be no *a priori* deduction based on the concept of matter alone, for a "mere concept is a word without meaning."[29] The concept of matter is never anything more than those determinate interactive situations, which we, as spiritual beings, experience in our relation to our world. Matter is always manifested as a qualitative *this* or *that* and so cannot be separated from the act of intuiting those determinate qualities.[30] This, however, does not mean that Schelling is turning to a solipsistic phenomenalism, for the self does not create its *own* opposition in the form of the world. There *is* something outside of the self that resists the self and that the self describes as "its world," only it is not material in nature, but rather spiritual. The idea of a self without a "World" set against it is impossible to Schelling.[31] Fichte's primordially positing ego had no content because it actually had nothing to posit. Schelling's standpoint now is no longer the simple positing self, but, instead, what would later be characterized variously as *the Absolute*, *Spirit*, *the World Soul*, or *the World System*. The self itself is constituted out of a "primordial activity" that lies beyond the represented self.[32] The self becomes aware of this unconditioned activity whenever it experiences its own limitations, for, in the experience of limitation, it simultaneously experiences the possibility of transcending that limitation. Yet, it can only approach that primordial activity, which, because it is the condition of intuition, must be inaccessible to intuition itself. It is, instead, what he calls "that X," autonomous in itself but heteronomous to the self.[33] Kant's thing-in-itself now becomes an activity instead of a "dead object" for Schelling.[34]

The Analysis of Causality

The problem of causality, for Schelling, is not the traditional problem of establishing a justification for our idea of a necessary connection between two events; rather, it concerns the question of how the very *idea* of a necessary connection comes to be thinkable for us in the first place. In fact, at one point he remarks that the problem of establishing the *idea* of necessity in human thought is the major problem of all philosophy.[35]

In Schelling's view, as long as the problem of causality is defined in the way Hume had defined it, the only solution to it must be found in Humean skepticism. If we begin with the empiricists' genetic and reductionist account of knowing, then no possibility exists for deducing from the premises of psychological atomism the idea of a necessary connection. And insofar as Kant himself only allowed sensory intuition to be the source of the material of concept formation, his answer to the problem remained in the psychological domain as well. In this vein, G. E. Schulze's *Aenesidemus* had argued that Kant had not solved Hume's skeptical challenge to knowing, simply because Kant's empiricist epistemology could never establish the conditions necessary for synthetic *a priori* judgments.[36] In all likelihood, Schelling, who had read Schulze's book, was in agreement with this line of criticism.

Schelling's own analysis of the problem begins with the distinction between three kinds of successive relations: one, the relation said to exist between objects; another, the relation said, by empiricists, to exist between the object and its idea; and a third referring to the order and connection among ideas themselves. Inasmuch as every determinate phenomenon [*Erscheinung*] manifests itself as part of a given determinate succession, the question then becomes one of deciding whether the order and connection of the succession of phenomena arise *outside* of or *inside* of the mind.[37] In the former case, there is a real connection among objects [*Dinge*] as well as a direct connection between each object and its idea. In the latter case, there is a genuine connection among our ideas alone, though, for Schelling, this will not imply that the connection between ideas is merely subjective, for he assumes that his task is to outline what sort of conditions for a genuine causal relation would justify our idea of a necessary connection, whether that connection exist between ideas or things. For this reason, the condition he rules out is that in which no connection could be established between objects and ideas. In that case we could not speak of *succession*, but rather "merely an ideal sequence of ideas."[38]

Schelling suggests the writings of Reid and Beatti as examples of philosophies that argue for the first kind of succession. From the point of view of common-sense philosophy there is supposed to be a *real* connection among objects, existing independently of the mind. Yet, how the mind can experience the connection is not established by them. It is not enough to claim, as did Reid, that an "inductive principle" given to man by God had to be the source of our idea of a necessary connection, for a justification of such an assumption would involve more than an appeal to common-sense notions. Schelling finds nothing "common" about common-sense philosophy, remarking that it is a philosophy that, in fact, exists in no man's head.[39] As long as we limit the treatment of causality to the external world, there will be no hope of establishing the justification or even the possibility of our idea of a necessary connection. Even if we can determine that each idea is directly caused by its object, this is not sufficient to establish the idea of a necessary connection among these ideas, unless we could somehow be sure that physical causality is deterministic as well. The only recourse, then, is to seek to establish the idea of a necessary connection in some condition of the mind. This, in Schelling's view, is what Kant and Hume had attempted. However, both attempts ended in failure because neither of them could free themselves from the dogmatism of the common-sense view. They both remained committed to the idea of a nonmental reality and, therefore, could not establish a basis for the idea of a necessary connection in the mind alone. It was to Hume's credit, at least, that, unlike Kant, he realized this most clearly.

Philosophers like Kant and Reinhold, who continued to maintain a dogmatic belief in things-in-themselves and yet who believed that they had established an *a priori* basis for causality, produced, in Schelling's words, "the most quixotic system that has ever existed."[40] This contradiction was, to Schelling, so manifest that it required no refutation. Kant's account is "subverted from the ground up" because it is a "deep secret" not only how the causal relation arises *a priori*, but also how, in the first place, a *unity* of apperception is achieved to bring about the perception of definite objects.[41]

In his later *System des transzendentalen Idealismus* Schelling developed his criticism of Kant in more detail. Here the problem of causality is defined as a problem of establishing those criteria which govern our concept of a particular thing. The causal relation is not seen by him to be problematic in relation to a world of individual bodies, but rather the finiteness of individuals itself becomes problematic without some concept of causal interconnection.

For Kant there were three conditions for the possibility of "knowledge of the object" — the manifold of pure intuition, the synthesis of the manifold through the imagination, and the unity of the synthesis through concepts. Pure intuition is primordial and spontaneous and, as such, inexplicable in itself. Of the power of imaginative synthesis, Kant remarks: "Synthesis in general. . .is the mere result of the power of the imagination, a blind but indispensable function of the soul, without which we should have no knowledge whatsoever, but of which we are scarcely ever conscious."[42] It is to the concepts of the Understanding — the categories — that we must turn to find the actual structures of these unifying tendencies.

Significantly, in the second edition of the *Critique* Kant claimed that the table of categories was capable of supplying "the *complete plan of a whole science*," part of which, we can presume, had already been accomplished in the *Metaphysische Anfangsgründe*, written since the first edition appeared.[43] It was one of the "nice points" of the table that "in view of the fact that all *a priori* division of concepts must be by dichotomy . . .it may be observed that the third category in each class always arises from the combination of the second category with the first."[44] Thus, "*community* is the causality of substances reciprocally determining one another."[45] Another such "nice point" is that the table can be divided into a "mathematical" and a "dynamical" set of categories, the former concerning the "objects of intuition, pure as well as empirical," and the latter concerning "the existence of these objects, in their relation either to each other or to the understanding."[46] The category of *community* belongs to the latter set, for Kant speaks of a "dynamical community" among substances as the basis for coexistence.[47]

From Kant's discussion of the category of *community* in the Third Analogy, it is clear that *community* as a "causality of substance" was not regarded by him as a category in the same sense as were *substance* and *causality*. Yet he must have realized that if he had included only the first two categories (as "inherence" and "consequence") under the heading of *Relation*, he would have been far from setting forth the conditions for the possibility of our experience of a *world*. For the synthesis of the imagination unified what the Sensibility intuited. This meant, in effect, that only *one* object could be presented in experience at a time. Causality would then link one object with another succeeding it. But at no time could *two or more* objects be present in our experience. This restriction was clearly counter to our experience of being aware of two or more objects existing simultaneously, or of a whole ensemble of them constituting a "world."

The synthetic power of the imagination does not include the ability to unite two perceptions; consequently, coexistence must derive from the ability to, for example, "direct [one's] perception first to the moon and then to the earth, or, conversely, first to the earth and then to the moon."[48] The discussion of the first two Analogies posed a problem that necessitated the Third Analogy—namely, the problem of how the experience of the coexistence of substances becomes possible. In fact, in the second edition of the *Critique* the extreme importance of this problem for Kant becomes apparent in his remark that the possibility of coexistence actually is "the condition of the possibility of things themselves as objects of experiences."[49]

Kant's solution to the problem is that for two substances, A and B, to coexist, there must be a reciprocal and dynamic interaction between them. In this case I can either perceive A and then B, or just as easily, B and then A. Without such a dynamic interaction the first one perceived could only be understood as preceding the second in time. So Kant concludes, "there must, therefore, besides the mere existence of A and B, be something through which A determines for B, and also reverse-wise B determines for A its position in time, because only on this condition can these substances be empirically represented as *coexisting*."[50] Now, inasmuch as causality is the *only* form of determination Kant allows, he must conclude, in order to establish reciprocal interaction, that "each substance. . .must therefore contain in itself the causality of certain determinations in the other substance, and at the same time the effects of the causality of that other."[51] However, the problem of how such dynamic interaction is possible remains to be solved, for it would plainly beg the question to establish reciprocal interaction by simply postulating that each substance within itself can determine the other and vice versa. Instead, Kant must look for a *medium* of interaction. Appealing to common sense, Kant notes that "only the continuous influences in all parts of space can lead our senses from one object to another," and this is not possible "unless matter in all parts of space makes perception of our position possible to us."[52] This implies that there is no empty space, or if there is, Kant argues, "it may exist where perception cannot reach."[53]

To Schelling this answer would have been clearly unacceptable. In order to establish the condition for the possibility of a community of substances reacting reciprocally with each other, Kant does indeed beg the question by postulating that very community in the form of "continuous influences" of a plenitude. In what way, however, could such a dogmatic claim be transcendentally established? Kant must be stood on his head, in Schelling's view, that is, it must be argued that the category of community is actually a more *fundamental* category than either of the categories of substance and causality, and not that it is a hybrid of the first two, as Kant had argued. Kant's failure to establish a basis for our experience of community is perfectly understandable, given his reductive treatment of our knowledge of the world. As he set out the problem, no solution is possible. The only recourse, then, is to reject Kant's entire procedure.

Our very concept of a *thing* cannot be separated from the notion of interaction and reciprocal determination, for, as Spinoza observed, every determination is a negation. Consequently, to Schelling, something is what it *is* only in relation to what it is *not*. It has the qualities it has only in comparison to those it does not possess.[54] A *thing* is actually a locus of activity, resulting from the interaction of several or all parts of the community. In *Process and Reality* Whitehead remarked, against Kant's First Analogy, that "in the philosophy of organism it is not 'substance' which is permanent, but 'form.' "[55] For Schelling, the "form" Whitehead speaks of would be, instead, the formal activities of the fundamental nature of spiritual reality. "All categories," he notes, "are modes of activity," through which objects themselves initially arise for us."[56] No comparison of relative qualities among substances is possible unless there is a consciousness to link and compare those qualities in the first place. Unless we *start* with consciousness as the primordial condition of existence, we cannot derive it from spontaneous and "blind" faculties, as Kant had attempted to do.

In a similar fashion, whenever we judge B to be the effect of A, we must be able to judge A's relevance to B *after B* has occurred. We cannot deduce the causal order of succession simply from the anisotrophy of time as an *a priori* condition of perception. Kant thought that the time relation was sufficient to establish a causal relation because he had assumed that if there were nothing in the character of individual perceptions that could establish an order of succession, all that would be needed to give them order was an *a priori* determination of time.[57] However, our perceptions do not occur in the form of a simple necessary succession, and a causal relation cannot be established merely in this manner. Interestingly enough, Kant himself seems to have realized this: "At this point a difficulty arises with which we must at once deal. The principle of the causal connection among appearances is limited in our formula to their serial succession, whereas it applies also to their co-existence, when cause and effect are simultaneous."[58] In fact, Kant argues, for the majority of cases the cause is judged to be simultaneous with the effect. Yet, somehow "the relation [of time] remains even if no time has elapsed."[59] How is this possible? Kant's answer is that it is simply an observable fact that we notice certain sorts of phenomena before we notice others. I observe a falling ball impressing a hollow in a pillow, but I never observe a ball being propelled upwards by a hollow in a pillow. Kant is appealing to the contingencies of empirical experience and not to the conditions for the possibility of experience *in general* to justify the causal relation; and he is using the asymmetry of the causal relation to establish the order of time-direction, whereas he claims he is simply establishing the *a priori* condition demanded by the transcendental unity of apperception.

The connection between the cause and effect is supposed to be established by the continuity of time, while the asymmetry of the causal relation is supposed to be established by the anisotropy of time. Yet, continuity and asymmetry can only establish a continuous *serial* relation.[60] What is lacking is the judgment that it was *A* that *caused B*, and not something that existed simultaneously with *A*. The time-relation cannot by itself supply this.[61]

In general, then, for Schelling both the causal relation between substances and the relationship of accidents adhering together to form a substance are possible only if a reciprocal relation between the items related is grasped by the "primordial consciousness." Then the categories of substance and causality become only "ideal factors," while the category of mutual interaction [*die Wechselwirkung*] alone is "real" [*Reelle*].[62] It is not, however, the coexistence of just *two* objects that is possible for Schelling; for, to admit only this would again lead to the same difficulties that resulted from the possibility of perceiving only one object at a time. Now the difficulty would be how these two objects could relate to a third, fourth, and so on. To say that the cagegory of community is the only "real" category is to maintain that the awareness of a *totality* of coexisting objects is possible. Schelling calls this totality "the Universe," or at times simply "Nature."[63] The categories of substance and causality become possible only *within* a world. *Things* are found in a world surrounded by other things that constitute their environment. And causality is the dynamic interplay of events emerging through the selective interest of consciousness out of that environment.[64]

The need for the Analogies derived from Kant's assumption that in our experience "perceptions come together only in accidental order, so that no necessity determining their connection is or can be revealed in the perceptions themselves."[65] The *unity* of apperception, however, demanded that, in the absence of an intrinsic construction, unity could be found in the time-relation. In Schelling's view, this assumption, coupled with Kant's claim that the Analogies only concerned the *existence* of appearances in relation to each other, and not with the nature of the appearances themselves, was the source of Kant's difficulty.[66] His reductive analysis of experience could not make possible the resynthesis of experience out of that sort of knowledge of appearances. In this respect Kant's analysis was helped considerably by Kemp-Smith's translation of "in the appearance" [*in der Erscheinung*] as "in the field of appearance," for the synthesis of appearances achieved by the schema of the Understanding is formed out of the data of sensuous intuition, which itself cannot be represented *to the Understanding* as a manifold.[67] Consequently, the synthesis of appearances based on the time-relation must itself be the condition for the possibility of knowledge of a field of appearances; it cannot simply synthesize appearance out of such a preexisting field. Yet, a field of appearances or even a "field of experience" is not derivable from the assumptions of the Analogies.[68] Kant was correct in noting in the second edition that the principle of the Analogies was that "experience is possible only through the representation of a necessary connection of perceptions."[69] However, that "representation" could be assumed in the possibility of a *field* of appearances; it could not be derived from the time-relation in the manner Kant had wished to derive it.

Because Kant assumed that the synthesis of the imagination revealed only one percept at a time, he had to derive coexistence from a reciprocal interaction of substances.[70] Yet, he reveals in a footnote at the end of the Third Analogy his view of the importance of community. There he notes that "the unity of the world-whole" is a "mere consequence of the tacitly assumed principle of the community of all substances which are co-existent," and significantly concludes that coexistence is "a merely ideal relation," while community is a "real relation"; the reason for this, he goes on, is that "if they [i.e., appearances] were isolated they would not as parts constitute a whole."[71] Schelling would maintain that Kant is not simply subverting the work of the Analogies in this remark, but is, in fact, admitting that the whole procedure of the *Critique* has been a failure. For if, as Kant notes in that footnote, "community is really the ground of the possibility of an empirical knowledge of coexistence," then for Schelling this means that it is also the ground for knowledge of causality and substance as well. The task of transcendental philosophy, then, must be to seek out the ground of community itself.

Turning now from Kant to Hume, Schelling considered the latter's account of causality to be the most respectable possible within the dogmatic tradition, and therefore actually an improvement over that of Kant. Hume had shown plainly the philosophical bankruptcy of psychological atomism insofar as he argued that it was impossible to establish an objective order to our perceptions. All we could do was to establish a reason for the erroneous belief in a necessary connection.[72] Yet, Hume did not go far enough in his view. While he could explain our belief in causality with the idea of *custom*, in Schelling's view it remained to be shown why it was that past experiences precisely followed in the order in which they did; in short, it remained to be determined whether the sequence of past experiences was the result of the objects [*Dinge*] themselves or whether it derived from some internal factor.[73] Unfortunately, in Schelling's view, this is the matter that Hume should have focused upon.

In fact, Hume *did* give his attention to this question. For, though he held that we infer the existence of a given object following on the appearance of another because we have been accustomed to do so in the past, he went on to observe that we have not "acquired any idea or knowledge of the secret power by which an object produces the other."[74] In Hume's opinion he was merely describing the "mental geography" of the mind, which involved "the delineation of the distinct parts and powers of the mind";[75] so that in speaking of "custom" in relation to the mind's propensity to remain committed to the inductive principle, he observes that "by employing that word, we pretend not to have given the ultimate reason of such a propensity."[76] Hume's epistemology could not supply an answer to the question of the basis for "secret powers," for such powers could never be observed. Yet, in posing the question of the "ultimate reason" for our inductive judgments, Hume was raising a transcendental question. He even ventured an answer to that question, an answer that was unacceptable to both Kant and Schelling, though for different reasons. Abandoning the standpoint of "mental geography," Hume amazingly noted: "Here, then, is a kind of pre-established harmony between the course of nature and the succession of our ideas; and though the powers and forces, by which the former is governed, be wholly unknown to us; yet our thoughts and conceptions have still, we find, gone on in the same train with the other works of nature. Custom is that principle, by which this correspondence has been effected."[77] For both Kant and Schelling it was the ground of a pre-established harmony that had to be established. Rejecting Kant's answer, Schelling turned instead to Spinoza and Leibniz.

The problem of an objective necessary connection arises when it is maintained that a thought is caused by an external object. In other words, the *problem* of causality is, in part, an outcome of the correspondence theory of truth. It is a mystery how external objects can affect one another, as Hume's arguments had shown. And it becomes impossible, once knowledge is regarded simply as the *result* of an encounter of the mind with external reality, to establish whether or not knowledge honestly reflects that reality. However, once this duality is overcome, the problem of causality dissolves as well. And so the whole question of the condition for the possibility of knowledge must, in Schelling's view, *begin* with the insight that knowledge is possible only if the knower and known are in some way connected. For in asking how it is possible to have knowledge of a necessary connection between two events or objects, we are also questioning the very possibility of there being knowledge at all, insofar as knowledge itself is a necessary connection between thought and object of thought. If we assume a separation between mind and external reality, then in asking for knowledge of a necessary connection we are asking for knowledge to operate in the absence of a condition that makes it possible. In short, the particular form of necessary connection manifested in the knowing-relation cannot be assumed until the question of whether or not there are necessary connections *in general* has been answered. But this rules out the possibility of knowledge at the outset. The object of knowledge must have the character of knowability, and this means it must in some way be *ideal* as well as *real*. If it is ideal, then it must share common elements with a knowing spirit.[78] This is what Spinoza suggested when he made *idea* and *object* attributes of one ideal reality. Unfortunately, in Schelling's view, Spinoza "lost himself in the idea of an Infinite Being outside of us," and so ended up destroying the personal self. Instead, he should have regarded reality as a dynamic interplay of connected centers of consciousness, as Leibniz had. Then there would be no risk that his monism would become simply an undifferentiated uniformity with no explanation possible for our awareness of being and becoming.[79] In Leibniz's concept of the individual, the idea and object are united as concomitant modes of action in the receptivity of perception and in the activity of appetition. In this way the unity of idea and object is established while the status of an irreducible self opposed to a world is maintained, for, to Schelling, "only a perceiving being [*das vorstellende Wesen*] has within itself the source and origin of its existence."[80] Yet, even with Leibniz, there is dogmatism. The latter's pre-established harmony that orchestrates the interplay of perceiving monads is rejected by Schelling as a claim that cannot be transcendentally established. Instead, philosophy must stay within the limits of a *"natural science of our spirit."*[81]

Since the interplay between finite and infinite emerges as self-consciousness in the form of a unity of the finite and infinite (the finite *Spirit*), perception itself becomes an active process instead of a passive one. "We observe," Schelling writes, "the system of our ideas not in their *being*, but in their *becoming*."[82] Schelling saw no need to resort to a preestablished harmony to guarantee the truth of perceptions, for the perceived was not "hidden" from the perceiver. Leibniz had defined perceptions as "the passing state which involves and represents a multitude in unity."[83] The only transcendental ground that could establish the possibility of this sort of activity was one in which the ultimate factors at work in the world were synthetic and organic, and not simply mechanical and causal. Schelling had argued that Kant's treatment of substance and causality depended on the analysis of community; now the problem of causality points in the direction of his philosophy of organism for its fullest solution.

The Analysis of Organic Form

Schelling's analysis of matter and causality led him away from the dogmatic and critical standpoints and toward his own version of transcendental idealism. Our notion of a *thing* presupposed a community of interacting processes, while the concept of causality presupposed an awareness of the totality we call *the world*. In short, the order of the presentation of the Analogies is actually an order of discovery, not an order reflecting the transcendental nature of reality. The order of reality is just the reverse, in Schelling's view. And consequently, the argument justifying the reality of organic communities must be considered a cornerstone of his idealism.

The only way of unifying a cause with its effect that does not lead either to dogmatism (Reid, Kant) or to skepticism (Hume) is to assume that such a relation can be interpreted as the sort of relationship that exists among the parts of an organic entity. In this case, cause and effect are not distinct events. In an organic totality, it makes no sense to speak of one part by itself having an effect on another part. Rather, because all parts are internally related, we can speak only of the individual parts effected by and affecting the whole. This is because as a genuine unity each organic form is governed by a *concept*, which determines precisely what the interaction among parts is to be.[84]

This concept contained in each organization cannot be analyzed into inorganic notions, however. We make a mistake, Schelling remarks, if we regard organic entities as works of art. For then we are led to believe that the governing idea behind the work can be separated from the work itself, inasmuch as such an idea existed before the artist realized it in its material form. If we proceed this way, we are left wondering how the two—material and form—can be made to combine into a true unity.[85] This difficulty can be avoided only if we refuse to separate form and content at the outset and, instead, judge an organism to be a true unity of various parts. This unity, for example, cannot be achieved on its material side through some life-giving *substance* such as protoplasm. Instead, it must be a "conceptual unity," and this implies that it be a unity produced by an intuiting and self-reflecting being, for it is only through a judgment (*ein Urteil*) that a relationship between part (*der Teil*) and whole can be established.[86]

This condition that organic unity derives from a conceptual unity has led some to believe that since the concept of purposiveness [*Zweckmässigkeit*] arises in the mind, this must mean that no ground can be established for the judgment that things-in-themselves are in fact purposive, and that, as a result, teleological judgments must be essentially *arbitrary*. For Schelling, however, the question to be answered is how it happens in the first place that putatively subjective judgments come to be made about putatively objective realities.[87] As was the case with the question of establishing the basis for the habit of inductive inference, Schelling is seeking the condition for the possibility of a teleological judgment. He also wants to know why, if teleological judgments are arbitrary, we do, in fact, appeal to criteria for distinguishing organic from inorganic forms. Certainly, if the criteria themselves are arbitrary, we do not apply them arbitrarily.

Following Kant, Schelling rejects any attempt to establish teleology by an appeal to divine creativity and intentionality. This approach simply pushes the question of determining the basis for our judgments to a more remote question of uncovering God's purpose, and we are essentially back where we started. Besides, he notes, this puts the purpose of nature outside of nature and thereby destroys the very organic quality of nature that a teleological judgment is designed to explain.[88] Those who demand a theological explanation for teleology no longer have the capacity to look at nature itself as its own ground of activity and organization. This ability, Schelling notes, recalling his early essay, *Uber Mythen*, was possessed by men of earlier times when a sense of the communion of man with nature was stronger.[89] What an analysis of organic being must accomplish is a reunion of Spirit and Nature, and a rethinking by man of his relation to the totality of which he is a part.

In *Von der Weltseele, einer Hypothese der höheren Physik zur Erklärung des allgemeinen Organismus* (1798) Schelling acknowledges the importance of Kant's analysis of teleological judgments in the latter's *Critique of Judgment*. And like Kant's analyses of matter and causality, Schelling finds Kant's approach to this question suggestive in spite of its limitations. Kant, in his view, was correct in seeking a transcendental ground for our teleological judgments. However, this task, too, must fail because of the underlying, but decisive dogmatism involved in the noumenon/phenomenon distinction, and in Kant's insistence that only sensuous intuition was possible.

In the "Analytic of the Teleological Judgment" of the *Critique of Judgment*, Kant set out the condition whereby an entity may be considered to possess genuine purposiveness "without the causality of the concepts of rational beings external to itself," the condition being that the entity be a unity of reciprocally interacting parts, or, in other words, a *self-organizing being*.[90] Such a condition rules out the possibility that a mechanical organization could be considered purposive in this sense. For as Kant notes, the "producing cause" of a machine lies outside of it, and therefore a machine does not have the capacity to regulate itself internally or to reproduce its kind by itself. The machine lacks the *"formative* power of a self-propagating kind."[91]

Assuming this distinction between internal and external purposiveness, Kant then sought the condition whereby a judgment of internal purposiveness could be possible for Reason; he concluded that such purposiveness had to be an "inscrutable property."[92] An organic being could not be considered a work of art, for that would at once destroy its *self*-organization and make it a mere machine. On the other hand, if we attribute its organization to an internal soul, we still divide the organism into soul as artificer and purposeless machine wherein the soul resides. The only other possibility is to "endow matter, as mere matter, with the property which contradicts its very being (hylozoism)."[93] This possibility Kant rejects without further comment. And so he concludes, "the organization of nature has in it nothing analogous to any causality we know."[94] Among other things, this means that the *concept* of a self-organizing being is not one that results from the concept-formation of the Understanding in the usual manner. Instead, Kant calls it "a regulative concept for the reflective judgment," a "maxim," and a "guiding thread for the observation of a species of natural things which we have conceived teleologically."[95]

An internal unity of parts is what the regulative maxim demands in any judgment of a *natural* object. This means that a natural object cannot be regarded as part organism and part machine, and also that *nature* cannot be composed of both organisms and machines. It also means that if the maxim is to serve as a methodological principle of natural science, to seek the ground of purposiveness in a transcendent God would destroy the "internal consistency" of that science.[96]

However, a conflict arises between this maxim and the judgment that nature be explained mechanistically, a conflict that results in an antinomy. Unlike *determinate* judgments, which are transcendentally formed by the Understanding as a result of the subsumption of the data of sensuous intuition under the categories, a *reflective* judgment is based on a law "not yet given."[97] Consequently, "the reflective judgment must in such cases serve as a principle for itself."[98] As a result, it becomes possible for the differing maxims of the reflective judgment to conflict with each other. The harmony guaranteed to the usual judging capacity of the Understanding does not carry over to the employment of reflective judgments as well. Reason is not in need of reflective principles when it utilizes the categories of the Understanding; it is only when it wishes to formulate particular laws of nature that it must supplement the determinate judgments with maxims. To further complicate matters, the Understanding itself suggests one of the maxims of reflective judgment, and, then, because the maxims are of two kinds, *a priori* and *a posteriori*, they "seem not to be capable of existing together, and consequently a dialectic arises which leads the judgment into error in the principle of its reflection."[99]

The *a priori* law prescribed by the Understanding concerns "the *universal* laws of material nature in general" and because of this takes the form: "all production of material things and their forms must be judged to be possible according to merely mechanical laws."[100] However, the counter-maxim, supplied by Reason, makes a claim for the justification of regarding organic entities autonomously in the sense just described. In spite of the differing origins of the maxim, Kant finds the conflict between them to be one only "in the legislation of Reason."[101] As such they do not involve a contradiction. According to the first maxim, I *must* always judge nature according to the principle of mere mechanism, for without the use of this maxim "there can be no proper knowledge of nature at all."[102] This is in line with Kant's observation that the *a priori* maxim pertains to "nature in general." Yet, because the *use* of these maxims is exclusively regulative, inasmuch as we lack *a priori* empirical laws, this does not prohibit us from using the maxim of Reason to explain "certain natural forms" in terms

The Theoretical Groundwork of the Philosophy of Nature 73

of final causes. What *cannot* be established, however, is whether there is "in the unknown inner ground of nature" a basis for the unity of teleology and mechanism.[103]

In reading the "Critique of the Teleological Judgment" it is difficult to avoid the impression that Kant's sympathy lies clearly with the first maxim. The very fact that the maxim originates in the Understanding *a priori* conveys to it a kind of transcendental prestige that the second, originating from Reason, cannot possess. Also, the first maxim is supposed to apply to universal laws of "material" nature in general, laws that Kant considers "objective" and the result of a *determinate* judgment.[104] The second maxim, on the other hand, is the result of "particular experiences" of Reason in its encounter with nature.[105] Kant even suggests that the natural objects that prompted these experiences — organic forms — might in actuality be subject to mechanistic laws; yet, he does not suggest that the opposite might be true — that mechanistic laws be subsumed under organic ones, and that understanding nature consists of accounting for those experiences where mechanics was applicable, rather than where it was not. In short, the first maxim must be applied universally, while the second only "if opportunity offers."[106]

Varying interpretations of Kant's "solution" of the antinomy has been given.[107] His remark that the antinomy results from a confusion of the *autonomy* of the proposition of the reflective judgment with the *heteronomy* of that of the determinate judgment has led some to conclude that Kant is simply noting that there can be no conflict among the maxims of reflective judgment. However, he is actually saying more here. It is clear that the two maxims are not of equal importance, for the autonomy of the teleological judgment results from its being "a guide to reflection" and of "mere subjective validity," while the heteronomy of the mechanistic principle derives from its being "an objective principle prescribed by reason," which, however, "must regulate itself according to laws . . . given to it by the Understanding."[108]

In one sense, then, the antinomy is resolved simply by virtue of the way Kant sets up the distinction between mechanical and teleological judgments. There is, however, another resolution. Kant notes that if we confine our speculation "within the bounds of mere natural knowledge" we can apply both maxims with what seems to be unlimited freedom.[109] In other words, there is enough material in nature for study along either mechanistic or teleological lines, so that with a proper division of disciplines (physics and biology) these maxims need never come into conflict. The problem with this approach, which is limited to the realm "as far as human powers reach," is that the resolution of the conflict remains, as Kant himself correctly notes, "quite undecided and unsolved speculatively."[110]

We may ask what Kant could have meant by the problem's remaining unsolved *speculatively*. In contrast to a speculative solution there is the solution involving "speculation within the bounds of mere natural knowledge," which Kant suggests instead. It seems, then, that the speculative solution he is seeking is one that must be found beyond *human* Reason itself. Very likely the reason Kant thought it necessary to speculate about a more serious solution of the antinomy was that the two maxims somehow were experienced as being in conflict, whereas they should not have been if the only factors operating were those derived from our own "human powers." This could mean, then, that factors *outside* of our faculties were influencing Reason in some way. This interpretation makes plausible Kant's otherwise astounding remark that "there is, then, indeed a certain presentiment of our Reason or a hint, as it were, given us by nature, that, by means of this concept of final causes, we go beyond nature and could unite it to the highest point in the series of causes . . . ."[111] Perhaps, Kant is wondering, teleological causality has a ground as *fundamental* as that of mechanical causality, though, he concludes, it lies "too deep for our investigation," and, in fact, even to consider the possibility of a genuinely teleological causality opens up "a wide field for difficulties."[112]

If such a ground were possible, then the solution within

the bounds of empirical knowledge would not resolve the antinomy. The two maxims each imply a systematic consistency that is at odds with the other.[113] However, the possibility of such a ground does furnish Kant with a possible resolution to the conflict between the maxims. In the idea of a *natural product* there is at once the notion of *contingency* (being a product) and *purpose* (being natural). These notions could avoid conflict as long as the condition for the possibility of final causality were grounded in the supersensible.[114] Unfortunately, in Kant's view, while there may lie within the supersensible realm a justification for regarding the regulative principle as a determinate judgment, *we* ourselves can never establish that justification, for since natural causation "cannot be derived from experience and also is not requisite for the possibility thereof, its objective reality can in no way be assured."[115]

Throughout, Kant's Newtonian bias is obvious, as, for example, in his observation that "nature as a whole is not given as organized (in the narrow sense of the word above indicated)."[116] And as long as he rejects hylozoism "because lifelessness, *inertia* constitutes the essential character of matter," it is also inconceivable that "inorganic" nature could somehow come to be seen as displaying purpose as well.[117] In effect, it was simply contrary to the nature of human intelligence that it be able to establish an a priori ground for purposiveness. For in every teleological judgment there is an element of contingency and particularity that cannot be derived from universal laws *a priori*.[118] This means that to Kant the regulative principle must *remain* regulative for human intelligence. To *another* sort of intelligence, however, particularity may be derivable *a priori* from determinate principles, in which case—given Kant's bias—such an intelligence "might find the ground of the possibility of such products of nature in the *mechanism* of nature."[119] Human intelligence experiences external objects only as phenomena, and from these phenomena no teleological explanation can be established.

Generally stated, Schelling's objections to Kant's treatment are as follows: (1) mechanistic causality is actually no less inscrutable than is teleological causality, so that Kant's prejudice in favor of the former is unfounded; (2) matter is not inertial by nature, but rather dynamic and relational, as Kant's own *Metaphysische Anfangsgründe* had suggested; (3) an objective basis for teleological judgment may, indeed, be *postulated* on the very basis of the "presentiment" or "hint" given us by nature, to which Kant himself had referred; and, in connection with these points, (4) Kant's unsuccessful approach to teleological judgments further adds to the case against the theory of intuition upon which it is based.[120]

Together, these objections free Schelling from the necessity of even defining the problem of final causality in Kant's manner. Now he need not consider it essential that the problem be worked out from a mechanistic starting point. In fact, he argues that as we employ an idea of an organic being in our judgments of nature, we must give up the possibility of ever explaining such beings mechanistically.[121] The conflict in the idea of a *natural product* that Kant correctly described as one between contingency and purpose—between, in other words, heteronomy and autonomy—need not be resolved in the manner Kant suggested (as a result of conflicting cognitive tendencies in human intelligence). Instead, the conflict can be transcended altogether [*aufgehoben*] if a more fundamental idea can be found that incorporates the notion of contingency and purpose into itself. In this case, what had been separated by a distinction of *human* intelligence can be reunited by that same intelligence, thereby putting intelligence and experience in harmony with each other once more. The concept Schelling selects to replace the dogmatic notion of a *natural product* and to bring about a union between free activity and activity in conformity to law [*Gesetz-mässigkeit*], is the process-concept of *natural impulse*.[122] The essential character of natural products is that they display a creative impulse [*der Bildungstrieb*] in one form or another. However, by appealing to the concept of natural impulse, Schelling does not mean to imply that the concept must be regarded as an uninterpretable notion. It is not an *explanation* for organic activity, and does not contain in itself an explanation for any particular organic structure. Being simply a "synthetic concept," it must be further analyzed into those conditions which makes the phenomenon of natural impulse possible.[123] For to simply postulate a *will* as the true thing-in-itself in place of an object is, to Schelling's way of thinking, no more acceptable as an approach to nature than was Kant's *a priori* rejection of teleological causality. What must be sought are entirely new fundamental principles of nature that apply to *all* organized material in general, and not simply to organisms as they are dogmatically understood. For more than anything else, Kant's difficulties resulted ultimately from the narrowness of his distinctions, and from the empiricist epistemology out of which he formed them.

The Structure of Schelling's Argument

The general structure of Schelling's case for his form of idealism can be put in the following manner corresponding to *modus tollens: if the world were as the dogmatist describes it, then our experience would be quite different from what it is, Hence, dogmatism is false.* If, in short, the dogmatist fails to establish his claims about the world, the error must lie with his assumptions. Kant, for example, argued for a concept of matter in terms of opposing forces, but then also tended to think of matter as a substantial and noumenal reality. This was because the critical approach of the *Critique* and the dogmatic intent of the *Metaphysische Anfangsgründe* could not be brought into harmony. Schelling, instead, chooses a radically critical approach and argues that what we call *matter* is nothing but force, and that because there is no force not involving the intent and experience of a spiritual, conscious being, the various structures of matter are actually the various forms of the self-reflection of that spiritual being. Formally, the argument could be reversed to establish spirit as a form of matter.

However, the inner *reality* of self-consciousness, which, as with Fichte's transcendental ego, cannot be destroyed by the self, rules out this possibility. In a similar vein, the flat dogmatic assertion of the existence of a noumenal reality of material substances independent of a knowing spirit is ruled out as philosophically gratuitous.

The same approach is taken in the causality argument. Kant had attempted to show that a causality of substances could account for our concept of a community of substances. However, he failed to prove even that we could derive a concept of coexistence from a causality of substances. Without a concept of coexistence no concept of community could be justified. Consequently, if we assume a causality of substances no concept of community can be established. But, to Schelling, the experience of community is undeniable, and therefore Kant's assumption that efficient causality is the primary mode of interaction is incorrect.

Hume also begins with empirical assumptions and is led to deny any justification for the inductive process. Yet, even he realized that his answer could not be a final one. For if objects do exist independently of the mind, and if the mind's undeniable adherence to the inductive principle is based on what it customarily observes, then there must at least be a preestablished harmony between the mental and the physical, if not, as Schelling would argue later, an essential and reciprocal relation.

Finally, in the third argument, given Kant's Newtonian starting point, teleological judgments were given no status; however, because, once more, it is contrary to our experience to reject the employment of such judgments, Kant's position must be rejected instead.

Schelling's approach in these arguments is synthetic and holistic rather than analytic. The facts of human experience must be accounted for in terms that leave the meanings of those facts *as experienced* intact. This means essentially that reality consists of *relations,* and not of objects or isolated experiences. To explain something, then, is not only to show of what parts it is comprised, but of what wholes it is a part as well. Not only must the parts be delineated in the thing to be explained, as they are in the traditional empirical approaches to the study of nature and intelligence; *how* the parts can interact as they do must be explained as well. And to do this we must look beyond the object itself to the broader reality of which it is a part. This means, in effect, that "there is no analysis without synthesis."[124] Analysis by itself leads to the dead end of atomism and leaves the *explanandum* unexplained.

Synthetic explanation does not avoid the use of principles of broad generality. For if the *explanans* were more complex than the *explanandum,* it would not explain it. However, the principles must contain within themselves the potential to explain complex relations in nature such as those involved in growth and intelligence. To do this they must be able to differentiate between simple and complex processes, something the mechanistic approach cannot do. Here the answer for Schelling lies in setting forth principles that supply a rationale for *dialectical processes*. The notion of a *hierarchy* and a rule for moving from one level to another takes the place of the static mechanistic view. In this way the *higher* need not be explained in terms of the *lower*, but rather in terms of the still higher of which it is a simpler manifestation, and toward which it strives. Synthetic explanation, then, seeks to *transcend* the *explanandum* by appealing to such principles. We now turn to Schelling's discussion of these.

3

The Idea of Nature

Fundamental Principles

The attack on mechanistic thinking embodied in the arguments on matter, causality, and organic form opens the way for the possibility of a *Naturphilosophie*. As such, the attack has so far merely a negative result: it points to the flaws in the idea of mechanical explanation and it challenges classical Newtonian conceptions of nature. Unless such thinking could be called critically into question, any other paradigm of science would in all likelihood not be taken seriously. Now Schelling must show that his own paradigm of science is a more desirable one. This is the positive side of his task.

In his work prior to the *Ideen zu einer Philosophie der Natur* (1797) Schelling was concerned with the critical question of how philosophy is possible. In his earliest works, that question was treated within the limits set for the most part by Fichte. Yet even then Schelling showed a desire for a more *detailed* development of the idea of an autonomous self positing a nonself. Gradually he abandoned the point of view of a *radically* transcendental self as too one-sided and abstract. Philosophy, he came to believe, must give a complete account of what we take to be *real* in the broadest sense of the word. It cannot, in effect, assume that our common-sense beliefs are utterly without merit, which is what an anti-dogmatic critique involves in its simplest form. Rather, a more thoroughgoing criticism must be undertaken that sheds light on why it is that we have the experiences, and the beliefs about the experiences, that we in fact have. This is what a truly critical philosophy must involve.

This early quest to establish the credentials of philosophy really constitutes the link between Schelling's early writings and his *Naturphilosophie*. For the condition for the possibility of philosophy as *Wissenschaft* is also the basic principle of *Naturphilosopie*, namely, that *what is real is also ideal, and what is ideal is real.*[1] Without this assumption, genuine knowledge is not possible. Without a kinship of some sort between the knower and the known, the knower would be enclosed within his own phenomenal world. Even the *idea* of a thing-in-itself would be unthinkable under these circumstances. The real as being-in-itself must possess the character of intelligibility, and intelligence must contain the capacity for knowing the real. It is simply, in Schelling's view, self-stultifying to deny this; as a fundamental principle this identity need not be proven for "it is the assumption upon which all true science is founded."[2]

The fundamental principle also serves as the starting point of *Naturphilosophie*, for if the real is actually also ideal, then this ought to be shown by uncovering the idealistic kernal within the outer hull of empirical science. This is what Schelling first attempts to do in the *Ideen* and *Von der Welt-seele*. Later, in his *System des transzendentalen Idealismus*, the task would be just the reversed—instead of the ideal being uncovered in the real, the real would be shown to reflect the ideal. In his lectures *Über die Methode des akademischen Studiums* (1803), Schelling characterizes the identity of the ideal and real in the following manner: "The Ideas are the souls of things and the things are the bodies of the Ideas; in this sense the Ideas are necessarily infinite, the things finite. But the infinite and the finite cannot become one until they have achieved internal and essential equality. Consequently, where the finite, as finite, does not contain and express the whole infinite and is not itself the objective aspect of the infinite, the Idea cannot function as its soul, and the essence is not manifested in itself but through something else, namely, an existent."[3] By making the modality of the real and ideal the *finite* and the *infinite,* Schelling now has a way to link the fundamental principle with the study of nature, and to interpret that study idealistically. The influence of Spinoza is once more apparent here. Just as thought and extension were, for Spinoza, aspects of one Substance, for Schelling the real and ideal were united as identical from the point of view of the *Absolute.*[4] The Absolute comprises the ultimate totality of things as the unity in variety, and as the basis for a reciprocal interplay between the universal and particular. Schelling also characterizes it as a primordial *will,* which expresses itself in various worldly forms.[5]

Schelling's next task is to establish in more detail the conditions for the possibility of knowledge of the Absolute, based on the preceding fundamental principle. Knowledge, in this case, means the understanding of the necessary and sufficient conditions of what is known; it consists of the sort of knowledge an inventor has of his invention. Empiricism cannot supply such knowledge, for the standpoint of empiricism allows only for the "mere seeing" of objects in their *being.* It produces only *history* as the acceptable form of knowledge, i.e., only a chronology of sensory observations.[6] Hume, in Schelling's view, had shown what such a method of acquiring knowledge must come to. Instead, genuine knowledge begins when objects are understood in their *becoming,* and this results only when knowledge of *relations* is made possible.[7]

To achieve this knowledge the results of scientific experimentation must be explained in terms of *a priori* principles. Schelling characterizes experimentation as "an invasion of nature . . . through freedom." Genuine science begins only "when we ourselves begin to produce the objects of that science."[8] An experiment, then, is not simply a question put to nature, for "every question contains an implicit *a priori* judgment; hence, every experiment that is an experiment is a prophecy," that is, is tied to a particular theoretical outlook.[9] Then, because "we *know* only the self-produced," the capacity to control phenomena makes possible experimentation, and experimentation makes possible genuine knowledge.[10] However, unlike the empiricists' use of experimentation, the *speculative physicist* recognizes the essential and decisive role of *a priori* principles in the formulation of scientific knowledge.

Schelling suggests the following six principles as those, which, along with the fundamental principle, must be accepted for science as *Wissenschaft* to be possible:

(1) *Nature constitutes a System:* all phenomena are interconnected through "intermediate links," which derive from the "ultimate conditions of Nature."[11] The idea of a system demands that there be such ultimate conditions, for without them the systematic unity of nature could not be established.

(2) *Nature involves both process and product:* this "universal duality" of nature cannot be transcended in favor of one or the other. If nature were simply product, the condition of its productivity would lie outside of it, which, given his definition of nature as a self-contained system, is impossible for Schelling. On the other hand, because the absolute condition for its productivity lies within itself, as in Spinoza's system, without a postulated duality nature would be at "absolute rest."[12] If nature were pure process alone, there would be nothing toward which it strived; no product would be produced to resist the further encroachments of process, even if temporarily, and so there would be no process in the first place.

(3) *The relation between product (natura naturata) and productivity (natura naturans) is ultimately one of identity:* if nature is a system and, therefore, a unity within which a duality of productivity and product must be maintained, this can be possible only through the underlying communion and reciprocal interplay between product and productivity.[13] In other words, the idea of nature cannot be entertained exclusive of the ideas of reversibility and feedback. This principle also

implies that "absolute continuity" in nature must be assumed as well, for without continuity the transition from product to productivity and vice versa could not be guaranteed in principle. However, this continuity can be intuited only intellectually and cannot be the result of *reflection*, which is based on the operation of making discriminations and establishing boundaries. While it is through reflection that the permanence of the product is established, it is through the intellectual intuition of connections that continuity is apprehended.[14]

(4) *The activity of nature results from the interplay of opposing forces:* if all forces in nature were in harmony, nothing could hinder the process of nature from moving rapidly to completion; in fact, nature would already have achieved harmony and rest by now. Yet, Schelling notes, in the idea of *becoming* there is contained the idea of an evolution *by degrees.*[15] Even a provisional permanence must imply a "retarding agent" of some sort, which holds the productive forces of nature at bay during the duration of the product's existence, no matter how brief that duration may be.[16] This means that in some way nature must be at odds with itself. For again if, Schelling argues, we assume that nature is pure productivity in harmony with itself, then no determination and individuation would be possible for it. If the principle of determination lies outside of nature, however, this renders nature at once a mere product and so destroys its absolute productivity. Either alternative is undesirable for him because each undermines the idea of nature as a dynamic relation between *natura naturans* and *natura naturata*. Rather, we must assume simply that there is a "primordial sundering in Nature itself." All scientific explanations must begin with this antithetical character in nature. Without being able to explain this antithesis itself, all science can do is reduce all the phenomena of nature "to that primordial antithesis in the heart of Nature, *which does not, however, itself appear.*"[17]

(5) *The opposing forces of nature are themselves equal:* here Schelling simply remarks that "there is no reason for supposing them unequal."[18] However, there certainly is a reason

for thinking them unequal; if they were equal, then nature would either be in a state of perpetual equilibrium or would already have been annihilated, but this appears contrary to the idea of nature as a dynamic process. For example, if the opposing forces of nature were, say, embodied in matter and antimatter, there would have to be some reason why annihilation has not yet taken place, such as that these forces have had different origins and have not yet come into contact. However, this would undermine the notion of nature as a unitary system. Consequently, there must be something *in* nature that makes dynamic change possible. Schelling could simply have postulated a condition of inequality somewhat analogous to the Second Law of Thermodynamics to explain the absence of equilibrium.

There are probably several reasons why he did not choose such a source. Ultimately, nature was regarded by him as a system of identities. To assume one of the opposing forces greater in magnitude than another would be to destroy this identity. What he required was that *inequality emerge out of ultimate identity*. The origin of such a fundamental inequality would, instead, have to be derived from a condition outside of nature. Also, in postulating such an inequality Schelling would have to admit that he was not *deducing* the principles of *Naturphilosophie a priori* from the idea of nature, for in this case the inequality of opposing forces would derive only from what we *empirically* observe. Then the inequality of nature, or, in other words, its *time's arrow*, would not be established *a priori*. Consequently, he is faced with a dilemma, or what he prefers to call a "contradiction."[19] If the forces are unequal, then he can account for change, though not in an *a priori* fashion; if they are equal, he explains persistence and harmony, but this leads to the annihilation of nature itself as a *dynamic* process.

Schelling's answer involves the concept of a *dialectical* relation between the opposing forces as a way of explaining how inequality emerges out of equality. First, the opposition between change and persistence is overcome: "No *subsistence* of a product is thinkable *without a continual process of being reproduced*. The product must be thought of as *annihilated at every step*, and at *every step reproduced anew*."[20] Persistence implies activity and, in fact, constant change, but in a context where no change is observed. There is, then, nothing *essentially* persistent about the stability of a product that only *manifests* itself as persistent. All processes of equilibrium are disruptable in principle because the equilibrium involved is not maintained internally but, rather, externally. It is clear, however, that Schelling has to be speaking here only of *natura naturata*, and not of the *whole* of nature, which is dependent on nothing lying outside of it. With respect to the totality of nature only an internal equilibrium is possible in accordance with the idea of nature here being developed by him. How, then, can Schelling avoid the conclusion that a genuine persistence in nature as a whole must result in an ultimate statis and inactivity? He finds the answer to this difficulty in the final principle.

(6) *Nature is structured hierarchically and its activity is in accordance with laws of evolution*: if the equilibrium of the whole is not to result in an equilibrium among all parts, this could occur only if natural processes were in some way aspects of an evolutionary process. For it is in the idea of evolutionary dialectic that the conflict of persistence and change is fully overcome: "This seeming product, which is reproduced at every step, cannot be a really infinite product, for otherwise productivity would exhaust itself in it; similarly it cannot be a finite product, for it is the force of the whole of nature that pours itself into it. It must, therefore, be both infinite and finite; it must be only seemingly finite, but in infinite development."[21] In other words, the *part* reflects a particular moment in the development of the whole. "In every product," he continues, "lies the germ of the universe."[22]

In this process of evolution nature builds on what it has hitherto accomplished; in short, it constructs itself hierarchically: "The product evolves itself ad infinitum. *In this evolution, therefore, nothing can happen which is not already a product (synthesis) and which might not divide up into new factors, each of these again having its factors.*"[23] This process must be open-ended in principle because, if it were not, the universe would tend to resolve itself once more into "original and simple activities."[24] The variety and proliferation of qualitative differentiation prove, according to Schelling, that there is a tendency in nature to combine these simple activities into ensembles of complex activities. This also means that qualitative distinctions, in his view, cannot be deduced from quantitative ones, for we can never explain *why* it is that certain quantitative factors produce the qualitative ones that they do.[25]

Schelling's next task is to display in more detail "the successive steps of the *transition of productivity* into product."[26] The difficulty that confronts the interpreter of his *Naturphilosophie* at this point, however, is that between 1797 and 1806 Schelling produces at least six major reformulations of his system. In general, however, we can say that the development of his thinking during this time proceeds from the concrete and piecemeal to the more abstract and architectonic. His *Erster Entwurf eines Systems der Naturphilosophie* (1799), for example, reflects Schelling's first effort to give systematic clarity to the more haphazard work he had set out in the *Ideen* and *Von der Weltseele*.

One obvious conclusion derived from the above principles is that rule-governed activity can be seen in the actual processes of nature. Among other things this means that similar conditions will produce similar results. If nature is truly a system and if no extra-natural factors are allowed, this means that we could expect a deduction from abstract principles to concrete phenomena to be possible. For at any given level of development in nature, Schelling argues, there must correspond to that level uniquely characteristic forms [*Gestaltung*] that cannot appear under any other conditions.[27] These forms ultimately correspond to the interplay between the opposing forces of nature as the infinite in finite development. It is this very condition that makes possible natural science as a genuine natural *history* insofar as it displays a rule-governed evolutionary process and so is more than a mere description of nature [*Naturbeschreibung*].[28]

Light and Gravity

The differentiation of nature into products is established initially through the agency of two complementary forces — *Gravity* [*Schwere*] and *Light-essence* [*Lichtwesen*]. Without these forces no communication among the forms of nature would be possible, and therefore no relations could be established. All of the particular forms of nature result from those two principles, which first combine to produce *matter* [*Materie*] in its various forms — solid, liquid, gas — and also the exchanges of energy, which *appear* within the system as heat, light [*Licht*], and electricity.[29]

A resolution of these forces is not possible, for there is no product resulting from their interaction that does not at the same time produce further oppositions within and without itself. Thus, the struggles in nature intensify with the proliferation of the products of nature itself.[30] It is only in "dead matter" that there exists no opposition, but then such matter could not generate activity and variety in the first place.[31] If A and B constitute, in Schelling's terms, the "one primary antithesis, between the limits of which all nature must lie," then the synthesis, C, of A and B, is capable of forming an opposition with either A or B, thus bringing about a fourth product, D, which, in turn, is capable of forming an opposition to the first three, and so on.[32] This dialectic is possible only if opposing elements are not entirely consumed (transcended) in their resulting product. *While* the product is being formed, it becomes at the same time a new condition for opposition among its own forming elements: "The Universe which forms itself from the center towards the periphery, *seeks* the point at which even the extreme antitheses of nature cancel themselves; the impossibility of this cancelling guarantees the infinity of the Universe."[33]

The force of gravity represents to Schelling the tendency of nature to move toward a *single* ideal point— a single center of gravity, and therefore a complete heterogeneity of being and nothingness. Light-essence, on the other hand, represents the opposite tendency, that of seeking a total uniformity and homogeneity in the form of absolute extensity. Its character is to move perpetually beyond itself unless checked by gravity. *Matter,* then, does not represent a substance, but a nexus of such opposing tendencies, an idea Kant had established earlier, though only in its abstract form.[34]

Interestingly, Schelling regards light-essence as the condition for unifying nature into a system that manifests unity in variety, and inasmuch as "the construction of *Naturphilosophie* could only be realized in the interconnectedness of the whole according to its necessity," light supplies the condition for such construction.[35] In the earlier *Ideen* Schelling appears, instead, to contrast light-essence with matter, as would Hegel later, stating that the combination of the two produces an *organism.* However, he is careful to note even here that both are "mere attributes" of something in-itself [*das An-sich*].[36] The question, then, of whether observed light is a material or a mere medium, which Schelling conceives to be the difference between the theories of Newton and Euler, is rejected by him as one-sided. In both cases the phenomenon of light is being sought in some particular kind of entity. What these thinkers overlook is that we, as observers and as part of nature, always investigate the phenomenon of light from a certain point of view. Hence, all we can say is that "all light of which we are aware is simply a *phenomenon of development*[*Entwicklung*]." It manifests itself to us only in the destruction of equilibria, and because of its unparallelled speed and its diffusion properties constitutes to us the "primordial motion" of nature.[37] Our idea of a material object, on the other hand, is possible only if we assume an equilibrium or stability in the object, so that the ideas of matter and light are fundamentally at odds with each other. For this reason what light is *in itself* as light-essence, or as "a higher matter" is unknowable, either as material or medium, particle or wave, and so we must be content with the characterization of it as "a primordial duplicity" as well.[38] Motion, however, must remain at least part of its essential character, for if one begins with an essentially materialist outlook, like that of Hobbes and Newton, then motion itself becomes inexplicable. For this reason Schelling calls light "the first phenomenon of the universal force of nature, through which motion is increased and maintained."[39] Light as a *phenomenon* of nature, however, must not be mistaken for something in-itself, though it does give evidence of the "universal force" of nature by virtue of its observable characteristics.

Both light and material objects, Schelling claims, represent on the phenomenal level those noumenal forces of cohesion and expansion, attraction and repulsion, without which nature would not be possible. It is no wonder, then, that this "primordial duplicity" of nature manifests itself in light as particle and wave and, in material objects, as matter and motion. Both conditions are needed for them to *appear* to an observer, for the interplay of forces between process and product produces perception as well. Unfortunately, Schelling does not always clearly distinguish between *Matter* as the result of the prephenomenal equilibrium of opposing tendencies, and *matter* in the form of material objects as we know them. We must keep in mind that matter "in the abstract" as gravity constitutes the opposing principle to that of light-essence,[40] and that this does not conflict with the analysis of matter *as the result of* opposing forces, given previously, for that analysis really constitutes an analysis of the condition for the possibility of *determinate* matter in the form of *material objects*. Abstract matter, that is, *mass*, is simply a concept used to explain momentum, which is itself the result of interacting gravitational forces.[41] It is, then, gravitational force that is the opposing force of the motion of light-essence.It was only after 1799 that this became clearly established in Schelling's mind, however.

In accordance with the dialectical process that results from the interaction of the opposing forces, the concept of

nature as a dialectical system must now be connected up with
the body of knowledge produced by empirical science. The
dialectic unfolds because of the tension between those parts of
nature at equilibrium and those processes which represent an
energy-exchange and thus threaten equilibrium elsewhere.
These two states Schelling characterizes as, correspondingly,
ones of "indifference" and "difference."[42] Any dynamic
process consists of a transition from one state of "indifference"
to another. Schelling then suggests the following schema to
reflect the dialectic of this process:[43]

Thesis:	Unity of a Product	Magnetism
Antithesis:	Duplicity of Products	Electricity
Synthesis:	Unity of Products	Chemical Process

Material objects, as we know them, do not appear in
either of the first two stages. The "products" referred to here
are probably the localized interactions of the two primordial
forces, for at this point we are not speaking of objects but of
becoming and of *reproducibility* [*Reproducirtwerden*].[44] What
the *thesis* is supposed to represent is "the continual sinking
back into identity in gravitation toward the universal indif-
ference-point." This process is continual because the indifference point is never reached. Instead, a state of *"pure difference
without substrate"* is achieved, that is, magnetic attraction.[45]

When two such magnetic forces come into contact and a
difference exists between them, polarity results. This difference is relative and transitory—"the products themselves
dissolve."[46] However, dissolution occurs only if there are no
further antitheses. When, however, the antithesis between
another intensity and the previous polarity is established, a synthesis is achieved that results in a product with a substrate. Instead of one pole's simply canceling the other, an equilibrium
is now achieved. "This struggle," Schelling concludes, "will not
cease until there exists a common product. The product, while
forming itself, proceeds from both sides through all intermediate links that lie between the two products."[47] What

products will be formed will depend on the conditions of formation, which can be accounted for entirely in terms of the forces available.

This dialectic of the dynamic process Schelling calls "the synthesis of matter."[48] It begins with those primordial forces and moves up through the hierarchy of subatomic, atomic, and molecular structures. With the chemical processes the initial synthesis of the dynamics of material nature is finally achieved. And so, "if further composition is to occur, this circle must open again."[49]

When the circle does open again, dialectical development leads to the evolution of *organic nature*. The general schema now reads:[50]

	Inorganic	Organic
Thesis: Light-essence	Magnetism	Sensibility
Antithesis: Gravity	Electricity	Irritability
Synthesis: Matter	Chemical process	Creative instinct

Using this scheme, Schelling wishes to show that all of the phenomena of nature "are interwoven into one great interdependent whole."[51] He suggests, for example, that even such a highly descriptive science as geology might contain laws that could be deduced from the laws of magnetism, electricity, and chemistry. The schema also reflects the view that there is no essential difference between the organic and inorganic. Rather, the differences that do exist are ones that derive from the *degree* of complexity of structure. The more evolution proceeds toward the complex, the more difficult it becomes for the evolved product to achieve a state of indifference. Once irritability in the organism is established, it will continually respond to changes in its environment and will, through further development, seek to overcome those changes with its creative instinct. Yet, "because life consists in nothing more than a continual *prevention of the attainment of indifference* (a prevention of the absolute transition of productivity into product)," life itself becomes "an extremely artificial condition . . . wrenched, as it were, from Nature—the subsisting against her will."[52] Life reaches out beyond itself to achieve wholeness, but the more it does so, the more productive it must become. However, the more productive it becomes, the more difficult it becomes to satisfy the increasingly complex requirements for maintenance and for the attainment of wholeness and indifference.

This means that while there is no material in the organic that is not found, at least in part, in the inorganic, it does not follow that the organic can be reduced to the inorganic. Organic forms are, by nature, forms in the process of perpetual reformation, never achieving indifference long enough to make them subject for study in the way inorganic nature can be studied. Out of the synthesis of matter emerges this "higher snythesis" of organic forms, which, in Schelling's view, shows that nature must be regarded as *"absolutely* organic," for it is in the highest, most complex products of nature that the essence of nature must be found.[53]

In his *Darstellung meines Systems der Philosophie* (1801) Schelling presented another exposition of his *Naturphilosophie,* this time more in the manner of Spinoza.[54] The following are some of the major propositions of the system:

(1) *Reason is the total indifference of subjective and objective.*

(2) *Outside of Reason there is nothing.*

(3) *Reason is One in the absolute sense.*

(4) *The highest law of the existence of Reason, and so of all existence, is the law of identity.*

(7) *The only unconditioned knowledge [Erkenntniss] is that of absolute identity $(A = A)$.*

(10) *The absolute identity is absolutely infinite.*

(13) *Nothing comes into being in itself.*

(14) *Nothing is to be examined individually.*

(20) *The self-knowledge of the absolute indentity is infinite and undifferentiated.*

(21) *The absolute identity cannot know itself infinitely without infinitely positing itself as subject and object.* This

proposition Schelling considers self-evident.

(23) *Nothing but a quantitative different is possible between subject and object.* This is one of the most crucial and perplexing of the propositions, one often singled out by Hegel for criticism. Schelling remarks that no qualitative difference could exist between subject and object; yet a preponderance [*Übergewicht*] in appearance [*Ansehen*] of subjectivity or objectivity is possible. In the identity $A = A$ there is no difference between each A in itself, but in the judgment "$A = A$" the former A contains a preponderance of subjectivity [*Überwiegende Subjectivität*], and the latter a preponderance of objectivity. In a later footnote Schelling attempts to clarify this notion, noting that the difference spoken of is actually a "formal" one; for example, between the pure idea *triangle* and particular triangles there is a difference, though not a qualitative one. Considering triangles in their totality, that is, in their most abstract form, there is no quantitative difference between them insofar as they remain undifferentiated; in their particularity, however, they are differentiated quantitatively. Analogously, *triangle* here is supposed to refer to Reason in its totality, while particular triangles refer to particular differentiated things.[55]

(25) *No quantitative difference is thinkable in relation to the absolute identity.*

(29) *Quantitative difference is thinkable only in respect to individual beings or things.*

(32) *The absolute identity is not the cause of the Universe, but is the Universe itself.*

(35) *Nothing individual has the ground of its existence in itself.*

(36) *Every individual being is determined through another individual being.*

(37) *The quantitative difference of subjective and objective is the ground of all finiteness.*

(38) *Every individual being is a definite form of the being of the absolute identity, though not its being itself, which is only in the totality.* This is supposed to follow from the notion that only a formal distinction between particulars and the

totality exists. The ground of specificity that establishes *"eine bestimmte Form des Seins"* has yet to be established, however.[56]

(39) *The absolute identity exists in the particular in the same form in which it exists in the totality.*

(41) *Every individual is a totality in relation to itself.*

(42) This proposition actually consists of two "explanations," usually an indication that Schelling is about to introduce an important distinction. In the second he sets out his idea of the *Potenzen* of nature. What exists, he notes, does so whenever there is an indifference between it and the remaining totality. When, then, an imbalance occurs and a difference is established, a *power* or *potency* occurs as well. At this point the object ceases to exist and the potency produces another. From the point of view of Reason, a potency emerges whenever there is a difference of subjectivity and objectivity.

(43) *The absolute identity only exists [ist] under the form of all potencies.*

(44) *All potencies are absolutely simultaneous.* This follows inasmuch as the absolute identity is eternal. We can also infer from this that, for Schelling, dialectical evolution does not take place in real time; thus any observable time's arrow in nature must be essentially illusory.

(47) *The constructed line is the form of existence of the absolute identity in the particular as well as in the whole.* Perhaps by this Schelling means that force is essentially vectorial, and therefore, so is the Absolute, insofar as it unfolds through opposing forces. Within the line, differentiation through segmentation is possible. Relative identities and duplicities become possible in this way, and also relative totalities (individuals). Terms such as *inner* and *outer, real* and *ideal* represent such relative duplicities. Schelling's intention, then, is to "construct the absolute totality through a real becoming [*Reellwerden*] of the subjective in all potencies, and the relative [totality] through a real becoming in the specific potency."[57] A reconstruction of Schelling's notation for the unfolding of duplicity out of unity is as follows:

1.	$A = A$	Absolute Identity
2.	$(A^1 = B) = (A^1 = B)$	Absolute Identity of Relative Identities.

Here $A^1 = B$ is a *relative identity,* which in identity with itself ($A = A$) constitutes an absolute identity; then letting $A^2 = (A^1 = B)$, differentiation within identity continues as,

   3. $[A^2 = (A^1 = B)] = [A^2 = (A^1 = B)]$, and so forth.

The first relative identity $(A^1 = B)$ is considered by Schelling to be the result of the force of gravity, though how this comes about is unexplained by him. As indicated earlier, a quantitative difference of forces would not do, because it would be left to explain how the forces became separated from the Absolute in the first place. For some reason, instead of making A equivalent to gravity and B to light-essence, which would at least present a parallel to his previous accounts, Schelling describes the duplicity of gravity and light-essence as $A^2 = (A^1 = B)$.

(62) *The A^2 is light.* Now, in an increasingly anthropomorphic vein Schelling writes, "light is an inner, gravity an outer intuition of nature."[58]

(65) *A and B in the relative identity of the second potency [A^2] exist in linear form.*

(66) *Matter as identity is composed of linear form, not only in particular, but in its entirety.*

(67) *The form of this line is the condition for Cohesion.*

(68) *The form of this line is that of Magnetism.*

(69) *Matter in its entirety appears as a magnet.*[59]

(74) *All distinctions between bodies result from the place they occupy in the Total Magnet.*

(80) *Every individual body strives to be a totality.* Schelling now introduces the potency manifested in electrical phenomena. The "difference" of two differing magnetic bodies that do not cancel themselves out by being equal and opposite produces the potency known as electricity. Hence, the schema for this potency is not a linear vector, but an *angle.*[60]

(90) *Heat conduction is an electrical process.*

(113) *The chemical process is mediated through magnetism and electricity.*

(122) *All so-called qualities of matter are merely powers of Cohesion.*

(143) *The absolute identity insofar as it exists under the form of A^2 and $A = B$ is efficiency* [*Wirksamkeit*], that is, the identity of force and activity. Schelling is preparing for a discussion of organic form, for *Wirksamkeit* becomes "the *indifference-ability* of the organism" where "organic indifference, the equilibrium of agitation, is health."[61]

(146) *The organism as organism is a totality not only in relation to itself, but absolutely.* This proposition appears to flatly contradict Schelling's distinction between relation and absolute totality.

(148) *Inorganic nature as such does not exist.*

(151) *Organization in particular as well as in its entirety must be thought of as arising through metamorphosis.*

From here Schelling goes on to describe the relations between the chemical elements, plants, and animals. His hierarchical approach leads to the formation of analogies such as *iron:water::animal:plant* and *north:south::plant:animal,* the latter of which Hegel would later criticize as both unscientific and unphilosophical.

4
The World System

The Problem of Individuation

Schelling's Spinozistic monism has a great deal in common with the view of nature implicit in General System Theory. Indeed, Schelling may be considered one of the first proponents of a systems point of view, inasmuch as he attempted to combine idealistic monism with the latest results of scientific experimentation. Like von Bertalanffy, Laszlo, Weiss, Koestler, and others, Schelling assumed that nature is an intelligibly organized unity.[1] As a *World System* nature must be understood as "a unity, which is self-maintaining, and which, contained within itself, requires no ground outside of itself for its movement and interconnectedness."[2]

Accepting this idea of nature has certain epistemological implications that are essentially anti-Cartesian in nature. For one thing, Archimedean objectivity must be abandoned, for we must consider *ourselves* a part of nature as well, and we must explain how it can be possible for us to formulate knowledge of the World System. Nature itself cannot be an object to anything that is a part of it, so that we must reject any explanation of nature that does not also contain a way of explaining the possibility of such knowledge without the Archimedean assumption. Mechanistic explanations not only called for a need to explain motion through some *external* condition, but also could not be accepted by Schelling because they were not capable of explaining intellectual activity, which itself was part of the phenomena of nature. Such explanations ruled out capabilities in nature that were clearly at odds with what we knew of the behavior and activities of the higher organisms.

Mechanistic explanations are possible and have enjoyed some success only because the *explananda,* material bodies in motion, belong to a realm of nature that need be explained only in a highly simplified and elliptical manner. Newtonian science represents such a surface view of natural events and is limited by its uncritical pluralism, reliance on sense-perception, and uncriticized belief in the uniformity of nature. It would be a mistake, in Schelling's view, to overlook these very specific conditions of mechanistic explanation and universalize the procedure for use in explaining not only more complicated processes but also the totality of nature itself. It is preferable, he argues, to speak of nature as a "universal organism" rather than as a mechanical machine.[3] However, it is still misleading to do so, because concepts such as *life* and *mechanical force* remain the result of an essentially pluralistic metaphysical outlook, as well as of a Cartesian espitemology. In a World System both the *organic* and *inorganic* are to be explained in terms of structural properties and functional relationships.[4] It is for this reason that Schelling maintains that "as soon as the idea of nature as a *whole* becomes possible for us, the opposition between mechanism and organism, which had blocked the progress of natural science long enough vanishes."[5]

What is needed, then, is a unified, interdisciplinary approach to the study of nature, of the sort outlined in the lectures on the method of academic studies, one overcoming the opposition between mechanism and organism by means of a *single* theory that would explain *mechanistic* and *organic* phenomena in nature. The only difference between such kinds of phenomena derives from the context and assumptions of scientific inquiry. In one sense, a leaf falling from a tree is a mechanical event, but in another sense it is an organic event involving, among other things, such complicated processes as seasonal variation, and the effect that decaying leaves will have on the fertility of the soils. The same may be said for the movement of land masses, erosion, chemical composition and decomposition, and so forth. In postulating nature as a mechanical clockwork, we restrict the level of explanation solely to that of simple, mechanical cause/effect between two single and isolated events. However, in considering nature to be a "universal organism," we can make possible explanations of more sophisticated interactions of events and subsume mechanistic laws under organic laws.[6]

Mechanical explanations result, in Schelling's view, from the assumption that nature can only be understood as a succession of individual events, and that only by using inductive inference can those events be structured. However, such a procedure contains no *principle of individuation*, which consequently makes it inadequate as an explanation of what we actually experience. Sensory experience is not a stream of perceived events, but a system of structured, coexisting wholes. In order to overcome the distinction between mechanical and organic processes, Schelling now introduces a form of the modern concept of *feedback* into his picture of the World System.

Whenever individuation occurs in nature, the "linear" sequence of cause and effect must be interrupted. The simplest idea of motion is motion in a straight line, or a force directed in a single direction. Organization occurs whenever a manifold of forces interact to produce an enduring product.[7] In fact, individuation and organization are one-and-the-same process. "*In nature,*" Schelling writes, "*what bears the character of individuality must be an organization, and vice versa.*"[8]

Yet, there must also be a *principle* of individuation, at least one that is understood in the context of some perceiver, even if it is not to be one that is eternally grounded in some absolute and enduring structure. In the early phases of Schelling's throught, that is, before 1799, the Absolute was what he called the "World Soul" which, like Spinoza's *Substance*, was largely regarded as ahistorical, eternal, and essentially changeless. At that time what unified the manifold of forces in nature, thus making possible individuals rather than "mere appearances," was a *concept* which Schelling often characterized as something fixed, resting, and unchangeable.[9] The function of the concept was to join together forces that could produce a product, that is, something containing form [*Form und Gestalt*], something not "fluid."[10]

This static explanation, however, did not satisfy him for very long. Having overcome the traditional pluralism embodied in an Aristotelian/Newtonian metaphysical outlook by means of Spinoza's monism, there still remained the problem of recasting that monism into a dynamic *Naturphilosophie*. As a start it was clear that if the World System was to be the true unconditioned, the answer to individuation would have to be found within it. Here Schelling chose to define the problem in epistemological terms, that is, as a problem of how *knowledge* of particulars could be possible. For, to ask *in general* how the infinite unfolds in a finite manner would imply that something outside of the World System could explain differentiation within it. With nothing outside of the World System, to explain differentiation and individuation is to explain it exclusively from some point of view.

Establishing the condition for individuation Schelling considers the "highest problem of all science," one that must be solved in a critical manner by a new kind of transcendental philosophy.[11] In answering it he utilizes the notions of *evolution, hierarchy,* and *structural isomorphism* introduced in the previous chapter. The World System is comprised of a hierarchy of subsystems, for if nature constructs its organizations in a dialectical manner, those organizations become interconnected hierarchically.[12] This evolution of complex systems from simpler ones Schelling characterizes as *dynamic* and *epigenetic*, while the devolution of complex forms becomes "an infinite *involution*" and an "*absolute involution.*"[13] Forms evolve and, through their interaction with the environment, possibilities of further evolution emerge. The more complex an organization becomes, the more its maintenance depends on highly complicated networks of subsystem/ World-System interactions. And as forms become more complex, indifference becomes progressively more difficult to achieve, for Schelling's "dynamic" evolution produces what von Bertalanffy has called "open systems," that is, systems that are capable of "metabolism, growth, development, self-regulation, response to stimuli, spontaneous activity," in contrast to closed systems, which do not interact with their environment and which are maintained in a static equilibrium rather than in a dynamic, steady state.[14]

It is in this context of a hierarchy of systems that the question of knowledge of individuals is now raised. Just as there is no substantial difference between the inorganic and organic in the World System, neither is there between the "mental" and the "physical." Each represents a certain configuration of subsystems in relation to other subsystems. Laszlo has described this position as "biperspectivism," as the view that mind-events and physical-events are "distinct but correlative types of events" in an overall psychophysical system: "Such systems are not 'dual' but 'biperspectival': they are single, self-consistent systems of events, observable from two points of view. When 'lived,' such a system is a system of mind-events, viz., a 'cognitive system'. When looked at from any other viewpoint, the system is a system of physical-events, i.e., a 'natural system'."[15] Each type of subsystem, because it is part of the overall system, displays structural isomorphism in relation to other subsystems, sharing properties like feedback capacity, energy-exchange, assimilation, dendritic structure, etcetera.[16] Within this approach, there cannot be said to be individuals in any absolute sense, for what is part of the perspective of one subsystem may not be of another. The subsystems themselves are individuals only in the sense that they reflect the various manifestations of the three dialectical structures—thesis, antithesis, synthesis—in the form of the three *potencies*. In other words, the true constants are the *relations* out of which the object as force, and the mind as idea, are constituted.

The Transcendental Deduction of the Real

Inasmuch as Schelling intended the *System des transzendentalen Idealismus* and the *Ideen* to be two complementary approaches to the World System as Absolute—one mental and one physical—his outlook can be considered biperspectival as well.[17] He notes, for example, that what the "primordial struggle of self-consciousness" is in the transcendental viewpoint, the "primordial struggle of the elements" is in the physical viewpoint.[18] Mind-events are themselves part of the epigenetic and dialectical development of the World System and it is for this reason that the *real* and the *ideal* can be ultimately the same. However, it was not until 1800 that he fully tried to work out this point of view.

As a result of his early Fichtean explorations, Schelling became convinced that consciousness of the self occurred simultaneously with consciousness of the nonself, and that it was mistaken to believe that the former was the condition of the latter. The primordial activity of a self-positing Fichtean ego could not be separated from the equally primordial activity of a nonself working on the self.[19] Consequently, the same "potencies" that are manifested as real in *Naturphilosophie* should also be found as ideal in transcendental philosophy. Schelling suggests the following schema for this:[20]

	Ideal	*Real*
First Potency: Unity in Variety	Self-consciousness	Quantity
Second Potency: Variety in Unity	Sensation	Quality
Third Potency: Unity in Varied Unities	Intuition	Relation

In relation to "cognitive" events the three potencies are manifested respectively as *reflection, judgment,* and *positing* [*die Setzende*], while in terms of "physical" events they are manifested as *substance, accident,* and *physical object.* Both "quantity" and "self-consciousness" are within themselves undifferentiated and nonqualitative (unity), while at the same time they refer beyond themselves to something that qualifies them in various ways (variety). With "sensation" and "quality" a definite character is presented, which then implies differentiation (variety), yet within the character itself no differentiation occurs (unity). Finally, in "intuition" and "relation" a single awareness (unity) of the relatedness among several qualities (varied unities) is established. Self-consciousness is manifested in "reflection," which is the enduring character (unity) we find in differing mental experiences (variety), while in "judgment" two qualities (variety) are linked together as one (unity). "Positing," on the other hand, is the act of relating and coordinating various sensations into the conscious unity of a material object. In all three cases the third potency is the synthesis of the first two. Just as a physical object, in Schelling's view, represents a unity of quantity and quality, intuition is the unification of self-consciousness with the data of sense-perception, and positing is the result of a capacity to make judgements reflectively. The ability to see the underlying unity of the objective and subjective, which Schelling attributes to "intellectual intuition," would be one example of such sophisticated reflection.

In the *System des transzendentalen Idealismus* Schelling attempted to show in more detail how the real could be understood from the viewpoint of the ideal. This meant that he had to begin from the standpoint of a knowing intelligence. This marked a return to the epistemological issues that had concerned him in the years before the development of his *Naturphilosophie.* Now Schelling argues once more that if knowledge is to be possible, a condition must be established for unifying the objective and subjective.[21] This condition, he concludes, can only be self-consciousness, in that no other condition could be established *by us as knowers.*[22] Self-consciousness itself involves an act of combining analytic and synthetic knowledge; in other words, self-knowledge has the necessity possessed by relations of ideas, but also the contingency of a matter of fact; in short, self-knowledge is synthetic *a priori*.

It is through the capacity of intellectual intution that self-knowledge can be possible for us. Its apodictic character is established because in intuitive knowing the object of knowledge is, in some way, identical to the process of knowing itself. Therefore, act and object are identical. Transcendental knowledge, then, which results from intellectual intution, takes the form of knowledge that "freely makes its object."[23] No condition outside of the self can be established for such knowledge. And because the self itself is known only transcendentally, it cannot be considered an object in its own right. For, to ask what the self is could not be a legitimate question for Schelling simply because the self is not the sort of thing that *is*.[24] In fact, it is only through the conscious experience of the self that things or objects are said *to be*. The very problem of the nature of the self results from the false alternative that *thing* and *no-thing* are the only two categories of reality. Schelling sees no reason why a third category, namely, *activity*, could not be just as primordial.

Up to now in his deduction of the real from the ideal, Schelling has argued that "self-consciousness is the absolute act through which everything is posited for the self."[25] Fichte had come this far as well. At this point, his problem is similar to the one he confronted and brushed aside five years earlier when he rejected the Fichtean standpoint as being onesidedly subjective, namely, how to expand the Fichtean transcendental standpoint, with its simple, distinctionless identity of act and object, into a philosophy that could shed light on the nature of the ideal in the real itself.

Schelling's answer is found in what he considers to be the capacity of consciousness to become reflective upon itself through the free act of simulation [*die freie Nachahmung*].[26] Consciousness can freely create its self *as object* and freely reflect upon that self, and then reflect upon that reflection. Formally, this notion is similar to Laszlo's "system's philosophy of consciousness." Laszlo argues that there is a tendency in human mental activity to generalize cognitive experiences of level L_n, thereby creating a higher level, $L_n + 1$: "The codes confirmed in L_n may in turn become the 'effective environment' of a cognitive circuit on level $L_n + 1$, the codes of which are mappings of the L_n codes; and so on. . . .Thereafter, the levels progressively reduce to increasingly difficult and unproductive feats of introspection."[27] However, instead of beginning, as in Laszlo's bio-cybernetic model of mind, from sensory experience and proceeding to abstract, reflective consciousness, Schelling's model reverses the procedure in accordance with the transcendental approach. Unlike Laszlo, who finds transcendental reflection to be the most unproductive activity of consciousness, Schelling is confident that he can dialectically generate from it all of the richness of human experience.

The dialectic begins with the claim that, in the act of "simulating" experiences in consciousness, we link together two experiences—the experience simulated, *A*, and the present awareness of simulating it, *B*. In so doing we demarcate and freely set limits to our experiences [*Begrenzung*], and establish a temporal order [*Zeitreihe*] between them. Time-consciousness, then, proceeds out of the distinctions self-consciousness makes. Once this "absolute synthesis" between *A* and *B* occurs, we can reflect upon that unity as well. However, now something *novel* emerges. With the introduction of a temporal order I see that the product of my free experience takes on the character of *necessity;* that is, I cannot freely reverse the order of *A* and *B*.[28] It is from this experience of necessity that the idea of the "real" first "evolves." Now for the first time consciousness comes to be at odds with itself, and it is this realization that produces in self-consciousness "an endless antagonism" with itself.[29]

The subsequent struggle produces a "history of self-consciousness" that follows a patterned development consisting of three "epochs." In the first epoch the encounter by consciousness of the "real" takes its most abstract form—as the awareness of a "mere stuff."[30] By reflecting on the nature of the distinction between *A* and *B* the self comes to conceive of the possibility of a subject/object distinction, and so realizes the possibility of regarding itself as either subject or object. The self now realizes that it is able to "intuit" an object; prior to this no object was raised to its consciousness to intuit, for "intuiting and delimiting [*Begrenzen*] are primordially the same."[31] However, at this stage in the first epoch, the self does not yet realize this; only *we as philosophers* can see the connection. What the self at that point assumes is that its act of delimiting the real is actually its innocent *response* to a determinate reality, which it calls *sense-perception*. However, this act of the self's limiting itself must result from the sheer self-deception, for there is no other way, according to Schelling, to account for an intuiting self's becoming convinced that the real must become the standard for its thought, rather than, as we would expect, just the reverse occurring.

While the self tends to judge "appearance" as contingent, every appearance, and in fact "the entire system of our perceptions" must occur necessarily as it does. This is because perception is not a process connecting two separate realities, but is rather the result of an orderly pattern of deductions from the original condition of the self as an unconditioned, intuiting being. However, once again, only the transcendental philosopher knows this to be the case at this point.

The self does not, however, stay for long in the stance of uncritical dogmatism. The question arises for it as to whether its perceptions are derived from the object or from the subject. In order for this question to become possible, the self must be able to reflect on the difference between the act of perceiving and the object perceived. That it can do this means that it has moved from the standpoint of sense-perception to that of "productive intuition."[32] The object, to the self as subject, is now not a "mere stuff" as in sense-perception, but a "thing-in-itself." At this point the self takes its first step into the realm of philosophy by raising the question of the adequacy of its knowledge. It does not regard the object of its knowledge as a merely passive quality, but as something active that *causes* the subject to know it. For the first time the conflict between the "real" and the "ideal" takes the form of a conflict between a self conscious of itself as a self and the "world" apart from it. Again, this self is not the philosophical self of the transcendental standpoint, but the "practical" self with its everyday concerns.

The "world" as the realm in opposition to the self comes to be seen by the self as a realm of "matter." To the practical self the opposition of things-in-themselves is precisely that they constitute a domain that is alien to the self, and when the practical self becomes more philosophical it characterizes this alien factor as something nonintelligent and material. Finally, however, the increasingly reflective self explores the nature of matter itself, as Leibniz and Kant had done, and then sees its alien character fall away through the insight that the idea of matter reduces to the idea of force, and that even a force in opposition to the self is not independent of the self. In this way "productive intuition" overcomes the opposition of the "real" and "ideal" embodied in the practical standpoint. It is with this insight that the first epoch in the history of self-consciousness comes to a close.

Having overcome the practical, common-sense standpoint, the self comes to see all opposition to it as really "for-itself," and with this the second epoch begins. Now the self realizes that all of its knowledge is really a form of intuition. It sees that its common-sense knowledge was really a form of "outer intuition," and so seeks a more fundamental connection between the "inner" and "outer," "real" and "ideal."[33] The first epoch becomes reinterpreted from the point of view of the second; sensuous objects become intuited objects.[34]

In its rejection of the materiality of substance, qualities alone come to be considered "real." Yet, in the transcendentally reinterpreted experience of sense-perception, the tension between the objective and subjective remains. For even within this standpoint qualities are not considered merely subjective. The fact of their differentiation points to conditions that have yet to be explicated by the activity of the philosophizing self. Consequently, the self must still seek a ground that would establish a connection between the objective and subjective. Having rejected as naive any answer that establishes that ground in some sort of material or otherwise substantial connection, the self now grasps a condition that is, in differing respects, both objective and subjective — *Time*. Whereas in the first epoch temporal order was the source of the first subjective/ objective distinction, in the second it becomes the consciously apprehended source of the difference between the intuiting (which is always timeless) and the intuited. The self now understands itself as "being present" and for the first time becomes conscious of itself not as a practical self, but as a "thinking" self. Time-consciousness, in other words, becomes, in turn, the condition for a full and developed self-consciousness.[35]

Having achieved the standpoint of its being-in-itself, the ideas of *coming-to-be* and *passing away* become possible for the self. In other words, the self now grasps the concept of a *causal relation*. Schelling's "deduction of causality," as noted earlier, did not begin from the point of view of psychological atomism, thus avoiding the problem of causality defined as the task of finding the link between two separate events. Instead, causality is conceived as the form the *a priori* structure of time-consciousness takes in experience; it is, in Schelling's words, "the necessary condition under which alone the self can recognize the present object as object."[36] This structuring of events in experience is *necessary* in the sense that the order of events is not subject to the discretion of the self. And because for Schelling being self-conscious is always the consciousness of *being present*, the consciousness of the object is a being present as well; hence, it is always the consciousness of that object's coming-to-be causally.

Yet, just as the object as object is grasped only on the condition that a causal relation be understood by the self, the notion of causality itself is possible only for a self that can transcend the present through its consciousness of the past's relation to the present. Here Schelling observes that the self as a thinking, self-conscious self must be timeless to itself *at the time* it grasps the connection between the past and present, otherwise it would be perpetually in the present, which, in his view, would be impossible; for in that case, having no notion of a past, it could not see itself as present, and, in fact, would not even be self-conscious.[37] To account for the possibility of this capacity of the self to be "timeless," Schelling argues that in some manner the self as past must be able to achieve an "absolute synthesis" of its experience into the "absolute totality" of the World System.[38] Such a synthesis makes possible the self's consciousness of its experience as occurring *in a world*. This does not mean that the self is conscious of this totality as if it could be a content of its intelligence; rather, this *nonthetic* consciousness is necessary for the self to be able to be conscious of objects *within* the totality that is the Universe.[39]

We are now at the point in the transcendental dialectic of the history of self-consciousness where Schelling attempts to answer the question posed previously, namely, how knowledge of particulars is possible. Because any *individual* is perceived on the condition that it is an organization, this question takes the form of a question concerning the condition that makes possible our knowledge of the organic. Empirical intelligence remains on the level of experience as a succession of ideas [*Vorstellung*] and consequently restricts knowledge to the study of mechanical causation. As such it does not recognize the capacity of intelligence to transcend the finite succession of experience in the absolute synthesis needed to comprehend a "world." The transcendental philosopher, on the other hand, considers that the capacity of intelligence to grasp a totality, manifested both by its understanding of a world and by its conception of the organic unity of natural objects, is evidence that the process of perception and intellection cannot be explained mechanistically. In effect, intelligence is able to conceive of an object because the processes involved in the formation of objects are similar to, and connected with, the very processes that bring an object to consciousness. A similar idea is found in Spinoza's *Ethics*.

For Spinoza the order and connection of ideas is the

same as the order and connection of causes, for the reason that both ideas and material causation were considered by him to be attributes of the single Substance.[40] The mental and the physical are, then, not really separate processes. In relation to that collection of attributes known as the *human being*, mind and body are what they are only through the interaction of each with the other, for "the mind does not know itself, except insofar as it perceives the ideas of the modifications of the body."[41] Individual objects are not the cause of ideas, however; rather, only God, wherein lies the true interconnection of ideas and objects, is the cause of our ideas. Our knowledge of individual external objects is really simply "an individual mode of thinking." As such, that knowledge is "inadequate," because the human mind, being the idea of modifications of the human body produced by other bodies, "does not involve an adequate knowledge of the external body."[42] Only God could have such knowledge, inasmuch as "the mind can only imagine external bodies as actually existing."[43] Spinoza then concludes:

> Hence it follows that the human mind, when it perceives things after the common order of nature, has not an adequate but only confused and fragmentary knowledge of itself, of its own body, and of external bodies. For the mind does not know itself, except insofar as it perceives the ideas of the modifications of body. . .
> *Note.* — I say expressly, that the mind has not an adequate but only a confused knowledge of itself, its own body, and of external bodies, whenever it perceives things after the common order of nature; that is, whenever it is determined from without, namely, by the fortuitous play of circumstance, to regard this or that; not at such times as it is determined from within, that is, by the fact of regarding several things at once, to understand their points of agreement, difference, and contrast. Whenever it is determined in anywise from within, it regards things clearly and distinctly. . . .[44]

In Schelling's terms, understanding things according to the "common order of nature" is the sort of understanding achieved by the common-sense, empirical standpoint, where perception "is determined from without. . .by the fortuitous play of circumstance." The transcendental philosopher, understanding that perceptions are "determined from within," seeks the source of that determinism in the underlying unity of perceiver and perceived.

An example of Spinoza's claim that the idea of every external object is a given mode of thinking can be found in Schelling's remark that "every plant is a symbol of intelligence" and is also "a complex tendency of the soul."[45] In effect, this means that the perception of a plant could not be explained according to the simple mechanical model of psychological atomism. For something like a plant to be perceived as a *whole*, there must be some condition that unifies certain perceptions into the ongoing succession of perceptions. The possibility for this condition for Schelling, as for Spinoza, had to be found in the unity of the perceiver and perceived, that is, in the totality of the World System itself. A plant is perceived as a unity because there is some logical structure or schema in the cognitive process of the perceiver that makes that perception possible.[46] The same primal forces of the World System operate in the physical as well as in the mental realms, for only in this way could any perceiving take place. If we knew what these underlying principles were, we would be able to *deduce* completely all of the forms of nature and their possible variations, just as, in Spinoza's system, being God would mean seeing beyond the duality of the mental and physical. How *natura naturans* emerges precisely as *natura naturata* would then be explained through the understanding of such principles. However, as *part* of the World System the human intelligence must be *passive* in certain respects, in the sense that there will always be some part of the World System employed in knowing, and hence unknowable itself in principle.

What, in Schelling's view, the transcendental philosopher can do is deduce *in general* the condition for the possibility of knowledge of particular objects (organizations) at all. This deduction always remains within the standpoint of human intelligence, however. It is such a deduction that Schelling next takes up.

Human intelligence at this moment in the dialectic of the second epoch is capable of viewing itself "in its productive transition from cause to effect."[47] Time-consciousness is simultaneously the transcendence of itself, for to be aware of the passage of time implies that in some fashion the self is capable of standing outside of time. "But," Schelling says, "it cannot do this without making that sequence permanent or depicting it statically."[48] Organization is precisely the outcome of the synthesis of the changing stream of perceptions with the static, timeless intelligence; then, because "intelligence is an endless endeavor to organize itself," the sole activity of intelligence becomes the structuring of the stream of perceptions into something *organic*.[49] In this manner Schelling can reject the stance that experience in its simplest form is a mere montage of static, pointillist sense-data. The time-relation invariably structures our perceptions as a succession, so that if stasis is to be experienced it must result from a capacity of intelligence itself, a capacity that unfolds through the self-consciousness of that intelligence.

The more intelligence can organize its experience, the more it approaches the "absolute synthesis," or total intelligence without the sort of passivity just referred to. The more organized intelligence becomes, the more organized the world appears. This correlation between knowledge and organization, Schelling observes, can be observed in the products of nature. The more complex an organic structure is the greater is its capacity to receive information from its environment: "The deeper we descend into organic nature, the narrower becomes the world which represents organization in itself (or, which organization represents in itself), and the smaller becomes the portion of the universe which coalesces in organization."[50] Schelling then continues:

For example, the sense of hearing is unlocked much sooner,

because the world of the organism is expanded only within a very close range. The divine sense of sight comes much later, because through it the world is extended to a breadth which even the imagination is incapable of measuring. Leibniz bore witness to so great a veneration for light that he attributed higher perception to animals purely because they are receptive to impressions of light. But even where this sense emerges with all its outer covering, it still remains uncertain how far the sense itself extends, and whether light is not purely light for the highest organization.[51]

Intelligence actively synthesizes the stream of perceptions into a given organic unity whenever the organization that makes that intelligence possible is as complex as the organism perceived. A more-organized intelligence can, as in Descartes's *scala natura*, gain knowledge of less-organized structures. In this way, nature appears as a hierarchy to each intelligence, the upper limits of which are determined by that intelligence:

> Now intelligence, however, should intuit not only the sequence of its ideas generally, but also itself, namely, as active in this sequence. If it is to become an object to itself as active in the sequence (outwardly, it goes without saying, for the intelligence is now only outwardly intuiting), it must regard the sequence as maintained by an inner principle of activity. Now the internal sequence, however, when intuited externally is movement. But such an object is called "living."[52]

This means that the concepts of *life* and *nonlife* are *contextual* in nature and depend on the degree of the intelligence making the distinction. Everything organized, simply by virtue of its being organized, must have life "in the broadest sense of the word, i.e. must have in itself an internal principle of movement."[53] Nothing is perceived that is not organized, and everything organized is in reality "alive" to that perceiver, though from the point of view of the absolute synthesis of the World System, these distinctions disappear. Schelling then describes the particular limitations placed upon *human* intelligence as a result of its place in the World System:

This gradation of organizations, however, merely designates different moments of the evolution of the universe. Just as the intelligence constantly strives to represent the absolute synthesis through the succession [of ideas], so organic nature will constantly appear as struggling toward the universal organism and in battle against an inorganic nature. The limit of the succession in the ideas of the intelligence will also be the limit of [its] organization. But there must be an absolute limit to the intuiting of the intelligence; for us this limit is *light*. For although our sphere of intuition extends nearly into the immeasurable, nevertheless the limit of light cannot be the limit of the universe, and it is not mere hypothesis that beyond the world of light there shines with a light unknown to us a world which no longer falls within the sphere of our intuition.[54]

Because of the limits placed on a specific form of intuiting intelligence, it cannot grasp anything greater in the evolution of the universe than what is possible given its own capability. A purely sensuous intelligence cannot understand anything greater than a sensuous reality, and so can see no evolution beyond an unfolding of sensuous experience. Human intelligence with its ability to experience self-consciousness can view the goal of the evolution of the universe as the fullest development of self-consciousness. For Schelling, the highest product of evolution that human intelligence could understand is the human being understood as an organic and thinking being. As such, human intelligence can have no adequate knowledge of the Absolute, for its intuition is limited by the condition that it can understand only what light is capable of revealing to it. When intelligence makes itself an object to itself, that is, when it reflects on what it is that manifests intelligence, it can only understand itself in its *human* form. The limitation of light makes it impossible for human intelligence to understand how higher intelligences can be organized. Nor could particular human intelligences have any comprehension of what it would mean for there to be a group mind or general intelligence.

However, in order to avoid inconsistency, Schelling must claim that human intelligence can grasp the *idea* of organizations of greater complexity through transcendental reflection; this means it is capable of understanding that, no matter what it is that lies beyond its ken, organization must be applicable to it as well. For transcendental philosophy maintains that our understanding of reality first begins with the categories of substance and accident, then sees the necessity to employ the idea of a causal relation between substances, and finally attains the idea of an interactive, reciprocal process, a process beyond which no higher degree of organization is possible. Furthermore, because a plurality of substances would make possible only a causal relation if reciprocity transcends causality, so must pluralism lead to the postulation of a single, all-encompassing organization, in other words, *the absolute organization*."[55] Human intelligence, then, knows that it is part of a single, absolute organization, even if it does not understand precisely how the higher structures come to reflect higher intelligence.

Schelling, of course, must maintain, as had Descartes, that human intelligence is not perfect intelligence, the reason being that human intelligence identifies itself with a particular organism (its body) and distinguishes its body from the larger context of its environment. For perfect intelligence, nothing could be understood as lying beyond it. "In the gradation of organization," Schelling writes, "one level must be found which the intelligence is compelled to view as identical with itself."[56] At this level intelligence, regarded as an "evolution from primordial ideas," and material organization, regarded as an evolution of dynamic forces, become *identical* from the transcendental point of view. In other words, certain material forces come into interaction with certain more sophisticated spiritual forces (ideas) in what is from the ordinary point of view a *self*. This means that I am simultaneously a body and mind, but only on the condition that the evolution of ideas and that of material forces achieve an equal development, that is, are structurally isomorphic. Schelling suggests the following example to elucidate this. A person whose material structure malfunctions at birth in the manner *we* characterize as *blindness* has no idea of light. To an observer accustomed to regarding sight as an inner experience not necessarily tied to a particular material structure, there is difficulty understanding why a blind person cannot "see" light with his "mind's eye" in spite of his purely physical disorder. What the observer does not understand is that he is comparing not simply inner and outer experiences, but experiences made possible through his own organism with those of a different sort of organism:

> The organism is the condition under which and only under which the intelligence can distinguish itself as substance or subject [a self] of the sequence [of its *Vorstellungen*] from the sequence itself or under which and only under which this sequence can become something independent of the intelligence. That it now seems to us as though there were a transition from the organism to the intelligence, namely [that] through an affectation [*Affektion*] of the former an idea is occasioned in the latter, this is pure delusion, because we can know nothing precisely about the idea before it becomes object to us through the organism; hence the affectation of the organism precedes the idea in consciousness and accordingly must not appear as conditional on it but much more as its condition. Not the idea itself, but surely the consciousness of it, is conditional on the affectation of the organism, and if empiricism limits its statement to the latter, nothing can be said against it.[57]

It appears that Schelling is involved in nothing less than a repudiation of idealism here, but this is not the case. For when he speaks of an "organism" he does not mean some sort of thing-in-itself, existing independently of intelligence and serving as its condition. The organism is itself "only a manner of intuition [*Anschauungsart*] of intelligence."[58] As in the case of Spinoza, it only *appears* to the intelligence that its ideas are produced by an independent body; in fact intelligence must first constitute such a body through an intellectual act. Empiricism is false, in other words, only to the extent that it does not take this into account. Without such an awareness of an organism, intelligence does not make its ideas conscious to itself. Somehow the "idea itself" first produces an awareness of an organism (the body), which simultaneously becomes the manner in which intelligence makes other ideas conscious to itself. It "chooses" this circuitous route, presumably, because if consciousness is to be possible as self-consciousness, then a subject/object distinction must be made by it.

One difficulty in understanding Schelling's dialectic arises from his failure to consistently distinguish two points of view. There is the standpoint of intelligence, with its essential ideas, and there is that of an actual intelligent *organism*, specifically the transcendental philosopher and his readers. As such, *"we can know nothing precisely about the idea before it becomes object to us* through the organism."[59] This is because we exist only as intelligence manifested in organic form. We are ourselves the *product* of a producing intelligence. Consequently, our knowledge of the world must derive from that intelligence and not from within ourselves. This is why associationist theories of the "origins" of knowledge leave unclear how *relations* come to be understood where there were initially only discrete sensory impressions. *Human* intelligence, in other words, is already programmed by the producing intelligence to follow certain *a priori* schemata. We do not perceive objects because they are there to be perceived; rather, they are there, they exist at all as individuals, because of the way we as perceivers are constituted. What we perceive as "external" is, then, really "internal." Thus human intelligence, while not derived from the organism, depends on it in that the organism serves as the outlet for such intelligence to become conscious of its ideas. We, as conscious selves, are rational organisms; and only as long as the interplay of ideas and forces harmonize in the form that we represent in the hierarchy can we be said to be *persons*, a harmonious state we unphilosophically characterize as *health*:

> The moment, for example, the organism is no longer the perfect reflex of our universe, it also no longer serves as the organ of self-perception, i.e., it is diseased; we feel *ourselves* diseased only because of that absolute identity of the organism with us. But the organism itself is only diseased according to the laws of

nature, i.e., according to the laws of the intelligence itself. For the intelligence is not free in its producing, but limited and constrained by laws. Consequently, when my organism must be diseased according to the laws of nature, I am obliged to view it as such. The feeling of illness arises from nothing other than the suspension of the identity between the intelligence and its organism; the feeling of health, on the other hand, if one can otherwise call a completely empty sensation "feeling," is the feeling of the total being-lost [*Verlorenseins*] of the intelligence in the organism.[60]

Intelligence made conscious of itself in human form regards itself as the paradigm of intelligence *in any form* as long as the organic form through which it is made possible remains transparent to it.[61] The condition of health is one in which the self distinguishes no separation of the mental and physical. This suggests Schelling's early interest in Schiller's notion of the natural man who loses his wholeness only with the advance of history and culture. However, it now appears that such a happy consciousness was never the destined state of human intelligence. Because the organism is a condition for intelligence in its human form and because "according to the laws of nature, a point in time is necessary when the organism as a mechanism. . .gradually destroys itself by its own power," human intelligence comes to understand its own frailty.[62] It must even, Schelling remarks, appear to itself as having been born at a certain time in the past, and through disease and weakness becomes aware of the possibility of a complete separation from its organic condition in the form of death. At such moments intelligence seems to have separated itself from its dynamic, producing side. Yet, without intelligence regarded in a passive way (as *natura naturata*), reflective consciousness would not be possible. Intelligence as pure *natura naturans* would never become conscious of itself as long as it did not have the capacity to produce finite products (bodies) and, in so doing, the condition for knowing them perceptually. In some manner it must be thrust back upon itself before self-consciousness is to be possible for it, yet in so doing, it experiences a separation it is never to completely overcome.

Now that the intelligence emerges in its human form, the ground of the "third epoch" has been prepared. In this epoch intelligence moves from reflection to unconditioned *willing*. A form of intuition, unknown hitherto, now emerges, one that constructs *concepts* and makes *judgments*; no longer must intelligence rely simply on the intuition that constitutes the perceptual object itself. This new intuition consciously operates under the rubric of a *schematism* that determines the use of concepts in judgment. Implicit in its operation is an awareness of the distinction between *concept* and *object* and between *noesis* and *noema*.[63] And out of this awareness language, for example, eventually becomes possible.

The previous form of intuition, which Schelling calls *primordial*, is itself *conceptless*. It is manifested, for example, in the prereflective awareness of *space*. However, only in "transcendental abstraction" does primordial intuition become objectified; space, for example, becomes the object of the study of geometry. At this point time-consciousness reenters the dialectic, once again serving as the condition for the possibility of unification — now, not of the experiences, but of the subject and object in the form of consciously made *judgments*. Schelling once more turns to the time-relation to make possible the next advance in the transcendental development of the intelligence, now recognizing it as the "most primordial" factor in the dialectic and as the ultimate "transcendental schema."[64]

Now the intelligence is prepared to enter the phase of its conscious *cognitive* life. It develops the capacity to make distinctions and exercises it with increasing competence. Out of this emerge categorial systems of greater and greater generality, and sciences of wider and wider applicability. In general, this period begins with the empirical phases of the life of intelligence, characteristic of pre-Kantian thought, then, grasping the insights of philosophical idealism, that intelligence develops transcendental categories and engages in transcendental abstraction. At this point, Schelling remarks, the cognitive side of intelligence manifested in the person comes to a close. For also at work in the dialectic is the *creative* force manifested in varying degrees in all natural bodies. Now, that force, coupled with the fruits of abstraction, unite into the life of *intelligent action*. It becomes clear that to Schelling it would have been one-sided even to consider theoretical philosophy set apart from willed activity, for even concepts, after all, were ultimately only "modes of activity" for him[65] Action itself is as primordial in the dialectic as is the reflection guiding intelligent creation.[66]

Finally, in artistic creation, the highest synthesis for human intelligence is achieved. Organism meets organism, and by their interaction they shape the further evolution of the World System through the production of new products that can further elevate the development of intelligence.

In summary, the "history of self-consciousness" just presented could be outlined in the following manner:

First Epoch

A.	Consciousness of Self as Mere Self	*Transcendental Subjectivity*
B.	Consciousness of *A*.	
C.	Consciousness of Relation between *B* and *A*.	
D.	Consciousness of Subject/Object Relation.	*Sense-perception*
E.	Consciousness of Relation between *D* and *A*.	*Productive Intuition*
F.	Consciousness of the Real.	*Common-Sense Dogmatism*
G.	Consciousness of Necessity of *F*.	

Second Epoch

H.	Consciousness of Relation between *F* and *G*.	*Idea of Time, Causality*
I.	Consciousness of Relation between *H* and *A*.	
J.	Consciousness of Self as Being Present.	

K. Consciousness of Relation between
    J and A.

L. Consciousness of Permanence.   *Organization*

M. Consciousness of Relation between
    L and A.

N. Consciousness of Self as an Intelligence.   *Life*

Third Epoch
(Life of Reflection and Action)   *Transcendental*
                                                    Reflection and
                                                    Abstraction
                                                    Willing

The method of the *System des transzendentalen Idealismus* appears to follow the dialectical pattern: Consciousness of *X*, followed by an awareness of that consciousness, followed finally by an awareness of the relation between the two. In the first a *subject* is posited, in the second an *object*, while in the third an awareness of the subject/object *relation* is achieved. Through this process intelligence grows and becomes more self-conscious and eventually penetrates most, if not all, of the World System with its spirituality.

At this point a general schema of the World System can be presented, one incorporating both *Naturphilosophie* and *Transcendental Philosophy*. Schelling himself suggested such a schema (Fig. 1);[67] however, his outline contains none of the

Figure 1

Schelling's Outline of His System

Relative-Real All		*Relative-Ideal All*	
Gravity (A^1)	Matter	Truth	Science
Light (A^2)	Motion	Goodness	Religion
Life (A^3)	Organism	Beauty	Art
The World System	Reason	History	
Man	Philosophy	State	

richness of his exposition; nor does it display, even though formulated after 1799, the unified evolutionary approach taken by him after that time. Very likely, however, no single outline can be given as definitive of all phases of his *Naturphilosophie* for, in many cases, in dealing with particulars Schelling appeared often to change his mind.

On the basis of the interpretation given here, which emphasizes the evolutionary component of his *Naturphilosophie*, and its relation to the transcendental deduction, the outline given in Figure 2 of Schelling's dialectic can be constructed.[68]

Figure 2

The Evolutionary Dialectic of the World System

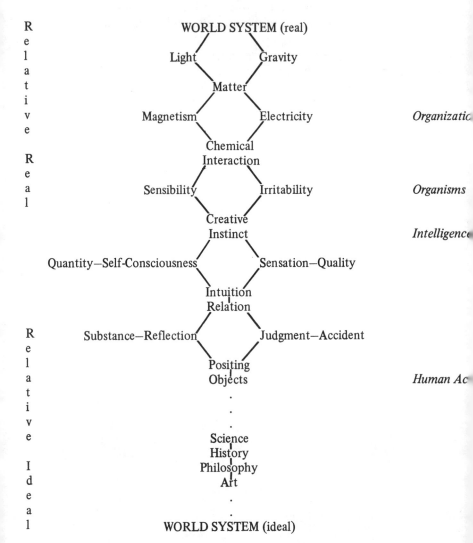

5

Science and *Naturphilosophie*

History has pronounced a harsh verdict on the school of *Naturphilosophie*. As a scientific approach it has been considered extravagant and damaging to the development of habits of true scientific investigation. Ueberweg noted that it was "mixed with erroneous and fantastical notions."[1] And Windelband explains it away as part of the enthusiasms of the time: "The systematic impulse. . .was due in good part of the desires of an audience in a state of high and many-sided excitement, which demanded from the teachers a complete scientific *Weltanschauung*."[2]

However, a proper interpretation of the historical role of *Naturphilosophie* is likely to depend on the philosophy of science currently respectable. In this respect, one of two tendencies of thought can be adopted — on the one hand, there are those who emphasize the importance of *theory* as a guide to research, and, on the other, there are those who hold empirical *observation* as not only the final judge of the soundness of a theory, but somehow the very source of theory itself. Clearly, the sympathies of the *Naturphilosophen* would lie with the former. And for anyone with like sympathies, the only criticism that could be leveled against them is that they did not execute the plan well enough, not that they had the wrong approach in the first place. Merz, in his history of nineteenth-century European thought, presents such a sympathetic criticism when he notes that *Naturphilosophie* "was a prospect rather than an achievement. The realization of it demanded volumes of research, in the course of which only gradually some definite features of the underlying scheme could reveal themselves."[3] Those who hold the latter position, of course, will maintain that achievement of the program could not be possible in the first place, for the theories of *Naturphilosophie* were untestable and systematically procrustean with respect to data. With their lack of specificity and undisciplined habit of metaphorical thinking, they could supposedly produce quick results in experimentation, but actually at the expense of information, and so would eventually freeze up the channels of free inquiry.

Rather than having to accept either position, a more accurate picture may be found in a *historical* approach to the relationship between observation and theory. In earlier times the careful use of the senses constituted almost exclusively the touchstone of scientific inquiry. For the folk sciences of husbandry, farming, navigation, and metallurgy to grow, the close observation of properties under varying conditions was necessary. At that point any theorizing short of simple conditional predictions would have been premature. Theories of excessive generality—if the early religions and creation myths may be regarded as such—made little if any contribution to the course the growth of knowledge was to follow. A certain amount of basic information about the terrestrial and macroscopic world would have had to be accumulated before theories of sufficient specificity to be fruitful could be formulated. Only at this point would systematic exploration into the more occult processes involving motion, combustion, growth, etcetera, be possible, and with this the emergence of modern science as we now know it. However, as our knowledge of the world becomes more sophisticated, theories exert a greater influence on the interpretation of what is observed, so that at some point the primitive data of science is already permeated with highly conceptual meaning. At this point the conflict is no longer between data and theory, but between one theory and another.

The recent history of science has been marked by periods of intense theoretical speculation, as well as by periods when theory merely guides from the background. Very likely in the former case a point is reached when the amount of information available increases beyond the capacity of the prevailing theories to reconcile all of it. New information is gathered, breakthroughs occur—sometimes through sheer coincidence or accident—and the prevailing theories, to those who are not emotionally wedded to them, seem almost overnight to lose their hold. Through all of this the drive for a unity of thought, that is, for science as ordered knowledge, can be seen operating. Without it new theories could be devised from new information, while the prevalent theories could remain suitable for the information left unchanged by recent discoveries. However, instead of theories increasing with the increase in our knowledge, the number of theories has diminished from the time when we could speak, say, of a "theory" of flint-chipping, or fishing, to the present, when we speak generally of physical theories, or biological theories, or, for some, simply "systems" theory.

The period of the flourishing of the Hermetic writings, the twelfth to the seventeenth centuries, could be interpreted as one of the first attempts to unify the knowledge and prevailing theories of the nature of man and the cosmos. Its view of reality as a unity of two principles (mercury and sulfur), combining in various proportions to establish a hierarchy of natural objects, makes it a crude forerunner of *Naturphilosophie*. And its guiding vision that, in the words of the Emerald Tablet, "what is below is like what is above," contains the later insight that the part reflects the whole, and that there is nothing that cannot be studied in the manner of an analogy to something else.

Between the period of the Hermetic writings and the *Naturphilosophie*, the vision of science as an encyclopedic endeavor came to dominate, no doubt largely as a result of the introduction of instrumentation into the process of exploration.

So much more of the world became accessible to observation that theory had to temporarily stand aside for description and classification. By the end of the eighteenth century, however, the need to bring the expanding horizon of scientific information within the limits of overall mental comprehension was again felt. To achieve this, generalizations would have to be framed, and an overall model would have to be constructed to serve as a guide for further research. This transition can be seen, for example, in the change in the approach to the study of nature found in Buffon and Erasmus Darwin, two writers to whom Schelling makes reference.

Schelling, however, would not be content with a unification of the life sciences alone. His dream, as should now be clear, was to formulate a general theory of all of nature itself, a theory that would unify the natural, life, and social sciences as aspects of a single, interconnected reality. To accomplish this, science would have to cease being empirical and discursive, and become "speculative" instead. I have traced this rejection of empiricism back to his Fichtean period, where Schelling began philosophy from the standpoint of the ahistorical transcendental self. Out of this he developed an interest in enriching the hitherto-bare subject/object relation, and so turned to Spinoza for a conceptual language that would give greater scope to that relation. The result of this elaboration was his *Naturphilosophie*, and later his transcendental philosophy. At no point in this period was the world of real historical time and of objective Newtonian space part of his perspective. Only his earliest essay on myths could be said to be historical, though even in this area he would soon replace the genetic approach with the transcendental approach of the later *Philosophie der Kunst*. Thus, without a clear and absolute separation of subject and object, and without the assumption of real time and space, empiricism becomes untenable. Instead, if the subject is part of the object through a higher unity, then it is only in understanding the nature of this connection that a proper perspective on our scientific knowledge of the world can be achieved. Science, then, must *begin* with certain transcendental truths or principles made evident through intellectual intuition, the main of these, as noted previously, being the unity of the ideal and real, the development of the real out of the structures of the ideal, and the priority of conception over perception. With empiricism no such unity of knowledge is possible. For the objects of empirical knowledge are finite, isolated structures of our experience that cannot be systematically interrelated with each other, or understood in their proper relation to the capacities of the knowing subject itself.[4]

Like Erasmus Darwin, Schelling had come to the conclusion that eighteenth-century science had become too haphazard and piecemeal by virtue of its lack of theoretical grounding, and that the time had come to change this. And given his contention that philosophy begins with transcendental reflection, it is not surprising that science too must begin with a theoretical model — *Naturphilosophie* — if it is ever to attain the level of *Naturwissenschaft*. "There is no reason for regarding the experimental investigation of nature as superior to theory," he writes, "for theory only guides it; without theory it would not be possible to 'put the question to nature,' as experimentation is described, since nature will give clear answers only to judicious questions."[5] Theory itself must be rigorous, unitary, and essentially philosophical, for "it is ridiculous to imagine that a theory has been established by stringing facts together, connected only by meaningless terms such as 'matter,' 'attraction,' etc."[6]

As the evolutionary approach came to dominate Schelling's point of view after 1800, he chose to interpret the very emergence of "speculative" science as an indication of the growth of Spirit and Reason in the unfolding development of the World System. Accepting this, it would be quite understandable that *Naturphilosophie* could not have been possible earlier. Now that the role of Reason in previous research had become evident, "to believe that intellectual changes, scientific revolutions, and the ideas they produce, as well as works expressing a specific scientific or artistic experience, reflect no necessity and are not produced in accordance with law but by chance, is

the highest barbarism."[7] As Schelling projects further development, later generations would eventually move beyond science.
Through *Naturphilosophie* they will come to see the incredible
simplicity of natural phenomena; they will contemplate the
rational laws of speciation and variability of form and, in
bringing nature totally within the ken of Reason, will subject
it completely to the realm of morality and beauty.

Before attempting to piece together some of the scientific
influences upon the young Schelling, it is useful to have an
overview of what he responded to in the scientific tradition of
his day. No attempt is made here to trace the detailed
development of his opinions on such subjects as the nature of
light, magnetism, combustion, and so forth, though Schelling's
observations here present a rich mine yet to be excavated by
historians of science. While he did study theoretical physics at
the Tübingen *Stift*, for the most part his studies were confined
to classical, philosophical, and theological subjects.[8] If we are
to speculate whether Schelling's scientific opinions derived
from contemporaries like Eschenmayer, Ritter, and Steffens,
or whether he came to them from his own perusals of published
work, in all likelihood the latter seems more plausible. Given
his already extensive philosophical background, we can expect
that he reacted negatively to much of the science he was
exposed to in his Leipzig studies of 1796. Having been trained
in the transcendental methods, he must have been disappointed
by the haphazard and uncritical character of the sciences of his
day. The influence of Eschenmayer and others first appears
after 1797, the year the *Ideen* was published.

Schelling was looking for two things in the sciences: in
the life sciences he found congenial arguments that justified
a holistic approach to organisms, but that were also based on a
dynamic evolutionary model and not on the acceptance of
specific vital entities like souls or entelechies; in the physical
sciences he would be dissatisfied with irreversible processes,
and arguments against the possibility of converting one substance
or process to another.

Early Scientific Influences

A. Life Sciences

As noted, Schelling seems to have been familiar with the biological studies of Buffon and Erasmus Darwin, with his greatest sympathy reserved for the latter. At one time Buffon's monumental *Natural History* was considered an advance over the Linnaean system because of its stress on the unity of natural forms. However, his molecular theory of life and his discursive and *ad hoc* explanations of natural phenomena made him at once too simplistic and unsystematic for the advocates of *Naturphilosophie*. Instead, a study of nature would have to begin with an answer to the question of how *natura naturata* emerged from *natura naturans*, before a true perspective of natural forms could be achieved. In the absence of the traditional theological answers, with their analogies to human generation, a new model to explain plant and animal life had to be found.

With the appearance of Erasmus Darwin's *Zoonomia* in 1794, a unified theory of the gradual transformation of all organisms from a single source came to the attention of the young Schelling. Darwin's work was motivated by a desire to propound a theory of organisms that would guide medical exploration, an interest he had in common with Schelling. In the Preface he rejects the mechanical model of the body as an approach to medical practice, and instead suggests that, because in nature "*the whole is one family of one parent*, [on] this similtude is founded all rational analogy"; and not realizing this, we have had "the want of a theory, deduced from such strict analogy, to conduct the practice of medicine."[9] He then suggests a fourfold classification of organic functions, with evident similarity to the one Schelling was later to produce—*sensation, irritation, association,* and *volition*—and goes on to describe how the symptoms and effects of various illnesses can be understood in terms of these functions and the particular "fibrous motions" producing them.

It was K. F. Kielmeyer (1765-1844), however, the speculative biologist, who is generally credited with supplying Schelling with a unified approach to animal organisms. In a lecture "On the Relations of the Organic Forces" delivered in 1793, he proposed the hierarchy of *sensibility, irritability,* and *reproduction* as the essential capacities of animal life.[10] However, it is doubtful Schelling merely took over his ideas, for in late 1797 he mentions in a letter to his parents that he was still working on his own theory of animal life.[11] Besides the unpublished lecture notes of Kielmeyer, which were passed among Schelling's circle, it is likely that Schelling was also familiar with the *Versuch über die Lebenskraft* (1795) by the physician and later *Naturphilosoph*, J. D. Brandis.[12]

J. F. Blumenbach's (1752-1840) pioneering work in comparative anatomy also came to Schelling's attention. His taxonomy of nature was considered an advance over that of Buffon, and his study of the races of men was the first approaching that of modern times. In his *Uber den Bildungstrieb* he also advanced an epigenetic theory of organic development in opposition to the preformationist views of Bonnet, and argued in a manner attractive to Schelling that the *Bildungstrieb* was a more essential and systemic life-force than either sensibility or irritability, and that therefore *organic* factors had to play a more important role in nature than mechanistic ones. For this reason, among others, Schelling opposed any attempt to establish the principle of life in a simple substance or force. Life to him was an interactive process involving a "free play of forces"; in fact, to become more organized meant that something had achieved greater freedom, for organization made possible selectivity and purpose, and the latter made possible genuine freedom.[13] Blumenbach's approach, then, was regarded by him as an improvement over earlier mechanistic approaches.[14]

Naturally, then, we would expect Schelling to side with Haller (1708-1777), the physiologist, in the latter's opposition to the materialism of La Mettrie. La Mettrie had argued, in effect, that the capacity of an organism to react to stimuli resided simply in its fibrous tissue, the proof of this being that parts of the body react to stimulation even when separated from it. Haller discounted this as the essential condition of life. Instead, he thought that irritability was the result of a network of interactions directed through the nervous system and on to the soul.[15] However, while Haller defended the wholeness of the body, he did so in a vague, almost Scholastic, manner and did not attempt to develop a general theory of sensibility and irritability of the sort Blumenbach was attempting.[16] Schelling had criticized John Brown's theory of excitability for being too simplistic, and this essentially would be his criticism of Haller's as well. Specifically, Schelling felt that Haller had attempted to account for irritability in terms of the structure of organs, and not in terms of their function and activity.[17]

In Goethe's *Versuch, die Metamorphose der Pflanzen zu erklären* (1790) Schelling encountered one of the most provocative accounts of organic form up to that time, seeing in it further evidence of his view of life as dynamic, evolutionary, and continuous. In that work, Goethe had argued, for example, that the leaves, petals, stamens, and pistils of the plant develop through a progressive structural evolution leading to the fulfillment of the plant in the form of its seeds, the mature plant being a "picture" of the stages of its entire lifetime. Schelling was later to generalize from this by arguing that all natural forms go through a similar process of "individualization."[18]

Also of influence on Schelling's theory of life may have been Franz von Baader's *Beiträge zur Elementar-Physiologie*, which was published in 1797.[19] Baader (1765-1841) is counted among those thinkers who are credited with turning Schelling's monism more in the direction of theology after 1801 and for a while each was writing works inspired by, and in response to, the other. In his *Beiträge* Baader rejects "dead mechanism," and instead puts forward a concept of force as a synthesis of a manifold of outer and inner sense. Outer intuition, he argues, occurs through mere addition and substraction, and therefore mechanistic processes must be regarded as crude approximations of nature, based only on quantity and arithmetic relation. The inner sense, however, operates through multiplicity and "exponentiation," and therefore is able to understand nature dynamically and qualitatively.[20] He also resolved matter into *Grundkräfte* and regarded the variety of natural phenomena as merely various forms of interrelation of the outer and inner senses, an idea that anticipates Schelling's later attempt in the *System des transzendentalen Idealismus* to deduce nature from self-consciousness and intelligence.

B. Physical Sciences

The influences of the mechanistic physical sciences on Schelling's organismic approach are understandably less than those of the life sciences. However, the less-understood phenomena of magnetism, light, electricity, and oxydation and reduction were of considerable interest to him. In fact, the larger portions of the two nonsystematic works of *Naturphilosophie*, the *Ideen* and the *Von der Weltseele*, involve Schelling's treatment of these processes.

G. F. Hildebrandt's (1764-1816) work in the chemistry of combustion is referred to by Schelling, as is the work of Guyton de Morveau (1737-1816), both antiphlogiston chemists. It was probably Guyton's views on equilibrium and conversion that were the most attractive to Schelling. For example, in Guyton's lectures of 1776, which were later translated into German, the introduction contains the remark: "all the theory of chemistry is in the two words *attraction, equiponderance*, and all the practice in the two words *dissolution, crystallisation*."[21] It was at this period that the laws of chemical combination were being worked out, and it was the belief that there had to be such relations among seemingly disparate substances, which contributed to their eventual discovery. No doubt Schelling must have found in Guyton's work support for his own view that nature must be understood in terms of harmonies and polarities, instead of in terms of irreducible ("imponderable") substances.

Fourcroy's (1755-1809) work, *Philosophie Chimique*, in German translation, is referred to by Schelling, as is Girtanner's (1769-1800) text in general chemistry, *Anfangsgründe der antiphlogistischen Chemie* (1792). De Saussure's (1767-1845) experiments on the oxygen-carbon dioxide cycle in plants eventually became known to Schelling, and appeared in later editions of the early works. To Schelling these antiphlogiston chemists were advocates of a "new system of chemistry," which eventually would lead to a comprehensive knowledge of the interaction of heat, light, and combustion.[22] However, there is reason to suspect that Schelling became less enthusiastic about the future role chemistry was to play in *Naturphilosophie*. In his lectures on university studies he characterizes that science as a "sanctuary for ignorance" because of the imprecision of its concepts.[23]

To defend his view that heat and light were essentially equivalent, though differing by circumstance, Schelling referred to the work of De Saussure, Pictet, and Rumford published in Friedrich Gren's (1760-1798) *Journal der Physik*, a periodical from which Schelling must have learned a great deal about current experimentation. However, not wanting to treat these subjects within the confines of the laboratory, Schelling coupled them with the cosmological views of Kant, Herschel, and Lichtenberg.[24]

For the application of physics and chemistry to animals, Schelling was familiar with the work of Alexander von Humbolt and Luigi Galvani, while, on the nature of electricity he refers to experiments by Cavallo, to the work of Aepinus attempting to show the connection between electricity and magnetism in tourmaline, and to the theories of Lichtenberg, Priestley, Franklin, Volta, and de Lüc.[25]

In his lectures on university studies, Schelling calls G. C. Lichtenberg (1742-1799) one of the most profound physicists of his time.[26] It is probably the latter's philosophical approach to the physical sciences that most appealed to him. We can expect that Schelling might have read with interest the following from among Lichtenberg's aphorisms:

> In nature everywhere we look for a certain determination, yet all this is nothing but an ordering of the obscure feeling of our own determination.

> The proper rules for the discovery of [scientific] truths are still without their Newtons and Herschels.

> The organization of the universe is certainly much easier to explain than that of a plant. The former corresponds more closely to cohesion and extreme crystallization. Even Diana's Tree grows, and so do the lovely ice ferns on the windowpane.[27]

Herschel's work on light and particularly Goethe's *Beiträge zur Optik* (1791) were used by Schelling in his theory to establish the primordial nature of light.[28] Goethe's experiments showing the optical behavior of the colors white and black were taken as evidence that in light the ultimate identity of unity and variety could be found. As a result of Schelling's enthusiastic support of his anti-Newtonian approach, Goethe became an advocate of *Naturphilosophie* and continued his speculative work in optics, finally producing his *Farbenlehre* in 1808.

One thing is clear from an investigation of Schelling's sources: even the idea of a *Naturphilosophie* could not have been possible were it not for the fact that for the first time the dissemination of scientific ideas had become more or less institutionalized. Surely men like Friedrich Gren and L. W. Gilbert as editors of influential scientific periodicals had as much to do with the rapid expansion of scientific knowledge in the nineteenth century as did those whose brilliant insights led to the great discoveries. Schelling was in a position to quickly assimilate, even if superficially, what had taken men years to produce, and in this manner, was able to see possible connections among experimental results, and so increase possibilities for theoretical development.

The School of *Naturphilosophie*

In a technical sense there was no "school" of *Naturphilosophie*. For one thing, Schelling's writings never achieved a final, polished result necessary for use by devoted followers. Also, Schelling himself moved into other fields, leaving the movement leaderless. However, there were those to a greater or lesser degree familiar with Schelling's work, who accepted the mandate of *Naturphilosophie* to seek interrelations among natural phenomena and to eventually bring about a unity of nature and culture. Each accepted in his own way the idea of the unity of nature as the basic principle of all research. Some, like Steffens and Eschenmayer, had been directly associated with Schelling either as colleague or student, while others were only indirectly touched by his work.

Oersted's discovery of electromagnetism has recently been attributed directly to the influence of Schelling's *Naturphilosophie*, and not, as has been thought, to a mere accident.[29] Oersted had been interested in *Naturphilosophie* as a youth, had written on Kant's *Metaphysische Anfangsgründe*, and was influenced by the work on galvanic electricity by Schelling's friend J. W. Ritter. Interestingly, one of the few pieces appearing in the *Kritisches Journal der Philosophie* not in the form of essays by Schelling or Hegel is a review of a work by Oersted, entitled in German *Ideen zu einer neuen Architektonik der Naturmetaphysik*, which contains an analysis of the dynamics of attractive and repulsive forces.[30] Oersted, however, would not have called himself a *Naturphilosoph* for the reason that he found sympathy only with its attitude toward nature, and not with its speculative approach to research.[31]

There are probably other such influences to be traced. The chemists Liebig and Schönbein, for example, were involved with *Naturphilosophie* in their youth, before turning to experimentation. Kuhn points specifically to the influence of Schelling on Leibig's interest in the equivalence of forces in chemical reactions, as well as on others involved in research on energy conservation.[32]

Heinrich Steffens (1773-1845)

Steffens says of himself, "I was the first professed naturalist who came to [Schelling's] views without halting and without reservation."[33] Born in Norway, Steffens came to Germany to study, later becoming a citizen. In his memoirs he speaks of how it felt to be part of "the dawn of a new scientific era" and recalls hearing one of Schelling's early lectures: "He had an air of decision, I must say, a half-defiant look."[34] In a letter to Schelling dated July 26, 1799, Steffens introduces himself and goes on to mention that he had been contemplating a "higher plan" to relate together magnetism, electricity, and combustion. Schelling's own replies have been lost, but in a letter a few months later Steffens enthusiastically responds to Schelling's *Einleitung* and *Erster Entwurf*, and again mentions his project to produce a "physiology of the universe."[35] This work finally appeared in 1801 as the *Beyträge zur innern Naturgeschichte der Erde*. In it Steffens argues that throughout the universe there are a series of polarities ranging from the elementary to the complex, and that each polarity, such as that between carbon and nitrogen, prepares the way for a higher level of polarity, such as between plant and animal. Schelling's provocative parallel between plant and animal, on the one hand, and the elements nitrogen, oxygen, and hydrogen, on the other, probably influenced Steffens here.[36] In a short piece in the *Zeitschrift für spekulative Physik*, Steffens acknowledges Schelling's influence: "Herr Schelling first showed us that vegetation involved deoxydation and animal processes oxydation. I intend to show the same for the process of terrestrial bodies."[37]

Probably of most interest in the *Beyträge* is Steffens's vision of a general theory of the universe. "All theory is by nature *genetic*," he writes, "all genesis synthetic." Therefore, to answer the question of how the earth was formed, we must develop a theory of the universe as a whole. Evidence indicates that Steffens was looking for a chemical theory of the evolution of the universe, rather than a physical theory that simply explained the motions of material bodies, and wanted to deduce the differentiation of elements from the "primordial homogenious mass."[38] Schelling was to characterize this attempt as the beginning of a genuinely "scientific geology,"[39] and in his lectures on university studies, he explains what he meant by this: "Now that the specific differences of matter have been grasped quantitatively and it is possible to represent matter as the metamorphosis of one and the same substance, through a mere change of form, the way is open for an historical construction of the system of material bodies already begun by Steffens." Schelling continues, "Geology, which must do the same for the earth as a whole, must exclude none of the earth's products and must demonstrate the genesis of all in their historical continuity and interdetermination, for the real side of science can only be historical. . . ."[40] It is clear that Steffens and Schelling wished to advance an evolutionary chemistry, which would explain the development of complex molecular structures from simple atomic ones, and eventually explain the evolutionary processes of the universe, and not, as in the case of physics, simply the dynamic interactions. With this scheme "old" chemical interactions could be distinguished from "young" ones, and in this manner, the course of planetary development could be charted. In his *Anthropologie*, written somewhat later but not published until 1822, Steffens constructs such a scheme by presenting a picture of the past geological history of the earth; in it he argues that the center of the earth had to be metallic, reflecting its earlier purely magnetic existence, and from there he moves up through the various geological eras to the emergence of animal life, and finally man. Like Schelling and Schiller earlier, he depicts man as having lost his innocence as a creature of nature, and as currently in the process of regaining it through *Naturphilosophie*.

Carl August Eschenmayer (1771-1852)

In the introduction of his *Grundriss der Natur-Philosophie*

(1832), Eschenmayer describes his early development in philosophy, beginning, as is so often the case with the *Naturphilosophen*, with Kant's analysis of matter, and leading finally to his exchange with Schelling in 1796. While he recognizes his debt to Schelling for giving him a "higher vision," he qualified this by saying, "I part from him not in the realm where law rules, that is, in nature, but rather in the realm in which freedom reigns."[41] For Eschenmayer felt that the World System could never account for the totality of nature; instead, he argued that there was a noumenal reality unable to be fully comprehended. This attitude was reflected early in a piece written at Schelling's request for the *Zeitschrift*. In "Spontaneität = Weltseele" Eschenmayer argues that the "principle of becoming" in nature is pure spontaneity and that only such a principle could rule out mechanistic explanation for good. Nature is regarded as just one tendency, the tendency toward individualization, one Eschenmayer felt that Schelling had overemphasized. The other tendency, that toward infinity, is manifested only by spirit, but it is in this that true spontaneity and freedom lie.[42] This means, in effect, that *Naturphilosophie* could never attain completion, and hence that its first principles would always be subject to revision. This would give an edge to empiricism, inasmuch as it would remain its task to describe the latest fruits of spontaneity, and so dictate how the principles were to be revised.

Eschenmayer's essay drew a critical response from Schelling. What he saw at stake here was a return to the subjectivism of Fichte. Eschenmayer, he argued, wanted to give priority to transcendental philosophy over *Naturphilosophie*; instead, this must be rejected because the "idealism of nature" is "primordial," while the "idealism of the self" is only deduced.[43] This means that the transcendental self is not the condition of nature, but is nature's condition insofar as nature is dynamic. In Schelling's view, Eschenmayer had remained in the standpoint of consciousness, not realizing that spontaneity is not merely a characteristic of spirit, but also of nature in the fullest sense, as *light-essence*.[44] Another reason Schelling questioned

Eschenmayer's grasp of his thought was the latter's belief that the laws of nature, in the form of the potencies, would be in need of further explanation. But this was impossible to Schelling; we cannot move outside of nature, for everything is contained within it, and so we must regard nature as its own lawgiver. Finally, because of his belief in the noumenal, Eschenmayer had said that it was much too early to be able to even speak of a "system" of *Naturphilosophie*, and that more experience (*Erfahrung*) was needed, to which Schelling replied, "experience is blind and must first learn to see its own wealth or poverty through *Wissenschaft*."[45]

In 1803 Eschenmayer published *Die Philosophie in ihrem Uebergang zur Nichtphilosophie*. In it he continues his critique of the *a priori* nature of *Naturphilosophie*, arguing that philosophy attempts to grasp the Whole as its subject, but to do this it must separate itself from the Whole, which it cannot do. Consequently, the only philosophy is a *Nichtphilosophie* that recognizes the impossibility of philosophy itself. The Absolute can only be a *symbol* of what cannot be fully comprehended, and for this reason can just as easily be regarded as the traditional God of theology. For example, Schelling's series of potencies do not explain how the identity separates into potencies, something that in fact is incapable of being understood.[46] However, in spite of this criticism, Eschenmayer and Schelling remained friends; perhaps because the former retained the substance of Schelling's *Naturphilosophie* and simply changed his attitude toward its full meaning. Schelling himself appeared ready to compromise with him by agreeing that in the Absolute no potencies are distinguished, and that "this Absolute is what you seem to call God."[47] At this time Schelling was working on his *Philosophie und Religion* and taking his first decisive steps in the direction of his second period. The System of Identity was beginning to break up, reflecting his suspicion that the antagonisms of nature, and those between nature and spirit, might be ultimately irreconcilable.

Eschenmayer's previously subdued mysticism finally became

clearly apparent in his *Einleitung in Natur und Geschichte* (1806). Both knowledge and action, the two human dimensions originally set into opposition by Fichte, are rejected by him as answers to the meaning of life. Only a recognition of the *beyond* in the form of religion is acceptable. Philosophy itself must be rejected inasmuch as it is capable only of developing the ideas (*Ideen*) of Reason and cannot understand the "total-intuition" in terms of these ideas. Nature and history become the two dimensions through which the transcendent operates, and this means that "the true in nature is not in the actual and the true in history is not in the present."[48] Yet Eschenmayer refused to abandon himself completely to fideism; for the world to be as intelligible as it is, we must conclude that Reason is somehow a copy (*Nachbild*) of the World Soul, and therefore it remains possible to at least move progressively closer and closer to the total-intuition of the Absolute. And this we do when we realize that Schelling's problem — how difference comes to identity, and relativity to the Absolute — can be solved by grasping the notion of the Absolute as a "self-objectivization of Reason" through knowing and willing, a process occurring in both nature and history.[49] Our own individual souls can only strive to be part of this process, an endless striving that for the most part takes the form of our spatial being.

In 1811 Eschenmayer became professor of medicine and philosophy at Tübingen and turned his attention to studies in animal magnetism. What are considered occult subjects today — hypnotism, clairvoyance, somnambulism, black magic — were seriously delved into by people like Eschenmayer, Kieser, Nasse, von Esenbeck, and even Hegel, because they felt that in such phenomena could be found a way of understanding the operation of Spirit in nature.[50]

Lorenz Oken (1779-1851)

Oken concerned himself little with the philosophical implications or difficulties of Schelling's system, and instead went straight on to fill in the details of the World System as it is manifested in the variety of natural products. It is probably for this reason that he won both renown and condemnation, and is probably the best known of the *Naturphilosophen*. Copies of his Würzburg lectures are said to have been made as early as 1802, some written in Eschenmayer's hand, so that some influence of Oken on Schelling also can be assumed. Essentially Oken's system is the same as Schelling's, but with specific scientific disciplines superimposed on it, so that it became at once a picture of the World System and a proposal for how to study it. His *Lehrbuch der Naturphilosophie* (1809), dedicated to Schelling and Steffens, contains a synoptic picture of the entire system he would expand later into the thirteen volumes of the *Allgemeine Naturgeschichte für alle Stande* (1833-44).[51] If nature is a process of composition and decomposition, of, in short, the production and destruction of individuals, then it must be studied in this manner; from this idea the three basic theories comprising the system can be outlined (Fig. 3).[52]

Mathesis is the condition of Schelling's Absolute Identity, wherein the first differentiation occurs. Abstractly considered, this is the separation of God and Nothing. This state Oken calls one of "relative zero."[53] Further differentiation occurs when the "relative zero" becomes *ousia* and *entelechy*, bringing rest and motion, and eventually light, gravity, and the other ether forms. With the ether the processes studied by *ontology* begin: the origin of the solar system through the processes of rhythmic polar expansion, the emergence of complex chemical reactions, and the gradual emergence of life. This latter point marks the return of the whole to itself through the individual, and becomes the study of *pneumatology*: the growth and expansion of sensation and consciousness, the emergence of science, art, and the rest of culture.

Suffice it to say that there is little that is directly recognizable as scientific theory in Oken's program. However, his *Allgemeine Naturgeschichte* was widely used, and his efforts to unify the institution of science through periodicals

Figure 3

Theoretical Outline of Oken's System

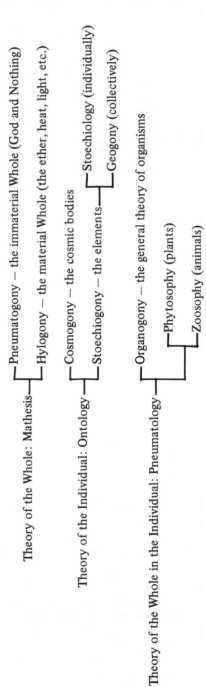

and conferences contributed to scientific development even where there was hostility to his mystical Swedenborgian flourishes.[54]

Gotthilf Schubert (1780-1860)

Schubert had attended Schelling's Jena Lectures on *Naturphilosophie* and several years later produced a dissertation on the application of Galvanism to deaf-and-dumbness. He is generally considered the "psychologist" among the *Naturphilosophen*. Of his many largely forgotten works, his *Die Geschichte der Seele* (1830) is usually considered representative of his thought. Like Eschenmayer and Schelling, Schubert turned *Naturphilosophie* more toward religion as time passed. Probably his *Ahndungen einer allgemeinen Geschichte des Lebens* is most characteristic of his *Naturphilosophie*. Like Oken, Schubert wanted to establish a cosmological scenario for the origin of life, except that in this case we get a mythic creation-drama of God—the "word," light, and fire—followed by gravity and its eventual outcome, individuation. Following a long discussion on the constituents and processes of the atmosphere, he takes up the question of the workings of oppositions within the All. Like Schelling, he maintains that all activity has its opposite, which itself cannot be further explained. This opposite is that which makes possible a striving beyond itself toward the infinite, and so guarantees frustration as well. However, in the whole of reality there is only rhythm and harmony and but a single living substance.[55] The third volume of the work contains a numerological account of the "periods" of "universal and particular life," with particular emphasis on the numbers seven, five, and ten as a measure of time, history, and organic structure. It is clear that Schubert embraced the Pythagorean vision of a universe governed by simple numerical relations, of which the more complicated physical laws were merely crude approximations lacking only sufficient generality.[56]

With his *Die Symbolik des Traumes* (1840) he leaves behind any pretense of being scientific for out-and-out mysticism.

To understand the truths of *Naturphilosophie*, he argues, one must become a poet and enter the "higher region" wherein lies the true ground of nature. Poetic associations in the form of *symbols* are said to describe the relations of nature more accurately than scientific laws. Certain plants and animals speak to us in different ways, as symbols, because we share with them the same forces of nature. Clearly, Schubert's reaction to Schelling closely follows that of his American contemporary, Ralph Waldo Emerson.

Johann Wagner (1775-1841)

Unlike Schubert or Eschenmayer, Wagner remained committed to the original project of *Naturphilosophie*, to study nature in order to reveal its hidden idealism, although like Schubert he tended to seek the unity of nature in the knowledge of mathematical forms. In the forward to his *Von der Natur der Dinge* (1803) he claims to be presenting, for the first time, a formulation of *Naturphilosophie* that combines both detail and principle, one that is based on a "pythagorean system of numbers."[57] However, this work, and his *System der Idealphilosophie* published a year later, indicates only that he had absorbed Schelling's system well and had remained entirely within its limits.

His *Ideen zu einer allgemeinen Mythologie der alten Welt* (1808) remained essentially an elaboration of Schelling's philosophical critique of myths. In it Wagner attempted to show that the cosmogonies of Greco-Roman, Indian, Tibetan, Persian, and Scandinavian mythology each reflect in poetic and symbolic language the structure of Schelling's system, thus showing the connection between history and nature, and the universality with which the ideal makes its appearance in the real. Only a passing reference is made in the Preface of the work to the need for the unification of mathematics and "objective intuition." A year later in his *Theodicee* he presents some idea of what he wants the role of mathematics in philosophy to be. All genuine knowledge must be able to be expressed mathematically, he contends. And if, as Schelling maintains, there is a symmetry and proportionality among the forms of nature and spirit, then in an abstract manner this can be expressed with the proportional identity, $a:b = c:d$. This means that each "factor" consists in a triadic relation with the others, and that four such relations are possible. This concept when fully understood, Wagner implies, will, for example, subsume as a special case the chemical laws of definite proportions.[58]

It was not until his *Mathematische Philosophie* (1811) that Wagner elaborated on his mathematical philosophy. Number and figure are supposed to be the first constituent of ancient man's cognitive grasp of his world. Even before the awareness of space and time, he argues, there had to be a consciousness of succession and linearity. The unity of man with nature in his prereflective state corresponds to the essential monadic nature of the world. With reflection a dyadic structure emerges, corresponding to the dyadic dimension of the world as a unity of opposites. Language, which is merely a localized arithmetic of the world with words standing as signs to objects, is formed to heal this rupture. So too with art, which must rely on the delineation and formation of color and sound. Static opposition is finally overthrown, not by a return to unity, but by a triadic mediation of opposites in the form of a "genus," "class" [*Geschlecht*], or "collective concept." Only dyads and triads are relations in the essential sense, all others being formed through the "reiteration" of these. However, a relation of sorts exists between Being as unity and Nothing as zero, so that from a metaphysical point of view the universe consists of a tetradic relation between *one* and *zero*, and between the opposites *plus* and *minus*. The numbers *zero, one, two, three,* are also said to represent these relationships: *zero* as the transcendence of any relation in the Totality, *one* as pure identity, *two* as opposition of like, *three* as opposition of differences.[59]

From these abstract relations the structure of nature can then be constructed. Some forms are parts of more complex forms. For example, we can say that *Brain:Nerve = Heart:Vein*, and on another level, *Nerve:Vein = Sensibility:Vegetation*. The structures change through a mathematical metamorphosis following definite proportions, so that if we knew the "laws of metamorphosis" fully we would be able to determine which structures would result from which modifications of the relations. These proportions are not so complicated as those which measure quantity alone, as in physics, but are more like logarithms. After illustrating these relations geometrically, Wagner presents a number of tetradic structures such as *Day:Night = Life: Death*, *God:Satan = Good:Bad*, *Hieroglyph:Word = Sense: Concept.*[60] Later this system was refined, though with less reference to science and *Naturphilosophie*, and more to traditional metaphysics; in this case the tetradic relations become part of a scheme of four "primary concepts," [*Urbegriffe*], each manifested in four ways (Fig. 4).[61]

Along with the above *Naturphilosophen*, who are selected as representative of some of the major tendencies within the movement, can also be included the following:

Johann Wilhelm Ritter (1776-1810), who is remembered for his work in galvanism and as the formulator of the electro-chemical table of chemical affinities. His *Die Physik als Kunst, Ein Versuch* gives his version of the Schellingian evolutionary scenario. At first, man is at one with Being, but then through a rupture his inner unity with nature is lost. However, this rupture is necessary to make possible a more spiritual unity between man and nature. Physics must go beyond *Wissenschaft* and become an art form, making possible the highest realization of life and action. Finally, man and nature become perfectly united once more in a Divine form.[62]

Friedrich Ast (1778-1841), as a cultural historian, placed his emphasis on the study of poetry and mythology. In the first volume of his *Zeitschrift für Wissenschaft und Kunst* he speaks of philosophy as "formalism" and "mere theory," which must be complemented by art and feeling; for life is a constant movement between the finite and the infinite, with science and art fully representing these tendencies.[63]

Figure 4

Wagner's Table of Categories

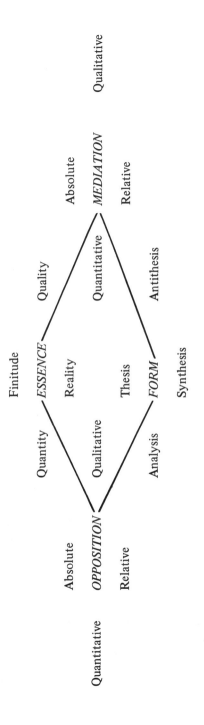

Georg M. Klein (1776-1820) also can be counted with those who extended Schelling's work in a mystical direction. In his *Betrachtungen über den gegenwärtigen Zustand der Philosophie in Deutschland* (1813) he quotes Schelling as saying that *Naturphilosophie* "is no theory, but a real life of Spirit in and with Nature" as a justification of his own emphasis on religion, poetry, and art.[64]

Joseph von Görres (1776-1848). His *Aphorismen* (1802) contains a great number of parallelisms and analogies reflecting two pulsating tendencies of nature—contraction and expansion. Such opposition is represented by the "battle" between the absolute and relative, the transcendental and the empirical, Jacobism and Royalism in politics, and phlogiston and anti-phlogiston in chemistry. The sexes, insofar as man represents phantasy, perception, and irritability, and woman, feeling, spirit, and excitability, also reflect this polarity. These tendencies can also be found in the productions of men—the telescope manifesting the expanding and ideal, the microscope the contracting and real.[65]

After 1805 Görres's interest turned more to poetry and religion. In his *Mythengeschichte der asiatischen Welt* (1810) he seeks the unity of all myths, and in this way, the hidden message in God's creation. The work itself is a kind of creation myth that attempts to show how cultural differences emerged from a common root. From this point on he moved away from *Naturphilosophie* and in later years joined Schelling, Baader, Schubert, and others in Munich as part of an anti-rationalist, politically conservative coalition.

Ignaz Paul Vital Troxler (1780-1866). Although only five years younger than Schelling, Troxler was one of his students at Jena, and for about the first five years of his work showed little disagreement with Schelling's early position. With his *Über das Leben und sein Problem* (1807) and *Elemente der Biosophie* (1807) he moved from *Naturphilosophie* to what he called *Lebensphilosophie*. In Schelling's identity theory Nature and Reason were the forms of the real and ideal. This was unacceptable to Troxler, who considered the concept of *life* to be essential for any theory of nature. In an identity there is no principle of becoming or animation; if, as Schelling argued, nature functions dialectically, then there must be an overall animating principle that drives the dialectic toward the realization of greater possibilities.

His differences with the earlier *Naturphilosophie* emerge clearly in his *Blicke in das Wesen des Menschen* (1812) where, in the introduction, he speaks of developing an anthropological metaphysics in place of the traditional *blossen Idealismus*. The influence of Hegel appears unmistakable in this work. "Spirit" as an "infinite living principle" is what comprises the Absolute, an eternal striving, unseating all oppositions and creating new ones. Man himself represents a perpetual shuttling back and forth between finite and infinite, as part of this *Lebensgeist*. Troxler considered this truth about man to be the basis for a theory of medicine, one that he says had been lost since the time of Paracelsus.[66]

Like Wagner, Troxler was also interested in drawing up a table of tetradic relations, a summary of which is given in Figure 5.[67]

Karl Christian Friedrich Krause (1781-1832) was another of Schelling's students at Jena. His dissertation in 1802 dealt with the relationship between philosophy and mathematics. A year later his *Grundriss der historischen Logik* appeared. In this work Krause regards logic as "the law of the activity of Spirit in thought," while "historical logic," in contrast to transcendental logic, involves the laws of development of thinking as it is actually thought by men. Here he argues that transcendental logic must be shown to be the basis for "historical" logic, and this ultimately means that intellectual intuition must be established as the basis for sensuous intuition. *Naturphilosophie* reveals the connection by indicating through transcendental reflection the ideal elements of the real. However, Krause rejects Schelling's idea of intuition as the identity of subject and object, saying "an absolutely first intuition is absolutely inconceivable." For, each intuition involves some form of activity that moves from subject to object, and this activity

Figure 5

Troxler's System of Tetradic Relations

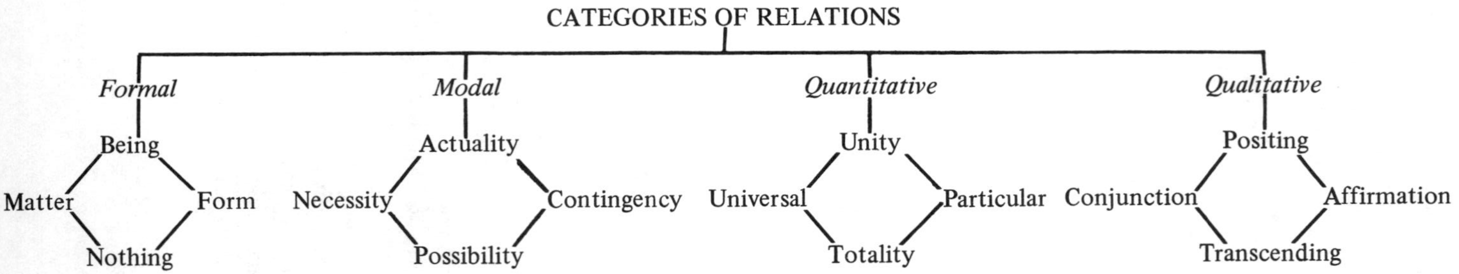

CATEGORIES OF RELATIONS

essentially involves reflection. However, there is no "pure or empty reflection," but only one, which involves a goal and will. This puts all of *Naturphilosophie* within a *human* context, and gives priority to the study of society and culture wherein the will of man operates. It also justifies a concern for traditional logic, to which Krause devotes the rest of the book.[68]

Out of this early work grew Krause's idea that philosophy would have to reconcile itself to an unresolvable tension between the objective and subjective. The transcendental standpoint, which attempts to establish unconditioned knowledge, eventually gives way to the genetic, subjectivist approach. This leaves a twofold course for philosophy — a "subjective-analytic" course involving analysis of the knowing human self in all its multiplicity of activities, and an "objective-synthetic" course, which strives to establish the condition for a pure theory of essence and an entirely unconditioned table of categories. His *Versuch einer wissenschaftlichen Begründung der Sittenlehre* (1810) is a description of the synthetic course of thought from the first *Urwesen*, through the development of the universe, and on to God, all in the form of a cosmology of creation, while a fuller statement of both courses is given in his *Vorlesungen über das System der Philosophie* (1828) in which he presents several tables of categories and uses a binary number system to illustrate how the *Urwesen* unfolds to become the divine spiritual community.[69]

Schelling's Later Period: Science or Religion?

During the decade, 1799-1809, Schelling's thought gradually turned from *Naturphilosophie* to a mystical theosophy. In one way, he was returning to the period of his own early essays; in another, he was giving due to the side of romanticism he had neglected and even spurned — its hankering after the numinous and ineffable. This is not to say that he was ever very far from mysticism. While notions like the *World-Soul, the Absolute,* and *Reason,* seemed tidy and rational enough in the overall system of *Naturphilosophie,* they were born out of what surely had to be mysticlike insights into the nature of the relation between the One and the Many. In spite of this, Schelling had the reputation of being a bit too rational for the Jena romantics, one reason for this being his opposition to the romantic revival of Christianity of Friedrich von Hardenberg (Novalis). In 1799 the poet Ludwig Tieck is said to have introduced Schelling to the writings of Jacob Böhme, and from this point on his interests began to expand into new areas.

Besides the outlook of Böhme, which was yet to have its strongest effect on him, Schelling had to contend with the gentle criticisms of Caroline Schlegel in the years 1800 and 1801. Caroline had interpreted the *Naturphilosophie* as not so much a product of reason as one of imagination; to her its insights were the result of a truly poetic capacity. We might suspect, then, that coming from the woman he was later to marry, these criticisms may have given Schelling a new respect for poetic insight, as well as for the general stance of the romantics. Yet it would probably be inaccurate to say that he was turning away from earlier views on this account. Schelling was too much of a creative philosophical thinker in his own right to have been decisively influenced in this manner.

As indicated, it was more probably the substantial arguments of Eschenmayer in "Spontaneität = Weltseele," in the work on *Nichtphilosophie*, and in *Einleitung in Natur und Geschichte*, that had the greatest influence on changing Schelling's perspective. Eschenmayer's criticism of the possibility of a *complete* rational system of thought, which anticipates Kierkegaard's later criticism of Hegel, forced Schelling to rethink some difficult questions at the heart of his System of Identities. For one thing, if the Absolute is One, how does it appear to be Many also? Does genuine differentiation occur, or is it simply a grand illusion? How, if there is one Reason, could there be several perspectives within the Absolute? Then there is the problem posed by Krug, which I shall note later, of how an idealistic system could account for and deduce the brute givenness of even a single object like *this* rose or *this* pen. And finally, and most importantly for Schelling, there was the lingering problem of explaining the notion of human freedom in terms of the System of Identities.

At this period Schelling had already been concerned with the question of whether Spinoza's Substance could justly be considered dynamic rather than static. Now Eschenmayer's critique drove home to him the importance of this problem. If there are genuine forces and drives in nature, and if they in part manifest themselves in the organic realm as *creative instinct*, then this requires something very much akin to a *Will* at the heart of the Absolute. But to argue in this fashion is to take a step in the direction of traditional theism, and away from a more abstract and static pantheism.

It was at this point that Schelling came to see his Absolute more in terms of Böhme's notion of the undifferentiated *Ungrund* or Abyss. Böhme had spoken of it as the *mysterium magnum* and as the *Eternal Chaos*, but he had also given to it the character of a primordial Will, which desires to will itself *as a something particular* (differentiation), from which it could see itself reflected as in a mirror. And so out of the *Ungrund* emerged the Idea as the catalyst that transfixes and goads the inwardly contemplative Abyss toward imaginative creation in the outer form of nature. In Böhme's hermetic vision polarity and strife (the principle of negativity) lie at the very heart of what there is; they are not resolved in a unitary Absolute, nor are they considered illusory as in a System of Identities. They are the inevitable result of the *Ungrund's* coming out of itself. Man himself grows out of this dark, wanton side of nature and must journey from the realm of nature to that of spirit, from necessity to freedom. In fact, all of the temporal realm of this earthly life becomes interpreted as a Fall from Eternity, a catastrophe and a temporary triumph of the dark forces of Negativity.

No doubt with encouragement from Baader, Tieck, and others, Schelling turned to Böhme's vision of the Absolute in response to the criticisms of Eschenmayer. And while there can be found certain theosophical tendencies in the *Darstellung* of 1801, it was not until his *Philosophie und Religion* (1804) that he first set out the direction for his later thought. There he tells us not only that the ideal and the real are no longer identical, and only formally distinct, but that the transition from the ideal to the real involves a complete rupture [*Abbrechen*] of the Absolute and a Fall [*Abfall*] of the real from the ideal.[70] This picture must have suited Schelling for several reasons. For one thing, it released him from the obligation of deducing with his *Naturphilosophie* the specific facticity of nature and experience, for now it would not be possible to proceed by rational degrees from the Absolute to the world as we know it. Also, it introduced the dimensions of Will and Desire lacking from his previous idea of the Absolute. In short, he came to agree with Eschenmayer on the question of spontaneity, for after all, "the ground of the possibility of the Fall lies in freedom."[71] Now there is no longer a chance of completing a deductive system in the manner of Spinoza's *Ethics*; creativity establishes that uncognizable factor, namely, spontaneity, which Eschenmayer believed must turn all philosophy into *Nichtphilosophy*.

More important, Schelling found in Böhme's scheme a way of more easily coming to grips with the human world of history and culture. *Naturphilosophie* pure and simple might have been suited to life in sylvan regions, but in the city it was apparent that it needed modification. Schelling had already discussed art in the *System* (1800) and in the *Philosophie der Kunst* (1802), but up to now he had devoted relatively little effort to a theory of history. With the concept of the Fall, he had a way of giving meaning to the process of history not available hitherto. The Fall marked the beginning of history, which itself would involve a journey away from and a return to the Absolute. Thus, in a well-known paragraph Schelling writes:

> History is an epic composed in the mind of God. Its two main parts are — first, that which depicts the departure of mankind from its center, up to its farthest point of alienation from its center, and secondly, that which depicts the return. The first part is the *Iliad*, the second, the *Odyssey* of history. In the first the movement was centrifugal, in the second it is centripetal.[72]

With this assumption, Schelling is now prepared to turn to an examination of the origins of human societies, religion, art, poetry, and the other forms of culture, all with the purpose of getting beneath their "outer form."[73] Recalling his earlier work on myths, he argues that in true mythology there can be found an indication of the revelation of the infinite in the finite. This sets for him a twofold task—the study of myths, as part of the story of the centrifugal departure away from the infinite center, and the study of revelation, as the vehicle for realizing the centripetal reunion of the finite with the infinite.

In writing *Philosophie und Religion*, Schelling was conceding to the romantics the importance of the study of history, and was joining the "Universal History" bandwagon, which would grow as the first decade wore on. Works like Fichte's *Grundzüge des gegenwärtigen Zeitalters* (1806), Eschenmayer's *Einleitung* (1806), and, of course, Hegel's *System der Wissenschaft: Erster Teil, die Phänomenologie des Geistes* (1807) were all proposing an evolutionary idealism as a way of best understanding the Absolute in its historical manifestation. Thus, Schelling was attempting to solve an important difficulty, that of reconciling his earlier *Naturphilosophie* with the growing interest in a general theory of human culture and history. In part, this difficulty had centered around the pantheism/ atheism issue as it pertained to the earlier writings, namely, in what sense could we speak of the Absolute as 'God' if it is, in fact, a System of Identities. Lovejoy put the issue well in his remarks on Schelling in *The Great Chain of Being*: "In much of his philosophizing between 1800 and 1812, it is true, he has still two Gods and therefore two religions—the religion of a time-transcending and eternally complete Absolute, an 'Identity of Identities', the One of Neoplatonism—and the religion of a struggling, temporally limited, gradually self-realizing World-Spirit or Life-Force."[74]

Schelling attempted to answer this seeming confusion more clearly in his *Philosophische Untersuchungen über das Wesen der menschlichen Freiheit* (1809). A careful examination of this work is beyond the scope of the present work, but relative to the status of the earlier *Naturphilosophie* it has some important things to say. Generally, the essay describes an evolutionary scenario now thoroughly impregnated with notions from the writings of Böhme. One of its central tasks is to reinstate the factors of freedom and spontaneity in the processes of nature and history. Here we are told that "Spinozism in its rigidity could be regarded like Pygmalion's statue, needing to be given a soul through the warm breath of love."[75] What Schelling is rejecting is the notion of a "block universe," to borrow a phrase from William James — one devoid of real possibility. Thus, "no matter how one pictures to oneself the procession of creatures from God, it can never be a mechanical production";[76] particularly in the more complex natural forms we can see that an "irrational and accidental element," and not "a geometric necessity" has operated in their emergence.[77] And so God "is not a System, but a Life."[78]

Jacobi and others saw difficulties in this transition from Spinoza to Böhme, but Schelling remained convinced that a *unified* formulation was still possible. He did not feel that *Naturphilosophie* was in conflict with the evolutionary picture, but rather was a necessary complement to it.[79] However, it would seem, on the face of it, that there is a considerable difference between a differentiation produced through the sheer interaction of primal forces (*generatio aequivoca*), and one resulting from a "desire" at the heart of Being to produce "life and love" and to seal away forever darkness and ir-rationality.[80] In this sense, Schelling had given as *eschato-logical* meaning to his earlier epigenetic theory, one that brought together to his satisfaction his scientific, religious, moral, and political interests. He would claim, no doubt, that he had merely unfolded the transcendental implications of the possibility of a *Naturphilosophie*, something Kant had approached only to be held back by his empiricism. One would have thought that in abandoning the "orthodox" concept of God as a youth, Schelling would have given up eschatology as well. Yet, it was eventually the need to come to grips with freedom and evil that pushed him over the brink—from epigenesis admitting reversibility, to eschatology—and that led him to give a religious, or, in any case, a spiritual preeminence to man, instead of granting him only a small place in the World System as he did earlier. At the end of the essay on human freedom Schelling seems to interpret his earlier *Naturphilosophie* as if it were itself a form of revelation: "We have a revelation earlier than any written one—Nature. It contains archetypes which no one has yet interpreted, whereas the written ones have long since received their fulfillment and exegesis."[81]

Whether, in presenting this Böhmean interpretation of the evolution of the World System, Schelling was turning completely away from science and toward personalistic religion, is a question that might be arguable either way. More accurately, it seems that he saw *Naturphilosophie* and religion as, instead, two roads leading in the same direction, in that each is a response to what are today still rather interesting questions—how variety emerges out of unity, if indeed it does, and if so, whether this emergence is accidental or nomological. Schelling considered that natural science had to be cleansed of its uncritical (mechanistic) assumptions and interrogated for its transcendental implications. But the same may be said for his approach to religious forms in his later years. He was not content to accept religion on face value, but sought to demythologize it so that, along with *Naturphilosophie*, he could produce what would emerge as "the only true system of religion and science."[82] This, we are to assume, would have involved a unified theory of the evolution and goals of both natural and social forms, of the sort attempted later by Herbert Spencer, and, in America, by Laurens Hickok and Charles Peirce, among others. It would almost surely have changed the meaning of religion from its traditional sense to one closer to what goes on in metaphysical speculation generally. Of course, Schelling did not succeed in formulating, during the rest of his long life, this one true system, and when one reflects on what it would have to contain, this is not surprising.

6
Schelling's Critics

By 1801 the major statement of Schelling's World System had been made in the form of the *Philosophy of Identity*. Hereafter his thought was to take the ultimately conflicting course of filling in scientific details of the system, while at the same time seeking a further ground for the unity of spirit and nature in something which, it became clearer, would have to be inaccessible to human reason. As indicated, it was in this conflict that the foundation for his later philosopohy was prepared. At this time also, critical works began to appear against the new Objective Idealism. Without realizing it, Hegel summed up a good part of this reaction when he wrote in the Preface to the *Phänomenologie des Geistes*: "One side insists on the wealth of its material and its intelligibility, the other side spurns at least the latter and insists on immediate rationality and divinity."[1] Kaufmann considers this comment a reference to the conflict between eighteenth-century *Aufklarung* and nineteenth-century romanticism, though very likely Hegel has Schelling in mind as an example of the former case.[2] Today Hegel's remark can be seen to fit, on the one hand, *his* reaction to Schelling's *Naturphilosophie*, and, on the other, that of the anti-idealists—the Kantians, common-sensists, and fideists.

160

The Anti-Idealists

Karl Leonhard Reinhold (1758-1823)

To Schelling, Reinhold had never left the Kantian critical tradition and for this reason had to be regarded as a "psychologist," and consequently as a "dogmatist" as well.[3] Not having grasped the implications of the *aufgehoben* of the thing-in-itself for epistemology, he could not enter the standpoint of idealism, but instead had to remain within the dualist epistemology of Kant. In turn, Reinhold considered the idealism of the "Fichte-Schelling School" to be an example of "*Philodoxie*," arguing his case in a short work, *Ueber die Paradoxien der neuesten Philosophie* (1799), and in the longer *Beiträge zur leichtern Uebersicht des Zustandes der Philosophie* (1802).

Reinhold's critique follows directly from his Kantian epistemology. Among other things, this means that *intellectual* intuition must be rejected as impossible; and from this it follows that the claim for the ultimate unity of subject and object cannot be established. Then, disallowing such unity, it becomes clear that idealism must be regarded as a mere form of subjectivism — hence his criticism that in *Naturphilosophie* nature becomes a mere appearance to the self.[4] Instead of a Kantian dualism and a Schellingian monism, Reinhold proposed a triadic relation of subject-representation-object, and sought an answer to the question of *how representations* are formed, rather than, as with Kant, from whence they arose. Then in order to overcome the Kantian difficulty over things-in-themselves, he considered noumena mere regulative Ideas in epistemology.

Schelling answered Reinhold's *Beiträge* in an essay that appeared in the *Kritischen Journal der Philosophie* in 1802.[5] His critique, as is so often the case with his polemical writings, consists mainly in a summary statement of his own position. In it he argues that Reinhold's approach further estranges the ideal and real, thought and being, by ignoring the question of the ontological status of the noumenon. It is not enough that the Idea of a noumenal reality serve as a heuristic principle in the study of knowing; the Idea must be grasped in its capacity as a condition for knowing itself, and this means in the fundamental unity of thinking and being. If one begins with a study of the content of consciousness, one can never move to the position of idealism; to begin, as does Reinhold, with an "empirical psychology" leaves no way out for an escape from dogmatism or phenomenalism.[6]

In short, to Reinhold it was Schelling who was the dogmatist, and to Schelling, it was Reinhold who was a subjective idealist. Schelling, with his concern for metaphysical questioning, found Reinhold's phenomenological approach superficial, while the latter found Schelling's claims critically unfounded.

Wilhelm Traugott Krug (1770-1842)

Krug's reaction to Kantian dualism was just the opposite of Reinhold's. Instead of underplaying the tension between subject and object in philosophy, Krug embraced it and made it the cornerstone of his work. However, unlike the idealism of Fichte and Schelling, which attempts to deduce the objective from the standpoint of transcendental reflection, Krug argued that the unity of subject and object could be found only in the standpoint of the common-sense thought of everyday life.

His attack on Schelling's *System des transzendentalen Idealismus* in his *Briefe über den neuesten Idealism* (1801) turns on his rejection of intellectual intuition. The transcendental philosopher, he argues, must in fact *assume* the unity of subject and object, and because of this his approach is essentially dogmatic as well.[7] He cannot deduce an "entire system" of thought or reality because this would be an "endless task"; in fact, it would be an accomplishment if the transcendental philosopher could deduce even a single rose. The latter claims to deduce the products of nature *in general*, but "a real object" remains incomprehensible to him, as it must for philosophy in general.[8]

In a similar fashion, Krug argues that Schelling's deduction of organic nature, in the *System*, from the cognition of a general Intelligence overlooks the fact that human intelligence is always the result of a *particular form* of the synthetic unity of apperception, and so no *general* deduction is possible. Here Krug refers to the obscure passage in the *System* quoted earlier where Schelling refers to the man born blind as an example of how the configuration of forces in a physical object determines how much of the total system is to be accessible to it. If the organism is simply a form of *intuition*, then having eyes that function would not seem to affect the capacity to experience such intuition. And yet the blind man, deprived only of the sensuous experience of light, does not know what we can know of organisms if we are not blind. Similarly, if the organism is ideal in nature, how is sickness possible? For Schelling, sickness arises when the identity of intelligence and organism is ruptured [*Aufhebung*], and yet the organism is supposed to be nothing material.[9] How then can it become estranged from what is its own activity?

Idealism to Krug is really a form of nihilism, because it pictures the ego as pure thought and not as a living person. If the ego is the unconditioned and is *something*, than an unconditioned something is a contradiction, he maintains; therefore, either idealism is incoherent, or else it leads to the negation of the ego. The transcendental philosopher overlooks the determination of his own ego, and thinks himself capable of discoursing on the ego in general.[10] However, the self that reflects on itself is not the same self as that which is reflected upon. The latter is abstract, but the former always is a real temporal, philosophizing subject.[11]

In *Über die verschiedenen Methoden des Philosophirens* (1802) Krug characterized three philosophical methods: the *thetic* method based on dogmatism and "philosophical despotism," the *antithetic* method, leading to skepticism and "philosophical anarchism," and the *synthetic* method (his own), based on criticism and "philosophical republicanism."[12] Fichte and Schelling are dogmatists inasmuch as they completely side-step the question of method in philosophy; instead, he argues, they seek quick results by transferring formal principles into substantive claims, and in so doing overlook their own dogmatic assumptions.

Friedrich Köppen (1775-1858)

With Krug representing a segment of the Kantian critical tradition, Köppen came forward representing the fideistic tradition of Jacobi in his critique of Schelling. In *Schellings Lehre, oder Das Ganze der Philosophie des absoluten Nichts* (1803) Köppen attacks the conceptual coherence of transcendental philosophy. This is to be expected, for a fideist is not prepared to deal substantively with the metaphysical claims of the idealist.

Köppen also accuses Schelling of nihilism, but this time because the latter's metaphysics lacks the concept of *substance*, and instead makes everything a form of dynamics.[13] Not only does the distinction between subject and object vanish, but also any reality to the world of our daily experience. Belief in the ultimate identity of subject and object is the error with which idealism begins, for the intuition of any identity is at best only a "merely logical" one; so that when Schelling moves from the intuition of $A = A$ to the distinction between A-subject and A-object, with a "preponderance" of subjectivity in the former, and of objectivity in the latter, he really was beginning his philosophy with a *non sequitur*. And from there it was easy to go on to develop meaningless analogies, such as that a line and angle are "forms of being" of the absolute identity.[14]

After having uncovered what he considered the bankruptcy of idealism, Köppen closes with a restatement of his own position: all knowledge must rest ultimately on belief and not on illusory faculties like intellectual intuition. What Schelling and, before him, Kant had called the "construction" of concepts was impossible for him, for personality and freedom cannot be "constructed" but must lie perpetually beyond such philosophical activity. Instead, what one must do is assent to a

Divine Intelligence as an act of faith in the fundamental rationality of reality.[15] What one cannot do is arrive at a comprehensive and systematic understanding of such rationality.

Franz Berg

Berg also focused his attack on Schelling's concept of intellectual intuition. In his *Sextus, oder Uber die absolute Erkenntniss von Schelling* (1804), he argues that Schelling's whole philosophy stands or falls on the justification he can give to his claim that absolute knowledge is possible. From this he attempts to show that all knowledge implies some form of cognitive mediation, and so mere intuition cannot support a knowledge claim, as Schelling maintains. In order to be sure error is not possible in an intellectual intuition, one must be prepared to judge that intuition using the canons of logic. But then he will not be intuiting, but instead thinking [*Denken*] and reflecting. Intellectual intuition is only a "phantasy," and is not the starting point of philosophy, but the product of a philosopher's mind. Instead, all philosophers must begin with "experience, thinking, reflection and even common sense."[16]

Even the logical identity $A = A$, which to Berg is all Schelling's claims amount to, is not an instance of immediate knowledge. For in the mental act of judging the A-subject to be identical with the A-object, one must reflect on the character of each before he can judge them identical.[17] And there is nothing immediate about this process. This means that apodictic knowledge of the sort Schelling desires in order to avoid dogmatism is not possible, and also that Schelling first must deal with all the traditional epistemological questions before he can establish his metaphysics.

Hegel's Attack

It is no credit to Hegel that we can now see the enormous debt he owes to Schelling. Direct references to his younger predecessor, when one considers the extent of the latter's influence upon him, are surprisingly few in number in his works, while references to Kant, Leibniz, Malebranch, Spinoza, and others far less important in his thought, abound. And when we consider that the great majority of indirect references to Fichte and Schelling are in the form of critical asides and insinuations, and not direct confrontations, we can suspect that perhaps Hegel wished it to appear to later historians that the other two were too obscure to be of any consequence to an interpretation of his own thought.

Without detracting from Hegel's own critical powers, there is reason to suspect that had he not had the benefit of Schelling's early writings on idealism, his thought would have developed in other directions, perhaps exclusively into juris-prudence or theology. H. S. Harris notes that in 1795 Schelling's interests were "more purely philosophical than Hegel's."[18] At this time Hegel was involved in traditional studies, which provoked Schelling's response in a letter to him that he had become "buried in the dust of ancient times" and instead should become more involved in the contemporary philosophical scene.[19] Indicative of the distance Hegel had to come was his reaction to Schelling's *Uber die Moglichkeit einer Form der Philosophie überhaupt.* In it he saw the destruction of the human personality and a challenge to his own classical humanism. Here Harris cites textual evidence "of Hegel's efforts to come to grips with this strange world of Ego and the non-Ego, and to relate it to the more concrete terms of the traditional moral psychology. . . ."[20] Even if the fragment *eine Ethik,* which has been attributed variously to Hegel, Schelling, and Hölderlin, was written in the summer of 1796 by Hegel, as Harris argues, there is very little in it that is not either directly or by direct implication found in Schelling's published work between 1793 and 1796.[21] The role given to myth in the fragment is developed in *Uber Mythen,* and the question posed by the author—"how must a world be con-stituted for a moral entity?"—is developed in the *Neue Deduction des Naturrechts* in some detail.[22] It is very likely, then, that it was Schelling who was calling the tune and Hegel learning to play variations of it, at least during this early period.

It has been argued that many of the critical asides, particularly in the *Zusätze* of Hegel's later works, were not intended against Schelling himself, but against his popularizers.[23] At one point Hegel does make such a distinction, and in the introduction to his *Naturphilosophie*, in speaking of the "considerable disfavor" *Naturphilosophie* had fallen into as a result of "crude treatment at unskilled hands," he does conclude, "it is on account of such charlatanism that *Naturphilosophie*, especially Schelling's, has become discredited."[24] Yet, these references are far outweighted by others more critical, which only seem to point to Schelling. How else, for example, are we to take Hegel's slap at "genius" as the current "rage in philosophy" in the Preface to the *Phänomenologie*?[25]

Hegel might simply have had an ambivalent attitude toward Schelling that he could never resolve. When compared to the anti-idealist critics, the two are kindred spirits, yet for some reason it was Hegel's wish to put as much distance between his work and Schelling's as could be possible given their similar starting points. We probably shall never know what feelings Hegel had about his relation with Schelling, for example in 1800, when at twenty-five Schelling was publishing the *System* and had achieved considerable notoriety, while it would still be a year before anything major of Hegel's would come before the public, and that in a journal in which Schelling clearly got top billing as co-editor. If it is not ambivalence that Hegel is reflecting in his May 1, 1807, letter to Schelling, then it could only be called hypocrisy, particularly in the light of the request he makes of Schelling. Making reference to the *Phäno-menologie* he writes: "In the Preface you will not find that I have gone too far against the shallowness that does so much mischief especially with your forms, reducing your science to a bare formalism" and finishes with, "Nor do I know anyone from whom I should rather see something to introduce this essay to the public and a judgment for my own benefit. . . ."[26] Schelling's reply six months later indicates that he was not altogether convinced of Hegel's intentions and sincerity: "So far I have read only the Preface. Inasmuch as you yourself mention its polemical part, having a just standard in my opinion of myself, I should have to think too little of myself to relate this polemic to myself. So it may and should strike, as you say in your letter to me, the abuse and babble of the imitators, although in this essay itself this distinction is not made."[27]

Hegel's criticism of Schelling seems to fall into six general categories: (1) Schelling's eclecticism, (2) his one-sidedness, wherein Schelling is made to appear as an earlier stage in the development of Hegel's position, (3) his belief in art as the highest human activity rather than philosophy, (4) his use of intellectual intuition, which leads to dogmatism, (5) his abstract formalism, which lacks the dialectical development of concepts, and (6) some of his specific views on gravity, magnetism, and light.

1. Eclecticism

Criticisms in this area are perhaps the most backhanded that Hegel presents, and they help create the suspicion of his desire to minimize the impact of Schelling's thought on his own. With few exceptions they are contained in the lectures on the history of philosophy. For example, in speaking of Kant's *Metaphysische Anfangsgründe der Naturwissenschaft*, Hegel notes that Kant "demands accordingly. . .a construction of matter from powers and activities, not from atoms; and Schelling still holds to this without getting further."[28] Once the dynamic concept of matter had been established, however, there was no further to go. What had to be done at that point was to point out its implications for the materialist outlook, and this Schelling did. Hegel was well aware of the difference between Kant and Schelling on matter. In the *Wissenschaft der Logik* he remarks that Kant's analysis of matter fails because "Kant from the start one-sidedly attributes to the concept of matter only the determination of impenetrability. . .," and in the *Naturphilosophie* he says of Kant that "he postulated the forces of attraction and repulsion, determinations of the reflective Understanding, as fixed mutual opposites, and whereas he should have made matter result from them, he presupposed it as something ready-made, so that what is to be attracted and repelled is already matter."[29] Both comments reflect substantially Schelling's own criticism of Kant's treatment of matter.

Then there are Hegel's remarks about the relation of Schelling to Fichte. While it was not until after 1800 that the break between the two became clearly evident to the public, Schelling had already departed from Fichtean idealism as early as 1796, and his works contain the sketch of a criticism of that system even earlier. Yet Hegel prefers to say that Schelling made "the only important advance upon the philosophy of Fichte; his philosopohy rose higher than that of Fichte, though undoubtedly it stood in close relation with it."[30] Hegel's comment is accurate only in the sense in which it could also be said that all the idealists stood in close relation to Kant, because it was to the latter's philosophy they all reacted.

After mentioning the work of Herder, Kielmeyer, and Eschenmayer on organic theory, Hegel remarks of Schelling: "It was only through what had been accomplished by these men that he was enabled to come into public notice so young."[31] Strictly speaking, Hegel's remark is accurate. Schelling had to rely on the work of others to be in a position to build their material into a *Naturphilosophie*, but the same applies no less to Hegel as well. The implication seems to be, though, that Schelling should get less credit for what he had accomplished than he was given at the time, and this is anything but accurate.

Finally, there is Hegel's final summation in the lectures on the history of philosophy of Schelling's work as "the latest form of philosophy which we had to consider, and it is a form both interesting and true."[32] Schelling's work is very recent history indeed, and unfortunately no attempt is made by Hegel here to show some of the connections between his own philosophy and Schelling's, though perhaps he did this in some of the lectures themselves. When we consider what Hegel thought Schelling's contributions were — that he had grasped the unity of the objective and subjective, and had shown nature to be a form of Spirit — it is surprising that he could refer to it only as the "latest form" and not as the cornerstone of his own philosophy, and therefore of genuine philosophy itself.

2. One-Sidedness

At times Schelling is made to appear one-sidedly subjective, at other times, one-sidedly objective. Here Hegel wishes to make it appear that Schelling's is an incomplete development of his own thought. He writes that after Kant "there was. . .to be found a yearning desire for content, for truth, since man could not possibly return to the condition of a brute, nor sink to the form of sensation, so that this yearning was for him the only thing that held good with regard to the higher life. The first requirement — consistency — Fichte sought to satisfy; the other — content — Schelling strove to fulfill."[33] The subtle implication contained in this passage is that Fichte lacked content and Schelling consistency, and that it was Hegel who first combined them. True enough, Fichte sought to give consistency to Kantianism, as other Kantians were attempting to do so at the time, but it is misleading to give the impression that Schelling was working on the same problems as was Fichte, only from another direction. Schelling was more concerned with the metaphysical implications of Fichte's critique of Kant, and Hegel knew this.

In his *Differenz des fichteschen und schellingschen Systems der Philosophie* (1801), written to defend Schelling against Reinhold, Hegel specifically attempts to show the radical break between Schelling and Fichte. Schelling, he argues, had gone beyond the subjectivity of Fichte's "subject = object," for "the principle of identity is the absolute principle of the *whole* of Schelling's system" and not, as with Fichte, limited only to his theory of knowledge.[34] At that point Hegel had realized that Schelling was attempting to build an idealistic *system* akin to that of Spinoza, and was not simply attempting to go beyond Kantian epistemology.[35] For some reason he later found it convenient to minimize this break with Fichte.

Schelling is given credit for *beginning* philosophy in the right way: "With Schelling the speculative form has thus again come to the front, and philosophy has again obtained a special character of its own. The principle of philosophy, rational thought in itself, has obtained the form of thought."[36] This marks the "time of birth and transition to a new period" in philosophy.[37] However, here Hegel does not make clear that Schelling belongs on his side against Fichte. Instead, pre-Hegelian philosophy is labeled "transcendental idealism," with no distinction made between the formulations of Fichte and Schelling. Transcendental idealism, Hegel argues, has not been liberated from the standpoint of consciousness, and this, he wants to imply, means that it has not been liberated from a one-sided subjectivism.[38] Yet, even as a description of Fichte's position, his argument is faulty: "the thing-in-itself being thus presupposed as the indeterminate, all determination falls outside it into an alien reflection to which it is indifferent. For *transcendental idealism* this external reflection is *consciousness.* Since this philosophical system places every determinateness of things both as regards form and content in consciousness. . . [it] is directly contradicted by the consciousness of freedom, according to which I know myself rather as the universal and undetermined. . . ."[39] It is more accurate to say that the thing-in-itself was *aufgehoben* by Schelling through intellectual intuition, and by Fichte through intuition and action, and it is precisely through the realization of this positing of object by the subject that the subject came to see its own freedom. At least in Schelling's case there was no world apart from the intuiting self, though as with Hegel also, there still remained the opposition of individual consciousness and the universal Spirit. And both Fichte and Schelling, from the earliest stages of the new post-Kantian idealism, adhered to the view that the free positing consciousness had the character of being unconditioned, absolute, and universal.

As part of his critique of previous philosophy in the Preface to the *Phänomenologie* Hegel writes: "Beginning with the subject, as if this remained the basis, it finds, because the predicate is really the substance, that the subject has moved into the predicate and has thus been transcended. Thus, that which seemed to be predicate has become the whole and independent mass, and thinking can no longer stray freely, but is brought to a stop by this gravity."[40] This remark seems to refer specifically to Schelling, and not simply to previous forms of idealism. In effect it constitutes an accusation that Schelling had lapsed into dogmatism; for after he realized the identity of subject and object in intellectual intuition, he transferred this to the identity of Nature and Spirit. Nature becomes unconscious, slumbering Spirit. It is here that "the subject has moved into the predicate" to Hegel, because Schelling regards Nature as also the realm of Spirit and not merely the collection of individual selves. The latter merely comprises part of the potency of Nature to reflect upon itself. Nature does become "the whole," but not as an "independent mass," for the opposition between self and Nature is merely one of part and whole, not one between freedom and necessity, life and "mass." Hegel himself must have understood this distinction, for it is the one upon which his own position is founded. And if Schelling's intuiting consciousness "can no longer stray freely," neither could the Hegelian conscious self contend with the cunning of Reason.

3. The Role of Art

The aesthetic standpoint marks the completion of the journey of self-consciousness in Schelling's *System des trans- zendentalen Idealismus*. This was disagreeable to Hegel, who thought that only *philosophy* could represent the highest form of spiritual activity. And so Hegel rejects Schelling's conclusion as a particular form of one-sidedness. For philosophy is the perfect self-realization of Reason, while in art the objective in its "stubborn foreignness" remains, to some extent, in the material upon which artistic creation must work. In the lectures on the history of philosophy Hegel expresses this view in his remark that for Schelling art represents the essential activity of intellectual intuition insofar as the latter is "objective sensuous intuition"; he continues, "but the concept, the comprehended necessity, is a very different objectivity," and therefore concludes, "but art and the power of imagination are not supreme. . .on account of this sensuous form of existence the work of art cannot correspond to the Spirit."[41] It is probably this sort of criticism Hegel had in mind when he said of Schelling that "he advanced only as far as the organism and did not reach the presentation of the other side of knowledge, the philosophy of Spirit."[42]

It is doubtful that Hegel would have been at odds with Schelling's approach to the history of art, for it was similar to his own. It is only the destiny of art that is at stake here. To Schelling this criticism would be unfair, inasmuch as it constitutes a subtle attempt to establish guilt through association, in this case with Kant. For Hegel makes it appear that "sensuous intuition" for Schelling means the same as for Kant, and that therefore Schelling is prey to all the difficulties involved in trying to extract the conceptual from the sensuous. However, Schelling's perspective is totally different from Kant's. For him the sensuous was not passive, and the imagination not blind. For Kant the *ens realissimum* was the noumenal realm; for Hegel it was Spirit as the Absolute; but for Schelling it was the World System in its self-creating activity. Hegel, he would argue, simply confuses the process with its result. The goal of the Absolute for both is greater freedom, self-reflection, and rationality, but the process for achieving this for Schelling involves artistic creativity rather than reflection on concepts. There is no "stubborn foreignness" for him, because nature is ultimately creative itself and works on itself in an aesthetic manner.

As noted earlier, Schelling's *Philosophie der Kunst* (1802-03) is his attempt to show this connection between art and *Naturphilosophie*. There he writes, "In the philosophy of art

I construe art not as art, as this *particular* thing, but I *construe the Universe in the form of art*, and the philosophy of art is the science of All in the form or potency of art." For example, "*music* is nothing other than the primordial [*urbildiche*] rhythm of nature and the Universe itself. The fully completed form, which the *plastic arts* produce, are the objective representative prototypes [*Urbilder*] of organic nature itself. The Homeric epic is the Identity itself, as it lays the foundation for history in the Absolute. And every painting manifests the intellectual world."[43] But this does not mean that art is superior to philosophy in doing what, in fact, only philosophy can do — that is, *comprehending* the nature of the Absolute. In the most obvious sense, Schelling regards himself as a philosopher and not as an artist, although he did try his hand at poetry on one or more occasions. His essential argument against Hegel here is that in the activity of philosophy we do not see how the Absolute operates, but only how it makes that operation understood to itself. *Content* for reflection remains to be established, and it is artistic activity that supplies this content. Schelling expresses this relation between art and philosophy in the following manner: "In the ideal world philosophy is to art, as Reason is to the organism in the real world."[44] This means that in the total identity of real and ideal contained in the Absolute — or, what now Schelling begins to speak of as "God" — art and philosophy each play their indispensable roles. Insofar as we as artists participate in this activity, we must do so by an interaction with nature, but in so doing we participate in the universal creative process by creating *symbols* as universals in particular form.[45]

Schelling's approach to art is more applicable to what Hegel calls *Objective Mind*. Here, for Hegel, Spirit finds its fullest expression. Yet even here philosophy does not proceed without art and imagination; instead, it becomes "the unity of Art and Religion."[46] Perhaps this means that philosophy itself ceases to be a cultural institution, or maybe that art and religion become essentially philosophical instead. In either case, Schelling wants to go even further and make creativity not only a character of Objective Mind, but an essential potency of the Absolute itself. This, of course, from the point of view of Hegel's more extreme rationalism, was completely unacceptable.

4. Intellectual Intuition

Hegel's criticisms of "intuition" could generally have been directed to any of a number of thinkers who held to some sort of immediacy in knowledge. This could include some fideists, those who appealed to common sense, and the transcendental idealists. That he was so indiscriminate in his attack may indicate that he would have been happy to have the leading intuitionists of the time — Fichte and Schelling — included among those he attacked. And surely, when he specifically criticized "intellectual intuition," most people at the time would have associated his remarks directly with Schelling. In the *Differenz*, where the germs of his own position can clearly be seen, Hegel seems to accept the legitimacy of claims based on intellectual intuition.[47] Yet, in the Preface to the *Phänomenologie*, instead of beginning with intellectual intuition and from there moving to an analysis of the dialectical development of concepts, he chose to single out the former for attack, and pitted one against the other. In the lectures on the history of philosophy, where he is speaking specifically of Schelling, he calls intellectual intuition "the Fichtean imagination," "the most convenient manner of asserting knowledge respecting anything one likes," and something "we may merely think we understand." Yet, he also calls it "the intelligent intuitive perception which all who wish to philosophize must have."[48] The following quotations may bring out the distinction Hegel wants to make between intellectual intuition and thinking with concepts:

> Intuition is consciousness *filled* with the certainty of Reason, whose object is *rationally* determined and consequently not an individual torn asunder into its various aspects but a totality,

a unified fullness of determination. It was in this sense that Schelling formally spoke of intuition. . . .But the necessity for going beyond mere intuition lies in the fact that intelligence, according to its concept, is *cognition* [*Erkennen*], whereas intuition is not as yet a *cognitive* awareness of the subject-matter, since as such it does not attain to the *immanent development* of the substance of the subject-matter. . . .Intuition is, therefore, only the *beginning* of cognition.[49]

We often find that philosophical exposition refers us to this internal intuition and thus spares itself the presentation of the dialectical movement of the proposition, which we demanded.[50]

And when thirdly, thinking unites with itself the being of the substance and comprehends immediacy or intuition as thinking, it still remains decisive whether this intellectual intuition does not fall back into inert simplicity and present actuality in a non-actual manner. . . .When the form is said to be the same as the essence it is plainly a misunderstanding to suppose that knowledge can be satisfied with the in-itself of the essence while sparing itself concern with the form — as if the absolute principle or absolute intuition made the explication of the former or the development of the latter dispensable.[51]

Here Hegel appears to be saying that Schelling's notion of intellectual intuition must be merely a *beginning* in philosophy and cannot take the place of cognition and the dialectical development of concepts, exemplified by both the *Phäno-menologie* and the *Wissenschaft der Logik*. But is there any reason for him to doubt that not only would Schelling agree with this, but that his philosophy, in fact, reflected such cognition, though not so powerfully as Hegel's had? In the same letter in which Schelling expresses his reservations about the intent of Hegel's criticism in the Preface he remarks: "So I confess that so far I do not comprehend the sense in which you oppose the concept to intuition. Surely, you could not mean anything else by it than what you and I used to call Idea, whose nature it is to have one side from which it is concept and one from which it is intuition."[52] To Schelling's way of thinking intuition is the act of intuiting and is immediate only in that sense; however, what it intuits are the *relations* between concepts such as *real* and *ideal, finite* and *infinite,* and the like, and out of a reflection on such relationships a transcendental philosophy emerges.

It is in the early pages of the *Wissenschaft der Logik* that Hegel's criticism ultimately stands or falls, for it is here, in Objective Logic, that philosophy must attain its absolute ground. After stating the historical problem involved in *beginning* a philosophy, he rejects starting his philosophy with first principles, a primordial substance, or an apodictic mental act, and instead chooses the concept of *Being* in its "simple immediacy" as "what is there before us" and as "an expression of reflection."[53] However, to Schelling, Hegel is saying nothing more than that the intuiting subject achieves an awareness of intuiting an object *as such*, for Hegel's *Sein* is already a being *reflected upon.* Hegel tries to minimize this when he goes on to remark that "we are not concerned in the science of logic with what is present only in *principle* or as something *inner.* . .," yet he cannot avoid the intuitive standpoint here. This applies also to his analysis of *Nothing*, for it is only through grasping Nothing *in consciousness* that it passes into Being.[54] Consequently, intellectual intuition remains indispensable to Hegel, and the impression he gives that his approach concerns the "outer" as well is unjustified. Perhaps he realized that he was drawing the issue between intuition and conceptual development too sharply when he added "True, intellectual intuition is the forcible rejection of mediation and ratiocinative, external reflection; but what it enunciates above and beyond simple immediacy is something concrete, something which contains within itself diverse determinations."[55] The intuition of the absolute identity, $A = A$, however, is not concrete; if this is what Hegel means by "simple immediacy" then Schelling has no quarrel. But even here Schelling's *System* is precisely his attempt to unfold the "diverse determinations" of simple self-reflection, so that it is clear he has not overlooked this fact. He would probably want to emphasize to Hegel that it is in the nature of the concepts themselves which way development is to proceed, but it is in intellectual intuition that the concepts become related in the first place. Ultimately Hegel must rely on it to establish the *aufgehoben* of Being and Nothing, Sameness and Difference, and Determination and Indetermination. Even so, to advertise this was to invite the same charge of dogmatism he brings against Schelling. In his lectures on the history of philosophy, where his argumentation just about approaches out-and-out propaganda for his position, he makes it appear that intellectual intuition cannot be a beginning in *any* sense, and therefore that his whole approach is opposed to Schelling's rather than being instead a clearer, more powerfully argued version of it. His remark that "in philosophy, when we desire to establish a position, we demand proof. . . .But if we begin with intellectual intuition, that constitutes an oracle to which we have to give way," applies no less to him as well.[56]

5. Formalism

Much of what has just been said bears on the charge of formalism as well, for to Hegel it is Schelling's reliance on intellectual intuition that leads to "monochromatic formalism."[57] This charge, which involves the bulk of Hegel's critical remarks against Schelling, is for him "the great difficulty in the philosophy of Schelling."[58]

To Hegel's way of thinking Schelling had simply *postulated* the identity of subject and object; instead, "it must be shown that the subjective signifies the transformation of itself into the objective." Schelling could not do this because he lacked "a definite logical method."[59] All he could do was dogmatically assert what the implications of absolute identity were supposed to be, but this is unacceptable because the geometric method "has no real application to philosophy."[60] Instead, Schelling must be satisfied with "abstract generality" and "monotony," which further leads to "a tangled mass of abstractions."[61] Hegel has in mind here Schelling's concept of the Absolute as perfect indifference and so as something that really does nothing.

Clearly referring to Schelling, Hegel writes: "To study anything as it is in the absolute here means merely that one says of it — 'to be sure it has just been spoken of as something, however, in the absolute itself, the $A = A$, there is nothing of the sort, for in the absolute everything is One.' To put this single piece of information, that the absolute All is One, against all the distinctions of knowledge, both attained knowledge and the search and demand for knowledge — or to pass off one's Absolute as the night in which, as one says, all cows are black — that is the naiveté of the emptiness of knowledge. . . ."[62]

Hegel elaborates his point further in the *Wissenschaft der Logik*:

> Thinking that keeps to external reflection and knows no other thinking but external reflection fails to attain to a grasp of identity in the form just expounded, or of essence, which is the same thing. . . .In its opinion Reason is nothing more than a loom on which it externally combines and weaves the warp of, say, identity, and then the woof of difference. . . .The truth is rather that a consideration of everything that is shows that *in its own self* everything is in its self-sameness different from itself and self-contradictory, and that in its difference, in its contradiction, it is self-identical, and is in its own self this movement from transition of one of these categories into the other, and for this reason, that each is in its own self the opposite of itself.[63]

This appears to be an exceedingly technical point against Schelling. The latter would not have wanted to *postulate* ultimate disharmony because he would have desired to establish a transcendental condition for such a possibility, which, insofar as it is the Absolute he is attempting to justify, would be impossible. Identity had the "self-sameness" that appeared to need no further justification. Besides, intellectual intuition was an example of such identity that we ourselves could experience. Yet even Schelling's Absolute generates oppositions "in its own self," for there is no other way they could result, so that Hegel's criticism here amounts to nothing more than that Schelling did not emphasize this point enough.

Actually, there is a deeper disagreement between the two. Schelling *begins* with the Absolute and then shows how differentiation comes to it. Hegel takes Schelling's Absolute and splits it into Idea and Spirit, and subjects both to a historical scenario, the development of the Idea toward the fullness of Spirit. He prefers to think of the Absolute as a "result" [*Resultat*], which, he admits, appears to be a contradiction. Some people, he says, abhor mediation in the Absolute itself and want to speak of it only as Absolute, whereas actually "mediation is nothing else than self-identity that moves itself, or is reflection into itself. . . ."[64] In one respect, Schelling does allow for such mediation as the differentiation of the Absolute. It would be wrong to hold, however, he would say, that the Absolute *in itself* as totality was subject to change; that would mistake our perspective as part of the Absolute for the whole of it. Hegel's Absolute for him would not be a *prius*, an essential characteristic of any Absolute. How it could *begin* only as Idea and through "the movement of positing itself, or the mediation between a self and its development into something different" become Spirit is never explained.[65] True enough, Schelling's Absolute first *appears* as simple (absolute) indifference, as Oken, for example, had interpreted it, and progressively moves toward greater differentiation. In this sense Schelling appears to present a cosmology in his *Naturphilosophie*.[66] However, this differentiation is not, in fact, conceived as *real*. Within the World System its reality is purely perspectival; from the point of view of the Absolute itself all distinctions collapse. To explain this Schelling would use the following mathematical relation:

$$0 = 1 + 1 - 1 + 1 - 1 . . .$$

Hegel prefers to characterize this motion of cancellation as "the life of the Concept," but for Schelling this metaphor and all those involving "movement" Hegel uses is deceptive.[67] The Absolute is not growing; nor does it feel itself become more self-conscious, at least in any absolute sense. It does separate itself, for example into light and gravity, and then into matter and motion, and so forth, but it cancels these, and returns to itself once more. For Schelling, the long and elaborate journey between Idea and the Absolute of which Hegel writes so much is actually only what the Absolute effects while it is moving from (+ 1) to (-1).

Schelling tried to explain this motion of the Absolute in his remark that all difference is only quantitative. Probably no other single remark provoked such a critical response from Hegel. Hegel had replied that "difference must really be understood as qualitative. . . .Quantitative difference is not true difference, but an entirely external relation."[68] In his own *Naturphilosophie* Hegel spoke of "the fundamental error of first defining the Absolute as the absolute indifference of subject and object, and then treating all determination as only *quantitative* differences. The truth is rather that the absolute form, i.e., the concept and principle of life, has for its soul only and solely the qualitative difference which transcends itself, the dialectic of absolute opposition."[69] Schelling would probably regard Hegel's comment here to be applicable only to ourselves, who possess life and rationality, and so as another indication of the latter's confusion of human philosophic understanding with the activity of the Absolute itself.

What, for Hegel, is this "qualitative difference which transcends itself"? In the *Wissenschaft der Logik* he attempts to show the primacy of the qualitative over the quantitative, but this attempt fails. At one point he remarks, "the difference of the *absolute* unity is supposed to be only quantitative; the quantitative, it is true, is immediate, transcended determinateness, but only the imperfect, as yet only *first* negation, not the infinite, not the *negation* of the negation. When *being* and *thought* are represented as quantitative determinations of absolute substance, they too, as quanta, become completely external to each other and unrelated, as, in a subordinate sphere, do carbon, nitrogen, etc."[70] Hegel characterizes the quantitative as "transcended determinateness" which *itself* must be transcended, so that either way determinateness is prior. One must turn to his discussion of the "Becoming of Essence" in order to see how he understands this process of transcendence. Here he takes up the transition of "determination of indifference" to "absolute indifference," and once again calls the latter "the *negation* of every determinateness of being," thereby giving priority to the former. Indifference is really "empty differentiation" involving "a mediation-with-self," negation, and relation.[71] This is precisely what Schelling would regard as *quantitative* difference, for Hegel is saying the same thing, but in a different way. Instead of speaking of the determination of indifference as being qualitative, he regards the indifferent as the negation of determination. And this determination for Hegel is *essentially* quantitative as well. For in his discussion of qualitative determination he maintains that such determination arises when "the two quanta" become related in a negative fashion, but *how* qualities become possible in this manner is never explained. All he says is "this relation is distinguished from the earlier inverted relation or inverse ratio by the fact that here the whole is a real substrate and each of the two sides is posited as having to be in itself this whole."[72] Schelling would not deny, for example, that the sensations of red and blue are each posited "in itself" as "whole" and "real," though he would deny that outside of such positings the difference can be anything more than quantitative. And it seems that Hegel himself must agree, for he concludes, "the one quality is through its quantum a *preponderant* in the one side, and so too, the other quality in the other side."[73]

Even without establishing his case Hegel accuses Schelling of presenting only "a dull semblance of differentiation" and a "formless repetition of one and the same principle."[74] Because Schelling regarded all relations as ultimately quantitative he used simple algebraic symbols to express the kind of relationship that existed within the Absolute. Naturally, then, Hegel is also in disagreement with this, characterizing it as "the puerile incapacity which again puts in place of thought determinations numbers themselves and number-forms like powers."[75] Hegel's complaint is that mathematical and logical notation does not "contain the Concept and therefore no problem for speculative thought, but [is] the antithesis of the Concept. . . .Because of the indifference of the factors in combination to the combination itself in which there is no necessity, thought is engaged here in an activity which is at the same time the extreme externalization of itself, an activity in which it is forced to move in a realm of thoughtlessness and to combine elements which are incapable of any necessary relationships."[76] There is no doubt that an analysis of quantitative relation such as Hegel gives in the "Objective Logic" is superior to simply writing $(A = B^+) = (A = B^-)$, but Schelling himself did not consider one the substitute for the other. Rather, he regarded the expression of such relationships as symbols, which Hegel himself, at one point, thinks to be "harmless enough," though not necessary in philosophy.[77] It is even open to question whether Hegel's distinction between symbols and concepts can be sustained, but this is not an issue between him and Schelling. If there is anything "puerile" about Schelling's approach it is not that he utilized symbols, but that his analysis of concepts was not so concretely developed as Hegel's.

Another facet of the formalism charge is Hegel's belief that Schelling used only the most superficial analogies in his *Naturphilosophie*.[78] Here Hegel can find much to ridicule: "Schelling and Steffens have likened the series of plants to the series of metals in a clever and ingenious fashion. This mode of representation is an old one. . . .Such allusions and analogies are external comparisons which decide nothing,"[79] and "this mistake of applying forms which are taken from one sphere of Nature to another sphere of the same has been carried a long way; Oken, for example, calls wood-fibre the nerves and brain of the plant, and is almost crazy on the subject."[80]

The use of analogies is essential to Schelling's outlook, for the structures of the Absolute are isomorphic in relation to each other. And Hegel himself makes analogous references between the Concept and a living organism, as well as between light and ideality. In fact, the whole *Phänomenologie* can be regarded as an illustration of how the forms of history and culture are analogous to the forms of self-consciousness. Hegel should have restricted his criticisms simply to his remark that "Schelling launched out into too many individual details, if he desired to indicate the construction of the whole universe."[81]

6. Differences in *Naturphilosophie*

For Schelling, initial differentiation comes to the Absolute with the separation of *Lichtwesen* and gravity, each representing the centrifugal and centripetal forces of nature. Then their interaction produces the provisional stability we know as matter. Finally, with the resolution of these opposing forces, a linear vector is formed, producing magnetism, and, from the further interaction of such vectors, as electricity, the particular forms of matter emerge. Hegel, however, opposed light with matter.[82] Gravity is for him "the being-with-self of matter" and "the Concept of matter."[83] Matter that is individualized Hegel calls "being-for-self developed within itself, and. . . .therefore determined within itself. Matter thus tears itself from gravity. . . ." Light, on the other hand, becomes the "universal *self* of Matter," and "physical ideality."[84] The differences between the two approaches, which perhaps only the most thoroughgoing devotee of *Naturphilosophie* can appreciate, is that in Schelling's system the interaction of the components produces the possibilities of further interaction, while in Hegel's a single component grows in self-awareness. This component is actually the Idea, which first appears as gravity. Matter in the abstract is self not yet separated from itself, and so is "selfless"; light, however, is "pure self."[85] It is clear, then, that the Idea takes the place of Schelling's *Lichtwesen* in Hegel's system, and gives it a more predetermined character. Schelling would not have felt justified in using the concept of *self* so early in the development of his World System. For the higher forms could develop through a metamorphosis recapitulating previous development, but not the World System itself, which would have to evolve through emergence, while in Hegel all development becomes simply the metamorphosis of the abstract Idea into concrete Spirit.

This overall difference affects the interpretation given other facts of their *Naturphilosophie*. For Hegel magnetism becomes "the clear active Concept, which however is not as yet realized," instead of, as with Schelling, a one-sided resolution of opposing tendencies.[86] The work of the Concept can also be seen on the organic level. Hegel observes that it was an advance to assert

> that nothing whatever can have a positive relation to the living being if the possibility of this relation is not in its own self, that is, if the relation is not determined by the Concept and hence not directly immanent in the subject. But of all the concoctions of external reflection in the sciences, none is more unphilosophical than the introduction of such formal and material relationships in the theory of stimulation as have long been regarded as philosophical, the introduction, for example, of the wholly abstract opposition of receptivity and active capacity.[87]

Schelling's method, in other words, lacking the Concept, could not be both "formal and material" at once. Organic activity emerges out of the dialectical extension of chemical reaction, first as sensation and finally as reproductive activity, and so must be an analogue of chemical interaction, though in a more complicated fashion. If there is a Concept here it is the dialectic itself, which re-creates itself at each level; however, it is a Concept that has no reality apart from nature itself. It does not "live" as does Hegel's.

7

Schelling's Influence in Nineteenth-Century America

In the early decades of the nineteenth century, German philosophy had to overcome two significant obstacles in America. First, it was "philosophy" in a strange and new sense, something very different from what Americans had been used to in the philosophical orthodoxy of the British schools. Here was a philosophy not "plain" and based on common sense, but "speculative," reflective, and transcendental. In 1810 Edward Everett warned his fellow students in *The Harvard Lyceum*, the first student publication of the college, to avoid the writings of "the mystical German,"[1] and as late as 1840 from the even more conservative *Yale Literary Magazine* came a criticism of abstruse philosophy generally, and of German philosophy in particular: "Cut loose from *common* sense, the followers of the Kantian system have found no scheme too vague, no plan too wild for their acceptance; allaying every doubt by the dream of a *transcendental* perception of truth, obviating every objection by the ready answer 'you do not understand us.' "[2]

Second, it was "German" philosophy, and as such shared in the rather pervasive ignorance of and bias against more recent German culture that existed at the time. Indicative of this is the fact that between 1817 and 1837 there was nowhere to be found in the curriculum of Harvard College any trace of German philosophy.[3] In 1820 the editor of the newly formed *German Correspondent* could justly complain that "it is very remarkable that in a country like the United States there is but little known concerning Germany."[4] The poems of Schiller and some references to Goethe do appear in the early Reviews and Quarterlies, but even these are outnumbered by "letters" sent back from exotic Italy by visiting Americans. However, perhaps because of this unfamiliarity, there was also a fascination with "German scholars" and with German university students, the latter of whom were said to beg in the streets and read their tomes by moonlight.[5] By about 1835 there were signs of change, and by 1840 a highly sympathetic audience for German thought had developed in America. Now *The Iris, or Literary Messenger* could speak of German scholars as profound thinkers — "they can rest at nothing but truth"[6] — while the *Boston Weekly Magazine* of 1839 would ambivalently complain:

> One Fulton, or Franklin, or Whitney, or Bowditch, is worth to *us* all the Professors the German Universities ever saw. . . we speculate, but not in the German sense. We study, but stocks much more than books. Few men are among us now of the class of Jonathan Edwards, who, slender as he was, devoted thirteen hours daily to his study, and ruminated over his treatises on horse-back besides.[7]

In this atmosphere it was inevitable that the New England Transcendentalists would become caught up in the question of the supposedly German origins of their philosophy. The writer of an article on Transcendentalism for the *Yale Literary Magazine* of 1844 summed up the situation well when he observed: "We believe ourselves perfectly safe in asserting that ninety-nine out of every one hundred declaimers against Transcendentalism use that term as synonymous with German opinions, whatever their character and source." To him this, however, was not the issue; the issue was not whether the new philosophy of Schelling and Hegel contained defects, but whether it could be an improvement over philosophical orthodoxy, for "one thing is certain; there is error or defect somewhere in the old system. Else why these interminable apologies, annotations, and qualifications of Locke?"[8] Still, Orestes Brownson saw fit to disassociate Transcendentalism from German influence. In an article in the *Christian Examiner* Francis Bowen had argued that Transcendentalism was an incomprehensible and dangerous doctrine, and that its proponents would benefit greatly by an education in Locke's philosophy.[9] Brownson replied to Bowen in the first issue of his *Boston Quarterly Review*:

> it would seem that these dangers consist in the fact that the Transcendentalists encourage the study of German literature and philosophy, and are introducing the habit of writing bad English. . . .So far, however, as our knowledge extends, there is no overweening fondness for German literature and philosophy. We know not of a single man in this country, who avows himself a disciple of what is properly called the Transcendental Philosophy. The genius of our countrymen is for Eclecticism.[10]

And in response to the criticism of Andrews Norton of Harvard that Transcendentalism represented a "German insanity," Brownson said of the members of the movement:

> Some of them embrace the Transcendental philosophy, some of them reject it, some of them *ignore* all philosophy, plant themselves on their instincts, and wait for the huge world to come round to them. . . .We have nothing to do with Hegel, or Schelling, or Kant, or Cousin, any further than our own inquiries lead us to approve their speculations.[11]

German philosophy remained, prior to 1835, a vast, uncharted, and exotic wilderness of ideas for most American thinkers. Not surprisingly, their first guides into this territory were English and French—Coleridge, Carlyle, Cousin, and Madame de Staël—and information began to filter through to them from British periodicals like the *New Monthly*

Magazine, which had an American edition, and the *Foreign Quarterly Review*. A few Americans like Edward Everett, George Ticknor, George Bancroft, and Frederic Hedge had studied in Germany as young men and had brought back a lively interest in German culture which, in most cases, remained all of their lives. Not to be discounted also were émigrés like F. A. Rauch and Charles Follen, the latter of whom had taught at the University of Jena and later took up a position at Harvard from 1825 to 1835, only to have his appointment terminated allegedly for spreading romantic and German influences.[12] By the late thirties anthologies of French and German literature began to appear. George Ripley's *Specimens of Foreign Standard Literature*, first published in 1838, contained selections translated by Ripley from Cousin, Jouffroy, and Benjamin Constant in its first two volumes. The third volume contained translations of Goethe, Schiller, and other German poets. *Selections from German Literature*, edited by B. B. Edwards and E. A. Park (1839), C. C. Felton's edition of Menzel's *History of German Literature*, and in 1849 Hedge's *The Prose Writers of Germany* all made significant contributions to the growing interest in German thought.

Transcendentalism

As indicated in Brownson's remarks, many of the Transcendentalists had a love/hate relation with the German philosophers. Nearly all were uneasy at the thought of being labeled a pure Schellingian or Hegelian. One important reason for this was that American Transcendentalism had strong religious roots and was in many cases advanced by ministers whose early interest in German thought began with German theology, biblical criticism, and jurisprudence; in almost all cases the more they learned about German philosophy the more impatient they became with its complexities and abstractions. George Ripley, who had taken to German philosophy in the 1830s, was to consider it by 1848 as merely providing "wonderful specimens of intellectual gymnastics."[13] Earlier, Brownson had said of members of Schelling's school: "they give us a magnificent poem which we believe to be mainly true, but which nevertheless is no philosophy and can in no degree solve the difficulty stated by Hume."[14] In all likelihood we can say that none of the Transcendentalists had embarked on a prolonged systematic study of German metaphysical idealism and had rejected it on that account. On the other hand, this does not mean that they had first formulated their position, as Brownson avers, and then turned to the Germans for corroboration. What seems to have happened is that Schelling's thought came to them first primarily through Coleridge and then through Cousin, and only later, when some scant primary source material became available, did Schelling seem to ratify their position.

In 1817 Coleridge's *Biographia Literaria* appeared in America and two years later it came into the hands of James Marsh, who was then a tutor at Dartmouth College; this encounter, along with Marsh's reading of Madame de Staël's *De L'Allemagne* (1814), led to an interest in German metaphysics. In 1826 Marsh was translating Herder's "Spirit of Hebrew Poetry" for the *Biblical Repertory*, and in 1829 he edited Coleridge's *Aids to Reflection*, including in the edition what was to become an important and controversial "Preliminary Essay." In this essay Marsh advanced for the first time a view of the compatibility of philosophy and religion, and of the importance of philosophical speculation about matters divine. "I should like to know," he asked, "how a man comes by any common sense in relation to the movements and laws of his intellectual and moral being without metaphysics."[15] At that time it was surely a controversial issue whether metaphysics was required for theology, and Marsh's claim that "every man, who has reflected at all, has his metaphysics" must have aroused suspicions in more conservative quarters. Even more, Marsh suggested that the Lockean and Scottish systems might actually be "injurious and dangerous" to theology, for "we have literally, if the system of Locke and the popular philosophy of the day be true. . .neither reason nor free-will."[16]

As he saw it, a better system was available to philosophers than the prevailing British one with its mechanistic and reductionist tendencies, and that system was the one that could be discovered behind Coleridge's reflections — the one implied in Coleridge's distinction, outlined in the *Aids*, between the Understanding as a faculty of judgment and Reason as the faculty of speculation. Doubtless, in presenting the argument of the "Preliminary Essay" Marsh had in mind what he had gleaned from the Schellingian theory of nature put forward in the *Biographia Literaria*, but, given the intellectual temper of his time, he evidently thought it more judicious to warm the public to the new German ideas slowly.

Later, as president of the University of Vermont, Marsh proposed a revision of the curriculum inspired by the architectonic approach to academic study of the Germans. Among his posthumous papers published by Torrey in 1843 is one entitled "Outlines of a Systematic Arrangement of the Departments of Knowledge, with a View to their Organic Relations to each other in a General System." Here Marsh gives an outline of a course of instruction that follows the hierarchical structure of the *Naturphilosophen*, beginning in this case with a study of space and time, followed by a study of Geometry and Chronometry, then to "Metaphysical Principles of Natural Philosophy," and on to physics and the life sciences, each building on what had came previously. Kant's dynamic theory of matter, and Fries's *Mathematische Naturphilosophie* are important influences in the essay, but its overall inspiration is pure Schellingian *Naturphilosophie*. The discussions of polarity, correlations between electricity, magnetism, and chemical affinity, and accounts of various organic "powers" clearly show the influence of Schelling, or of those, Oersted in this case, associated with him.[17]

Marsh could not be considered a *Transcendentalist* in the usual sense of the word, primarily because he was not an active member of that southern New England movement. In fact, he called the movement at one point "a superficial affair" and complained of its members: "they have many of the prettinesses of the German writers, but without their manly logic and strong systematizing tendency."[18] However, his influence must be measured by the way he first broke the ground for the reception of German ideas, and here it was probably more decisive than that of any other thinker of the time.

Frederic Hedge was both a member of the movement—so much so that the Transcendental Club was informally called the "Hedge Club" because it would convene whenever he would come down to Boston from Bangor, Maine, where he was a minister—and a scholarly thinker, who, like Marsh, also lamented the lack of sound American scholarship in German philosophy. Hedge went to Germany when thirteen years old in the company of George Bancroft, sent there by his father, Levi Hedge, who was then Professor of Logic at Harvard, for the purposes of improving his education. He returned four years later, in 1822, and entered Harvard soon thereafter.

In 1833 he wrote "Coleridge's Literary Character" for the *Christian Examiner*, and in years later recalled that this essay was "the *first word*, so far as I know, which any American had uttered in respectful recognition of the claims of Transcendentalism."[19] A disrespectful critique of idealism, entitled "Cousins Philosophy," had appeared two years earlier in the *American Quarterly Review*, wherein the author had warned:

> But at this moment, if we mistake not the signs of the times, philosophy has come to the birth even amongst us. The system which already prevails here, which has been intimated if not developed in a philosophical work—President Marsh's commentary upon Coleridge. . . .—this system is Idealism. We propose therefore to say what seems to us the wants and dangers of idealism.

After noting that "idealism is matured and bears its true and ripened fruit in Schelling's celebrated Intellectual Intuition," the reviewer goes on to indicate the danger of this subjectivism to our basic common-sense notions of God and creation.[20]

Hedge's review, on the other hand, indicates that he had

learned enough of German philosophy to begin to see patterns and implications. For this reason this work was probably the most important of the time in terms of informational content and concrete effect in moving the more liberal forms of Christianity closer to Transcendentalism.[21] He notes, for example, that the transcendental method "is synthetical, proceeding from a given point, the lowest that can be found in our consciousness, and deducing from that point 'the whole world of intelligences, with the whole system of their representations.' " After describing some of the basic notions of Fichte's philosophy, Hedge, as he would all his life, gives his highest praise to Schelling—"the ontologist of the Kantian school":

> Of all the Germans who have trod the path of metaphysical inquiry under the guidance of Kant, Schelling is the most satisfactory. In him intellectual philosophy is more ripe, more substantial, more promising, and, if we may apply such a term to such speculations, more practical than in any of the others.[22]

In his *The Prose Writers of Germany*, Hedge included selections from Boehme, Kant's *Critique of Judgment*, Fichte's *Vocation of Man*, Hegel's "Introduction" to the *Philosophy of History*, and Schelling's "On the Relation of the Plastic Arts to Nature." Here too he speaks of Schelling as "the richest genius and the widest influence. . . .His word is the breath of spring to the intellectual world of his time. . . .His philosophy is creative, as that of Kant is destructive."[23] Throughout the rest of his long life Hedge continued to incorporate idealistic notions into his writings. His *Reason in Religion* (1866) and *Ways of the Spirit and Other Essays* (1877) reflect throughout his concern for issues raised by Schelling. And in his *Martin Luther and Other Essays* (1888) he wisely observed of the idealistic movement:

> As a science of the *Absolute*, it has failed to redeem its high promise, and to place itself on a footing of equality, in point of demonstration, with the exact sciences. . . .But with all its faults, it will be found, in the final judgment, to have answered,

in its degree, the true purpose of metaphysical inquiry, in furnishing a new impulse to thought, and enlarging, somewhat the horizon of life.[24]

Some of the earliest accounts of the new idealism to appear in America are found in the unsympathetic and unsystematic reviews of Victor Cousin's *Fragments Philosophiques* and *Cours de Philosophie*.[25] The first sympathetic approach to idealism via Cousin, however, is found in the writings of Caleb Sprague Henry, who became Professor of Mental and Moral Philosophy at New York University in 1838, after a career as a minister. Henry edited Cousin's *Elements of Psychology* in 1834 and used the opportunity to inveigh against British empiricism and to advance Schelling's position in America. Besides editing the *New York Review* (1837-1840), which contained reviews of works by Ripley, Marsh, and Rauch, Henry translated from the French *An Epitome of the History of Philosophy* (1841-42), an important work at the time in that it presented, in the Appendix, a "Sketch of the History of Philosophy from Reid to the Present Time" and devoted about a dozen pages to a systematic account of Schelling's system. In all likelihood, this work became the most important source for Schelling's philosophy until the later, more scholarly translations would appear. Like Marsh and Hedge, Henry was more interested in studying German metaphysical systems for their own sake then in presenting his own version of Transcendentalism.[26]

Schelling's influence on Alcott, Ripley, Parker, and other of the more ideological Transcendentalists, while usually evident in their writings, is difficult to delineate precisely. They were a closely knit group of men and women, who passed around to each other books and manuscripts, and shared their ideas while still in the process of forming them. In the case of George Ripley, German idealism became part of his view of Christianity in the early thirties. His "Discourse on the Philosophy of Religion Addressed to Doubters who wish to Believe," preached by him in 1834 and published in 1836, was one of the first public avowals of idealistic philosophy in America. Amos Bronson Alcott seems to have been acquainted with the writings of Oken, Schubert, and Baader, and had attempted to incorporate Neoplatonic elements into Schelling's *Naturphilosophie*, while Theodore Parker had gone to Germany in 1843 and had heard Schelling lecture on the Philosophy of Revelation.

Emerson also came to Schelling's philosophy in the early thirties. In 1834 he wrote in his *Journal*:

> The Germans believe in the necessary Trinity of God — The Infinite; the finite, & the passage from Inf. into Fin.; or the Creation. It is typified in the act of thinking. Whilst we contemplate we are infinite; the thought we express is partial & finite; the expression is the third part & is equivalent to the act of Creation. Unity says Schelling is barren.[27]

But there is no evidence that he had studied much primary source material during this period. In the forties he had seen John Elliot Cabot's unpublished translation of Schelling's work on human freedom, and had written around that time — "How much now Schelling's [thought] avails, and how much everyday Plato! What storms of nonsense they silently avert."[28] Eventually, however, Emerson became disappointed in the German thinkers and confirmed for himself an earlier prediction — "leave me alone, do not teach me out of Leibniz or Schelling, & I shall find it all myself."[29]

In 1843 *The Dial*, the most important of the Transcendentalist periodicals, published a series of letters by Charles S. Wheeler from Heidelberg. Included with these letters was Hedge's translation of "Schelling's Introductory Lecture in Berlin." In one letter readers were given an interesting interpretation of the relation between the early and later Schelling:

> What Schelling taught in 1800, he still teaches. Man is the end and aim of creation, the spirit which moves in all, that to which all tends. But Schelling, who takes the history in its particulars and does not attempt a solution by generalization, acknowledges,

at the same time, that at the end of the Creation, the rest, which should be the result of this motion, did not by any means obtain; on the contrary, he sees a new process start up, and to understand this is his next task. It would be more convenient indeed to deny the fact of this unrest; for it appears so absurd 'that the world should topple together like a cardhouse, by a capricious blow of man's folly.' Yet such a fall has taken place, and therefore nothing but ignorance of History and Revelation, or caprice, can elude it.[30]

John Elliot Cabot, Emerson's biographer, was another contributor to *The Dial* who had a special interest in German philosophy. Besides translating Schelling's 1809 essay on freedom, Cabot had translated the Schelling selection for Hedge's *Prose Writers* and had attended Schelling's Berlin Lectures. He later expanded his ideas on art and nature in an essay for *The Atlantic Monthly*, and though he does not specifically refer to Schelling in this work, the latter's influence is apparent.[31]

Finally, Dr. William Ellery Channing can also be counted among those who, if not entirely influenced by Schelling and German philosophy, adopted it to support their own positions. "I have always found," he wrote, "in the accounts I have read of German philosophy in Madame de Staël, and in these later times, that it was cognate to my own."[32] In 1816 at Channing's request, George Ticknor sent back to him a description of the state of philosophy in Germany, which is quoted here at length for its general interest and probable accuracy:

[The] consequences of the success and failure of Kant, Fichte, and Schelling, is [*sic*], I think, in great measure to be traced [to] the present condition of metaphysics in Germany. Within the lives of the present generation of instructors, these three systems have had their respective triumphs, and of course every one who wishes to be thought a metaphysician must lay the very foundation of his pretensions in a thorough knowledge of them all. But within the same period, too, they have all been exploded, and of course every one who recollects the mortification of that fall will be careful how he exposes himself to a similar fate. The first makes them thorough, deep, and acute; the last makes them cautious. The consequence of both is that the number of powerful metaphysicians in Germany is at this moment very great, and that they are almost all eclectic.

I do not mean, when I talk of the overthrow of these three systems, that no adherents to them are now to be found. Far from it. In Leipsic, where revolutions in modes of thinking are effected with difficulty, perhaps the majority of those who examine such subjects are still followers of Kant. In Berlin, where Fichte still lives and has lately much distinguished himself by some very powerful pieces to arouse and sustain the Prussian spirit against the French usurpation, his philosophy has still some active friends. And, in Jena, the feelings awakened by Schelling's eloquence and enthusiasm have not yet grown cold.

But, after all, the number is comparatively small, and the spirit feeble; and if you go through Germany and take the whole mass of metaphysicians together, you will rarely, *very* rarely, find one who professes himself of either of the schools. Particularly at the universities, you will find that each one has a system of his own, collected from the *disjecta membra* of the systems of Kant, Fichte, and Schelling.[33]

From this brief account, it is evident that in those early decades of the nineteenth century American thinkers were reaching out to German philosophy for the needed insights that could be used to remold prevailing attitudes, and this meant at the time that they were turning to the philosophy of Schelling generally, inasmuch as for them, and to a great extent for all others outside of Germany, German philosophy meant Schelling's philosophy. However, with the possible exceptions of Hedge, Marsh, and Henry, it seems clear that Schelling's influence on the Transcendentalists was both diffuse and oblique. He gave to a highly individualistic and anti-scholastic movement more moral support than actual theoretical grounding. Yet it is also clear that without German *Natur-philosophie* and theology we would have had a reform movement in Transcendentalism, already small enough, which was even smaller and less confident of its position against established orthodoxy in church, state, and university.

Evolutionary Idealism

Nineteenth-century American philosophy was given over almost entirely to one form or another of idealism. With the demise of Transcendentalism in the forties there came, with the appearance of translations of Schelling and Hegel, the objective and evolutionary idealisms of Stallo, Hickok, Fiske, Snider, Henry James, Sr., William T. Harris, Peirce, Royce, and others. Now the influence of Hegel becomes more extensive, and inasmuch as eclecticism characterizes these movements, it becomes more difficult to separate out particular influences from any of the German idealists. In 1879 G. Stanley Hall, Peirce's colleague at Johns Hopkins, noted that "the influence of German modes of thought in America is very great and is probably increasing. . . .The market for German books in the United States is in several departments of learning larger than in Germany itself. . . ." He also observed that "outside of schools and colleges, philosophical interests have taken on the whole a wide range. Trendelenburg, Schleiermacher, Krause, Schelling, Fichte, Herbert and Lotze have all found more or less careful students and even disciples among men of partial leisure in the various professions, who have spent the last year or two of student-life in Germany."[34] In particular, writers of "mental philosophy" like Frederick Rauch, Francis Bowen, Laurens Hickok, Noah Porter, and James McCosh were helping to disseminate German idealist notions in one form or another, even if, as in the case of Bowen and McCosh, they were not always in agreement with them. McCosh, for example, complained that

> the man of genius, like Schelling, will create an ingenious theory, beautiful as the golden locks of the setting sun; the man of vigorous intellect, like Hegel, will erect a fabric which looks as coherent as a palace of ice: but until they can be shown to be founded on the inherent principles of the mind, or to be built up of materials thence derived, I wrap myself up

in philosophic doubt, as not being sure whether they may not disappear while I am gazing on them.[35]

Laurens P. Hickok can probably be counted America's first systematic philosopher in the European mold. His *Rational Psychology* (1849), *Moral Science* (1853), *Empirical Psychology* (1854), and *Rational Cosmology* (1858) present, when taken together, a transcendental philosophy and a *Naturphilosophie* on the grand scale of Schelling and Hegel. The success of these works has suggested to some that they contain a mere syncretistic rehashing of German idealism. But it is clear that while Hickok lacked the creative insight of Schelling, he understood well the core problems out of which the latter's idealism grew. *Rational Psychology* looks very much like a crossbreeding of Kant's *Critique* and Schelling's *System*. It presents the "transcendental science" of the mind from sensation, to understanding, and culminates in the transcendental faculty of Reason. At the outset we have Kant and at the close of the work Schelling and Hegel. Hickok seeks to overcome the opposition of the subjective and objective by finding a transcendental path between them. He rejects Schelling's earlier Identity Theory in favor of Hegel's growth model: "Beginning thus with simple absolute being, the law of self-development as mere *'reflective force'* sees its own inner essence, and thus objectifies all of itself."[36] The journey from unreflective sensation to transcendental Reason mirrors the larger unfolding of the Absolute as a unified, rule-governed system:

The nature of things as they exist is thus demonstrably an intelligible Universal System. Not an accumulation of atoms but a connection of things; not a sequence of appearances but a conditioned series of events; not a coincidence of facts but a universal communion of interacting forces. Nor is such a conclusion merely assumed; nor the credulity induced by habitual experience; nor the revelation of an instinctive prophecy; but a demonstration from an apriori Idea and an actual Law which logically and legitimately excludes all skepticism.[37]

For Hickok, as for Kant and the idealists, the possibility of science establishes transcendentally the idea of nature as a system, and this further makes possible "a Classification of sciences in an apriori Universal System of all science."[38] Hickok then unfolds this idea in terms of the notions of polarity, hierarchy, spontaneity, and eventually freedom and God, much as did Schelling and Hegel earlier; he continued this theme in *Rational Cosmology*, the purpose of which was to establish a *Naturphilosophie* in the form of "Laws of World-System," based on studies in physics, astronomy, and geology.

It is likely that Hickok had been aided in his preparation of *Rational Psychology* by Johann B. Stallo's *The General Principles of the Philosophy of Nature* (1848). Stallo came to America in his teens and studied German idealism while a lecturer at St. John's College (Fordham) between 1844 and 1847; eventually he would reject idealism and the use of metaphysics in science in his *The Concepts and Theories of Modern Physics* (1882). For a while, though, he considered Schelling "the legitimate child of this century" whose philosophy "became the soul of all intellectual exertions of Germany."[39] However, he adopted Hegel's notion of the Absolute, making the not uncommon mistake of failing to see the influence of Schelling's struggles after 1800 on Hegel. Thus, he wrote, "The Absolute, in which all things live, is not, as with Schelling, the abstract identity of two spheres; it is the eternal *spirit thinking itself* in nature and history."[40] From among the principles of *Naturphilosophie* put forward by Stallo are the following:[41]

Every individual organism is the activity of all-comprehending nature embodied in concrete unity, the life of the Whole reflected in a part.

The development of each particular organic form is a miniature reproduction of the formative evolution of entire nature.

The development of all individual forms will be spiral, characterized by *evolution* and *revolution, advance* and *retrogression.*

There is no absolute rest.

Motion is in itself necessarily dual.

Matter has no foundation either by or in itself; its nature is self-attraction.

The laws of mind are also the laws of material nature.

Every individual existence is but a living history.

An account of idealism in America in the last century could hardly neglect the Philosophical Society of St. Louis, formed in 1866, and its journals, *The Journal of Speculative Philosophy* and *The Western*. The Society became a forum of ideas that were less welcome in the Eastern universities, and its journals would publish important early essays by Peirce and Royce, among others. In 1858 William T. Harris, an educator in St. Louis, met Henry Brokmeyer, who had left Germany during the Revolution of 1848 and had been in contact with Hedge while at Brown University, and the two began what has come to be known as the "St. Louis Movement." Brockmeyer had translated Hegel's *Logic* by 1860 and the manuscript circulated among Harris and his friends. Eventually the movement included Thomas Davidson, an Aristotelian whom Denton J. Snider, another member, called "a jolly drifter and general free fighter, with much effervescence of erudition";[42] Adolf Kroeger, a Fichtean; and Louis Soldan, who was a follower of Spinoza and Dante. These were nonacademic men, generally, who had a taste for public affairs and current issues. Their philosophical journal published translations from Fichte, including the "Sun-Clear Report," as well as Davidson's translations of Schelling's *Einleitung* (1799) and the "Introduction" to the 1800 *System*. Probably no two better selections could have been chosen as an introduction to Schelling. However for them Hegel was the master, for by the sixties there was considerably more Hegel in English than there was Schelling. Sibree's *Philosophy of History*, Sandars's synopsis of the

Philosophy of Right in the *Oxford Essays*, 1855, and Stirling's *Secret of Hegel* had by then appeared and advanced Hegel's position considerably, thereby commencing the "Hegel interpretation" of Schelling, which has remained until recent times.

If Schelling was generally shunned by the St. Louis Hegelians, he was openly embraced by the man who is, in all likelihood, America's greatest philosopher, Charles Sanders Peirce. There are few areas of philosophy that Peirce did not investigate, and in all of those which he did, he made lasting contributions. In his philosophy the entire preceding idealistic tradition in America comes to fruition. As a youth in the enlightened house of his father, Benjamin Peirce of Harvard, who was an idealist in his own right, he had been exposed to New England Transcendentalism, had known Hedge and Cabot, had heard Emerson lecture on Nature, and had read Henry's *Epitome*, Schiller's *Aesthetic Letters,* Hickok's *Rational Cosmology*, the Swedenborgian critique of Kant found in Henry James, Sr.'s *Substance and Shadow*, and Meiklejohn's translation of Kant's *Critique*. With characteristic irony he writes of this early influence:

> I may mention, for the benefit of those who are curious in studying mental biographies, that I was born and reared in the neighborhood of Concord—I mean in Cambridge—at the time when Emerson, Hedge, and their friends were disseminating the ideas that were caught from Schelling, and Schelling from Plotinus, from Boehm, and from God knows what minds stricken with the monstrous mysticism of the East. But the atmosphere of Cambridge held many an antiseptic against Concord transcendentalism; and I am not conscious of having contracted any of that virus. Nevertheless, it is probable that some cultured bacilli, some benignant form of the disease was implanted in my soul, unawares, and that now, after long incubation, it comes to the surface, modified by mathematical conceptions and by training in physical investigations.[43]

Peirce also referred to himself as a "Schellingian, of some stripe," advancing a "Schelling-fashioned idealism which holds matter to be mere specialized and partially deadened mind," and in a letter to William James he wrote,

> My views were probably influenced by Schelling—by all stages of Schelling, but especially by the *Philosophie der Natur*. I consider Schelling as enormous; and one thing I admire about him is his freedom from the trammels of system, and his holding himself uncommitted to any previous utterance. In that, he is like a scientific man. If you were to call my philosophy Schellingism transformed in the light of modern physics, I should not take it hard."[44]

Anyone familiar with the broad scope of Peirce's ideas must be struck by the similarity of themes between him and the *Naturphilosophen*. Popularly he is known as a logician and pragmatist, and from this one would be inclined to think him hostile to idealism of any sort, let alone to the objective idealism of Schelling and Hegel. Yet Peirce himself saw no such conflict. For him logical investigation was a way of clarifying the methods of metaphysical analysis, something he thought even Hegel had failed to do properly; and pragmatic theory was for him a theory of how in particular, in the case of human activity, the process of synechism realizes itself in the long run.

Among the themes Peirce's thought shares in common with the *Naturphilosophen* is, first, that of the *unity of nature and history*. As we have seen, the transition from the early to the late Schelling involved primarily the attempt to unify nature and history in a general developmental pattern. Here Schiller's philosophical and aesthetic letters are a common influence on both thinkers. Peirce, particularly in his later years, speculated on the problem of a logic of historical development not bound to the assumptions of individualistic social explanation. The best indication of this is the fact that social events were included by him among the areas subject to metaphysical analysis, and as such followed the same triadic laws operating elsewhere in nature.[45]

Second, there is the interest in the *reclassification of the disciplines of knowledge* necessitated by the unified metaphysics of objective idealism. Schelling had first suggested this in his lectures on academic study, and Oken later had carried this scheme out in great detail. Peirce also proposed a reclassification of the sciences, recalling Marsh's earlier effort, in a way that gave priority to formal, structural, and theoretical considerations. Mathematics, "Cenoscopy," and Metaphysics remained in Peirce's scheme what Mathesis was in Oken's, or what Theology, taken in a broad sense, was in Schelling's. Peirce's scheme, however, is broader and more sophisticated, covering in more detail more of those phenomena we would consider "historical" in nature—those involving, for example, industry, economy, and commerce.

The priority given to theory in classification reflects a third similarity between Peirce and Schelling, their idea of *scientific explanation*. Schelling's *Naturphilosophie*, as indicated, was clearly a reaction to the descriptive methods of eighteenth-century science, and had attempted to bring comprehension to the growing body of experimental data. Likewise, Peirce emphasized the importance of *abduction* as the first step in scientific reasoning, and of the mind-dependent facility for asking the right questions in any scientific investigation. For him, facts abductively suggest a hypothesis through resemblance and analogy, an approach taken by the *Naturphilosophen* in their attempt to uncover similar structures in different phenomena. Thus, Peirce wrote,

> The scientific specialists—pendulum swingers and the like—are doing a great and useful work; each one very little, but altogether something vast. But the higher places in science in the coming years are for those who succeed in adapting the methods of one science to the investigation of another. That is what the greatest progress of the passing generation has consisted in.[46]

Science, then, involves induction, but it is not essentially inductive or Baconian in nature. It is not a contingent fabrication of the finite world of sensory experience. Even when we speak of the instinctive, inductive response to regularity, as does Hume, we must remember, Peirce contends, that "emotion is merely the instinctive indication of the logical situation. . . .it is evolution. . .that has provided us with emotion." For this reason we ignore irregularities that will take us nowhere in knowledge, for in science "solid truth, or reality, is demanded, though not necessarily existential reality." And so Peirce concluded that through science man "really penetrates in some measure the ideas that govern creation."[47]

Fourth, Peirce has in common with the *Naturphilosophen* a belief in the *logical and dialectical structure of nature*. There is an unmistakable similarity between his own metaphysical categories — *Firstness, Secondness, Thirdness* — and Schelling's triadic dialectic. Here Firstness would be illustrated by Magnetism and Sensibility, Secondness by Electricity and Irritability, and Thirdness by Chemical Interaction and Creative Instinct. Very likely, after his long struggle with logical triads leading to his "New List of Categories," Peirce must have found much to agree with in Davidson's translation of Schelling in the *Journal of Speculative Philosophy* of 1867. Generally, Peirce was of the view that the earlier idealists had failed to incorporate logic into their metaphysics and that this had been the main drawback of their system. Yet he was in agreement that metaphysics and logic should work together, and that "a metaphysics not founded on the science of logic is of all branches of scientific inquiry the most shaky and insecure."[48] While he would very likely have rejected the results, he would have endorsed the attempt, as unsophisticated as it was, to produce what Wagner and others had called a *"mathematische Philosophie."*

Finally, there is the matter of an *evolutionary cosmology*. An evolutionary scenario depicting the dialectical emergence of heterogeneity out of homogeneity, or, as Schelling put it, of Difference out of Indifference, was one of the most persistent themes in the thought of Peirce. A great deal of his effort in later life was given to developing his synechistic metaphysics, which was to be "a theory so comprehensive that, for a long time to come, the entire work of human reason, in philosophy of every school and kind, in mathematics, in psychology, in physical science, in history, in sociology, and in whatever other department there may be, shall appear as the filling up of its details."[49] A detailed examination would be necessary to investigate the similarities and differences between Peirce's own evolutionary theories and those of the *Naturphilosophen*. For present purposes it need only be said that he shares with them the view that evolution not only involves differentiation, heterogeneity, and complexity, but also that it involves an increase in spirituality, freedom, self-consciousness, love, sociability, and community.[50]

The last major American idealist of the nineteenth century was Josiah Royce. Like Peirce, Royce began his philosophic career with Kant, advanced to absolute idealism, also contributed to the *Journal of Speculative Philosophy*, and attempted to give precision to metaphysics by a study of logic. Generally, he felt that Schelling "lacked due self-criticism," and "did not take the trouble properly to digest his large store of information concerning the current physical science of his day. . ."; yet he also found in him "a fine instinct for essentially important leading ideas such as the science of his day was beginning to develop."[51]

Royce turned to the German idealists more as inspiration for his own personalistic formulation of absolute idealism. In this respect, while he compiled, as a professor at Harvard, the best American collection of works on Schelling up to his time, he seemed less interested in corroborating for himself some of the standard interpretations of Schelling and Hegel found in the secondary sources of the period. These opinions often carried into his own work, particularly in his *Lectures on Modern Idealism*. Of his own position he wrote:

The view that I have in mind is not Schopenhauer's doctrine of the Will in Nature, nor Schelling's *Naturphilosophie*, nor von Hartmann's theory of the Unconscious as manifested in physical phenomena. From such theories mine is to be distinguished by its genesis. It tries to avoid all premature dogmatism as to the inner aspect of the life of nature. But it conceives the possibility of a gradual and, as one may hope, a very significant enlargement, through the slow growth of human experience, of our insight into the inner meaning of nature's life, and into the essentially social constitution of the finite world.[52]

Surely this is true of Schopenhauer and von Hartmann, who brought a particular interpretation to their account of the relation of consciousness to nature, but far less so of Schelling, who had attempted, much as did Royce in "The Possibility of Error" and elsewhere, to present an undogmatic deduction of idealism critically employing only reflection and the facts of consciousness.

In tracing the course of American idealism in the last century, evidence seems to indicate that with the possible exception of the St. Louis Movement, the influence of Schelling and of his fellow idealists was not so extensive or decisive on American idealists as was that of the established Anglo-Saxon philosophers on the advocates of orthodoxy. Idealism in America has always had to contend with the dominance of the British philosophers: Locke, Stewart, Reid in the eighteenth century; Mill, Whewell, and Hamilton in the nineteenth century; and Russell, Moore, Ayer, Ryle, and the Anglicized Wittgenstein in the twentieth century. Consequently, it has been and continues to be a minority position in America. Yet, because of the relatively small influence from the Continent, American idealism probably represents on balance and over the long span from Edwards to Hocking, Hartshorne, and Blanshard the largest portion of America's own creative effort in philosophy.

8

Idealism in Recent Times

A Primer for Realists

Historically, idealism has taken many forms. Like a house with many mansions, or a family with many members differing remarkably in character, one is at first inclined to doubt that ways could be found linking each with any other. If an arid and careful rationalist ponders in the study, we can see no kinship with his poetical relative who keeps to his garret and dreams theosophical dreams. The numerous forms of idealism truly have shown during their long history an "immense array of internal differences," as Hartshorne puts it.[1] Yet, in spite of this there are bonds that unite all idealists, and avenues of thought from one philosophical mansion to another. In recent times idealism has suffered for its association with theism because so many of its advocates, particularly in their later years, devote a preponderance of their time to what, from a traditional standpoint, are discernibly theological questions. Today this is largely looked upon as a feeble way to go about philosophizing, and so their total efforts have been interpreted accordingly. When a philosopher goes soft-headed, it is often felt, he begins to philosophize as an idealist and looses touch with the community of critical thinkers around him.

A bias of this sort has many causes, not the least of which

is the connection between the fact that a philosophy is academic and what the character of that philosophy is. At least since the industrial and scientific revolutions academic philosophies generally have been tough-minded and have fawned upon the methods and prizes of the natural and social sciences. They have been philosophies that delineate a specific, relatively narrow domain of research—sensory experience, linguistic behavior, human action, and the like—and then discourse entirely within these limits, keeping the philosopher's perspective entirely out of sight. Seldom is the very standpoint of the philosopher problematic; nor would we expect it to be if it is part of the intent of these approaches to retain a steady, self-confident posture in a highly competitive academic climate. In this environment idealism is all wrong. It comes across either as a vestigial spiritualism hiding behind the cloak of secularism, or as a remanent of ancient Greek sophistry and subjectivism. Happily, there are signs that the situation is beginning to change. In fact, it may not be farfetched to suggest that a swing back to idealistic philosophy can be detected. Even Wittgenstein is being put in a more Teutonic cast, one suggesting that he had never been so easily confident as he had been made to appear in his statement that enduring philosophical problems could simply be dissolved away.[2] And works like Sellars's *Science and Metaphysics*, Rescher's *Conceptual Idealism*, and Findlay's *The Discipline of the Cave* have recently contributed to an understanding of central questions in idealism in a manner more congenial to the contemporary intellect.

The plausibility of a nontheologically formulated idealism begins with epistemological considerations. If we trace back the arguments of the realist and idealist to the point prior to where each parts company with the other and takes a separate fork in the road, we arrive at the question each poses and answers in a different way—*what is given immediately in experience?* Let us imagine such a philosophic "state of nature," prior to labels and philosophic ideologies. The person who eventually comes to be known as the realist answers either by saying that *sensory qualities* are what is given, or that *material objects* in space and time are immediately present. This is bedrock fact for him. He is not answering the question of *how* experience comes to be what it is; he is saying what it first of all *is*. We begin with primitive data—whether qualities or objects—and only from there does interpretation begin. For example, we might like to go on to inquire about the status of knowledge claims about the past or future, or about other minds, mathematical relations, and so on, but only after we stand on the firm foundation of the given.

Now, the proto-idealist finds nothing to disagree with in all this. He too begins with the same experiences that are available to the realist. He is not born a mystic with a self-evident realization that he is an eternally living spiritual being; rather, he begins with the same wonderment as the realist. And as long as the realist is content to give only a few exceedingly sparse descriptions of the world around him, the idealist does not rise to disagreement. Surely there can be nothing to argue over regarding the fact that seeing a red something is different from seeing a green something, or that feeling something touch me is not the same thing as my touching something. This is all innocent enough, and for that reason is *hardly philosophy*. For while we may wonder where experience begins, where the realist says it begins is surely not where philosophy itself begins. Philosophy, it seems, is an irreducibly cognitive and interpretive enterprise—at least as we have known it in the West, where we have never been satisfied merely with knowing smiles. And this means that in the very asking of a philosophical question we do not leave everything as it is in the common-sense or natural standpoint. We may have a philosophy of common sense, but not a common-sense philosophy. It seems, then, that the person destined to become the idealist has an inkling that this is so. For while the realist is certainly correct in asserting that qualities or objects are given in experience, and immediately so, this looks too much like a *general* philosophic pronouncement to the idealist, and less like a claim that within experience some things seem to have the quality of "qualitative givenness."

Inasmuch as philosophy is an endeavor to make fresh starts, the realist chooses these primitive simples as the starting point for philosophy as well, but almost immediately he runs into trouble because the starting point of philosophy is at cross-purposes with the starting point of experience. Rather, philosophy begins with a question — of the sort given above — and a question calls for an answer, in this case an answer about the state of affairs of the world. The idealist realizes that to have even a chance of supplying an answer it is necessary to distinguish between our momentary experiences, many of which are immediately given in a way we cannot question, and what we may say of these experiences in a way in which they may be philosophically understood, interpreted, and described.

At once the realist objects: While it is true that philosophy is an attempt to say something beyond what we can say at the moment (*ouch*, for example) about what may occur at the moment, it can still generalize without inconsistency to the effect that this is where experience and knowledge begin. It may in its pronouncements cut across large spans of time, but it may reveal that with regard to what we may know we must confine ourselves to what is immediately given. At this point, the idealist, wishing like the realist that there be as little controversy as possible, would be ready to accept this reply were it not for the quandary he sees implied in the realist's response. Either we should, as the realist suggests, confine ourselves within the moment as far as knowledge goes, and so somehow generate instantaneous and instantaneously obsolete philosophies, or else drop philosophy altogether, or else we could hold onto our philosophical position on the nature of immediacy as long as we explain why it is we do not have to submit it to the very standards of momentary knowing it pronounces as the only kind possible. We either embrace Pyrrhonian skepticism at the outset, or we clear up the question of the status of philosophical claims. These are our best alternatives.

Skepticism seems to embody a lack of commitment about those questions which would concern either a realist or idealist, and so only the second alternative remains alive in this discussion. The realist could maintain that philosophy *itself* is somehow part of the stream of experience by naturalizing it to the point where it is a matter of sentiment (Hume), or he could simply explain it as part of a primordial faculty of reflection (Locke), or he could ignore the question. The idealist experiences disquiet with each possibility. He finds that a statement like Locke's "*the mind* furnishes the understanding with the ideas of its own operations,"[3] is pushing the idea of givenness too far. What does such a statement mean, he wants to know? What, for example, does Locke mean by *internal sense* that justifies the parallel with sensory experience as the realist first began to speak of it? Too much is being passed over here for the idealist, and so he retraces his steps once more to the point where philosophy is first born out of common sense.

It is at this point that he discovers a hitherto unnoticed distinction. For at the very heart of the realist's assertion that such and such is given is a distinction between an *as such* and an *as given*, and in this he finds an interesting complementarity. What is merely and momentarily given is not a *such*, and what is a such is never merely *given*. Now, if philosophy is the attempt to say what are the sorts of things that are given, then it must deal with the *such*, and it must *also* deal with the distinction between an order of reality and an order of reflection. Here, once more, the realist may object *à la* Moore that it is one thing to make a knowledge claim about what there is, and another to give a correct reflective analysis of that claim. To this the idealist would reply that Moore's distinction surely applies to the very sophisticated, but seemingly simple claims like "There exists at present a living human body, which is *my* body"; in such a claim there are all sorts of *suches* that may be carefully *analyzed*. However, he continues, such a distinction also applies to whatever claim we wish to make about "what is," including claims about sensory experience. It is not just that our common-sense claims are unwittingly sophisticated; so are our supposedly bare-bones epistemological claims about what is immediately given. Moore seems to assume that in *making* a claim I am not doing anything akin to what I do in analyzing it correctly—a division of labor the idealist rejects. For to formulate a claim about a portion of our experience is to already analyze that experience in a certain way, and if so, we cannot claim to know anything in the absence of analysis, correct or otherwise. To simply *have* the experience, of course, is another matter altogether, and if Moore means that there is a difference between having certain experiences and giving a correct analysis of them, the idealist heartily agrees, and has been saying just this all along. Using these distinctions, the idealist takes as *his* philosophical starting point the view that experience in its broad dimension involves a twofold structure: a formal, conceptual structure and a material, perceptual structure.

And now a *new* question arises for him. The realist has by now traveled in his own direction and is dealing with questions like "Granted what is given, on what grounds can I claim to know other things (generalities, the future, etc.) based on what is given?" And so his books take the form of Locke's *Essay*, Russell's *An Inquiry into Meaning and Truth*, or Ayer's *The Problem of Knowledge*, all of which have the same argumentative structure. Here the realist is involved in a descriptive account of what are our natural attitudes formed in the course of our daily lives, and in the process he makes inroads for our understanding of notions like *belief, evidence, probability,* and other tools of comprehension we use in this practical manner. His philosophy is a taxonomy of practical life, and for this reason does have a "plain" quality to it; however it is decidedly *not* "historical" as well. It describes how we use certain notions on various occasions, but it does not explain anything about how these notions came to be formulated or given. It gives a fairly good account of whether, say, our idea of causality can be made to apply in certain circumstances, but it fares much more poorly on the issue of how we come to have such an idea. These "historical" or genetic questions are the ones taken up by the idealist, whose distinction leads him to pose his new question—how is it possible for knowledge to be an interconnection of formal and material modes?

The realist is aghast at such a question, for, he complains, how could we possibly answer it? If all that is given are sensory qualities or material objects, then what we can say must be restricted to these only. But the idealist is more confident. Indeed, in common sense these are what is given immediately, but now so also is philosophical questioning, with its distinction between form and matter, "given" as something to be explained. What is required, then, is to explore the conditions for the possibility of philosophy; and this is a task the realist himself cannot avoid, since he cannot consistently deny that he is asking a *philosophical question*, employing the distinction between *such-ness* and *givenness*, when he asks *what* is immediately given in experience.

At this point, an "immense array of internal differences" becomes possible for the idealist. He may begin with some rather abstract considerations on the very nature of the reflective standpoint such as is found in Husserl's phenomenology, or he could adopt and modify a paradigm from common sense such as the (theological) one found in Plato, Berkeley, and Edwards, which can account for the connection of form and matter. Or he could adopt the transcendental method of Kant, Fichte, Schelling and Hegel, which argues: *if* knowledge is possible, and if that knowledge takes the form of *science*, and if the connection between knowledge and nature is such that an ideational penetration of nature is possible, thereby enhancing control and predictability, *then* certain conditions in the nature of things must have been satisfied. The possibility of logic, mathematics, science, and, more recently, language reveals for the idealist philosopher the existence of *a priori* structures and functions, which in turn suggests that a systematic way could be found for explaining the interplay of form and matter in knowledge. Kant had indicated this direction when he rejected the account of knowledge given by Locke and Hume:

> Now this empirical derivation, in which both philosophers agree, cannot be reconciled with the scientific *a priori* knowledge which

we do actually possess, namely, *pure mathematics* and *general science of nature*; and this fact therefore suffices to disprove such derivation.[4]

As for what these *conditions* are — to describe them in detail is to tell the entire story of idealistic philosophy in all of its various forms and ramifications. Suffice it to say, from the perspective of Schelling's idealism, that Kant's attempt to restrict these conditions to functions within the mind of knowing persons was not successful. We may say that such conditions are found "in the mind," but then we can only wonder what the condition for the operation of the mind itself is. This too looks like an "empirical derivation" and it is no wonder that a pupil of Kant (Reinhold) would have taken critical philosophy in a psychological direction. However, Kant himself realized that the critique of pure reason would have to take place within a general *Metaphysics of Nature*, which would contain no less than an epigenetic account of such reason, and hence it is in this direction that the post-Kantian idealists set out.

In a sense, the realist is correct in noting that the idealist, in questioning the structure of knowing, cannot *directly know* how form and matter are united the way he knows that snow is cold or that two plus two equals four. He must "deduce" the connection from a theoretical model, and to do this he must first, as Kant would often remind us, *construct* such a model, one that would contain the requisite conditions for the deduction of knowledge and science. This means that much of the debate between the realist and idealist over the past centuries has been at cross-purposes. The idealist is trying to construct a metaphysics that would be required to explain the possibility of experience, while the realist generally has concerned himself with a descriptive account of that experience. The latter investigates and describes, in the form of empiricism, the workings of science, while the former speculates, in the form of a rationalistic metaphysics, on the conditions for the possibility of science. Insofar as realism is itself a metaphysics involved in the question of what there really is, then of course it is bound to collide at times with idealism, but probably far less frequently than is commonly thought today. For the issue is not between subjectivism and objectivism; in seeking the conditions for knowing, the idealist is not restricted to the mind of the individual person for his model—this is a common misunderstanding that will be corrected in the next section. In this sense, Rescher is certainly correct in recently noting that "historically, idealists have never made a reality a matter of wishful thinking that lets thought shape the world without objective constraints."[5] Such constraints are embodied in the particular metaphysical paradigm of the idealist. And while it is probably true that for a time in Fichte's and Schelling's early philosophy there was an attempt to transcend *all* constraints, both eventually came to see the impossibility of such an undertaking. Attempting to go beyond Kant, Schelling sought constraints in the idea of a World System as the ultimate condition for the possibility of mind, and then, finding this inadequate, he added a historical dimension that explained not only the interplay of form and matter in all stages of the evolutionary hierarchy, but the very possibility of philosophy itself as well.

The realist may point to the emphasis on "intellectual intuition" and on mystical, theosophical references in this and other idealistic philosophy, and for this the idealists are largely at fault. It may have been that at times Schelling gave the impression that his metaphysical system could be explained and justified by intellectual intuition; what he should have said was that his system, which itself was far from intuitively evident, was proposed to explain the possibility of intellectual intuition itself. Intellectual (that is, mathematical and logical) intuition is evidence for transcendental metaphysics, but it does not deductively establish such metaphysics. Here the idealistic approach must stand or fall the way any other approach does —by its intelligibility and its ability to fit the overall facts of experience. Historically, idealism has presented a problem for itself by more often than not turning to the language of theology to describe its paradigm. This is understandable, however, when we realize that it faces a genuine problem: it attempts to explain transcendentally what has been called by Wilfrid Sellars "the manifest image" of common-sense life, yet it cannot achieve its task simply by employing as used the terms and notions of that image, and so it must mint new conceptual currency (Peirce, Whitehead) or give new value to old currency (Hegel, Royce); and this generally is why it has been so often attracted to the wholesale use of theological vocabularies.

To a great extent, the above account of the *generative core* of idealistic philosophy follows the course of argument taken by Muirhead in the final section of his *The Platonic Tradition in Anglo-Saxon Philosophy,* aptly entitled "What is Dead and What is Alive in Idealism," and by Ewing in his *Idealism: A Critical Survey.* In both works it is the purpose of the author to show that idealism is not a philosophy that states simply that "the world is my idea," in short, that it is not opposed to realism by denying the reality the realist says exists. Thus Muirhead observes: "The idealism which is the subject of these Studies has from the first been as insistent as realism (*is* a form of realism in insisting) on the presence to consciousness of a non-ego."[6] What it rejects is the unknown thing-in-itself, which, as Bosanquet noted, becomes "more unknowable the more it is understood." For this reason Muirhead considered Kant's epistemology a "withered branch" of the idealistic tradition.[7] Since Kant, he maintains, a true Copernican revolution in thought has occurred, which has moved beyond simple subjectivism and dualism:

> Any philosophy which overlooks this immediate contact with Being is self-condemned. But the undifferentiated experience in which the world is thus given to sense and feeling is only the point of departure of the mind which, as continuous with the felt reality, is pledged to follow its movement as it expands into a form more adequate to express the fullness of the differences and the fundamental unity of its contents. To assert, with some forms of realism, that all reality is "out there," or with some forms of idealism that it is all "in here" . . . is to falsify the most elementary convictions of

common sense, the constructive work of science and the achievements of the human mind in the works of art, morality, and social life.[8]

Similarly, Ewing rejects idealistic subjectivism, or what he calls "epistemological idealism" because it does not account for the givenness or heteronomous aspect of experience, and because "a thorough-going idealist epistemology is quite incapable of working in any branch of knowledge."[9] As Ewing's overall argument implies, and as was indicated above, what is epistemologically given may not at all be metaphysically given. In his final chapter, entitled "Idealistic Metaphysics," Ewing recognizes that idealism can be made plausible as a general theory of knowledge and experience if it is able to "avoid conflict with common-sense and to retain the advantages of realism in regard to physical objects."[10] And this it can do in any manner that accounts for the interconnection of form and matter in knowledge in a way that does not make my knowledge claims about the world dependent on the workings of *my own mind*. Indeed, how could I make such claims dependent on the workings of my mind if it is only my experiences that are *mine*, if even these, and not the cognitive conditions making them possible? Here, any transpersonal idealism is in a position to suggest an explanation, whether it be an evolutionary theism or a Piercean and Roycean community of minds.

Historically, the name given for this form of idealism is Objective Idealism. The Hegelian version, called "Absolute Idealism," is actually one particular form of Objective Idealism, in that it does not limit itself to the standpoint of individual consciousness. Peirce described this general form of idealism well when he wrote the definition in the *Century Dictionary* for "ideal-realism":

A metaphysical doctrine which combines the principles of idealism and realism. The ideal-realism of Schleiermacher, Beneke, Trendelenburg, Ueberweg, Wundt, and others consists in acknowledging the correctness of Kant's account of the subjective origin of space, time, and the conceptions of cause, substance, and the like, and in holding, in addition, that these things have also an existence altogether independent of the mind. The ideal-realism of Ulrici, B. Peirce, and others consists in the opinion that nature and the mind have such a community as to impart to our guesses a tendency toward the truth, while at the same time they require the confirmation of empirical science.

A common thread can be seen to run through each of the various formulations of Objective Idealism, namely, its appeal to science as the most unambiguous evidence for the viability of such a metaphysical view. Rather than oppose science, the objective idealists took a far more wondrous view of it than did most of their realist counterparts. They were more inclined to see a genuinely revelatory character in scientific knowledge, while the realists preferred to stay closer to conventionalism. Where the idealists seem to wax theological is in their attempt to place the scientific process within a larger framework. They do not rest with scientific explanations of nature alone, but seek such explanations for the human world as well. In his "Continuity of the Idealist Tradition," Charles Bakewell, besides observing that "a realistic interpretation of nature is not only consistent with, but demanded by idealism," also remarked that:

> Philosophy differs from science simply in comprehensiveness. It takes all experience for its province. It must be judged, as science is, by its success in discovering the principle or principles that link all the facts of experience in a rational and orderly whole.[11]

Objective idealism probably has come the closest of any philosophy to presenting such a comprehensive theory of experience in its attempt to unite in a meaningful fabric man's scientific, social, and valuational endeavors. But it has done this at the risk of having appeared to confound the realm of facts and the realm of values, for historically the idealist has also been a consistent defender of the status of human values. A realism that limits the world to the world of immediacy and postulates no other possibilities for experience is more acceptable to the view that value is simply immediate gratification in the here-and-now, involving only something materially tangible. Thus we may have a loose but discernible connection between realism, materialism, and capitalism on the one hand, and idealism, spiritualism, and socialism on the other. In nineteenth-century America, at least, issues seemed to line up this way. To the extent that idealism appeals to forms beyond immediate sensation or perception, it has been a fertile ground for reform movements of many sorts, but particularly those in the field of education. Here the efforts of Schelling, Marsh, Alcott, and the St. Louis Hegelians come to mind.

If we borrow Muirhead's phrase and ask what is dead and what is alive in idealism today, we must generally and unfortunately conclude that a great deal of what has been vital in traditional idealism is also dead at the present.[12] What Blanshard called the "revolt against reason" and Findlay "the modern rejection of 'essentialism' " has had the effect that almost any position advocated within an idealistic framework has come to be automatically rejected.[13] However, Nicolas Rescher's *Conceptual Idealism* represents a modern attempt to restore much of what is sound in the idealistic tradition. It is his purpose to delineate those features of thought, experience, and reality which contain what he calls a "mind-invoking" dimension. As such, he wishes to avoid the usual pitfalls of ontological idealism by refraining from any commitment to the question of how reality is constituted in the absence of the philosophizing mind. Instead, he advances, much in the manner of Laszlo, a "transactionalist mode of idealism," which maintains that the encounter of subject and object is genuine and not one-sidedly passive or active.[14] The knowing self is not merely a spectator, nor is the object merely constituted out of mind. In this sense conceptual idealism is proposed as a remedy against the claims of naive realism and subjective idealism.

In establishing his position, Rescher appeals to much of

the evidence used by idealists since Kant; for him notions such as possibility, lawfulness, causality, individuation, and space and time necessarily imply the framework of cognitive assessment, and hence are incapable of explication in traditional realist terms. Reality *an sich* is not rejected in this analysis, but rather takes the form of a *theoretical* realm of constructs developed and employed in a scientific manner:

> We can have no experiential information regarding the properly constitutive features of things, but only *impute* such features to particulars in the *theoretical* interests of explaining their experientially manifest features. We cannot cross the gulf between the dispositional properties presumably present in experience and the proper properties of things by any inferential process whatever, but only by an *imputation* built into the systematic framework of a theory.[15]

In this case, the *theory* is the idealistic theory of nature, and the theoretical construct is simply that of a reality-as-a-whole-*an-sich*.[16] Rescher considers such an idealism "presuppositional," advanced for the purposes of "explanatory systematization"; yet while he generally eschews metaphysical idealism, we can find it peeking out from the pages of nearly every chapter. For no matter how subtle the methodological remarks about the nature of "mind-invokingness" are, in order to eliminate the possibility of a reductive phenomenalism a metaphysics of some sort must be introduced. And here Rescher does so, but gingerly. He notes, for example, that the "mind" of "mind-invokingness" is not a subjective, individual self, but "the generic, public, interpersonal capabilities of minds."[17] Yet he fails to make clear in what sense, given his self-imposed limitations, he can speak of a *common* world of public minds, one constituting an epistemological and linguistic community. The hard work of idealism *begins* at this point, rather than ending or being left hanging, as here.

Similarly, Rescher seeks the test of truth in the notion of "Concept-Darwinism," that is, in a pragmatic view that holds that concepts are more or less adequate to reality to the extent that they can explain, predict, and control that reality. This view is advanced by him as an *a posteriori* claim about what we can in fact observe about the functioning of concepts; here *practice* is supposed to be the neutral test. But again such claims, if recent arguments in favor of conceptual relativism have any bite, must be understood within, and are implied by, a specific normative framework. It is at this point, as Peirce surely realized, that the pragmatist must fish or cut bait. If he appeals to the workings of history, natural or otherwise, he must explain how history makes possible such desirable results. And if the results are desired only because they *are* the results in fact obtained, they lose their meaning when translated within a human context. We can surely sympathize with Rescher's reticence to make history a form of revelation, but there is room for maneuver between his position and outright theology. It might be argued that evolution involves certain mechanisms, which *ceteris paribus* conduce to the realization of certain highly adaptive forms, particularly those involving greater variability, complexity, and flexibility. *Why* it does this we may not be able to say, but it is certainly within the purview of science to consider such questions. The *ex post facto* approach of a simple pragmatic theory certainly lacks the conceptual richness that could make this question interesting. It is only at this point that the evolutionary process, if it is going to be appealed to at all, comes to have explanatory implications for what goes on in the human world of conceptual activity.

Concept-Darwinism, by itself, as Royce noted, does not get us anything like what would be required for a theory of truth. In this respect, Rescher's general coherentist position is a more adequate formulation of our notion of truth, and his remarks on the pragmatic sanction should probably be seen in this light. However, even here the coherentist view, as Blanshard's long and detailed arguments have shown, imply a total metaphysical perspective, and this is where conceptual idealism has considerable room for expansion. After all, there is no reason, if methodological and epistemological idealism can be considered presuppositional, that metaphysical or, more specifically, objective idealism cannot be, too. Surely nobody fears that transcendental reflection can create transcendent realities, and therefore there is no reason that it cannot assist in producing for us "the best theoretical systematization of our experience."[18]

However, while Rescher wishes to stop short of a Hartshorne style of idealism, much of what else he says can be taken to indicate what ought to be alive in idealism today. As for the question of refining a metaphysical paradigm, that may have to wait until we know a great deal more than we currently do about the workings of the universe. Here Rescher's transactional view is particularly compatible with whatever the course of scientific development might turn out to be. He notes that a causal materialism is not at all at odds with conceptual idealism, for the former involves the order of causation, the latter, the order of understanding and conceptualization.[19] However, it is at this point that Rescher's *a posteriori* approach is most seriously challenged. He does not want to rule out on subjectivist grounds the implications for idealism of discoveries in the area of neurophysiology and molecular biology, and so he is willing to concede that "nothing in the dialectic of the present discussion forecloses this prospect that the sort of mind-involvement in question is only one half of the story."[20] Surely idealism can say more than this. If mind-involvement is to come to be seen increasingly from a heteronomous point of view, then it can only be as a result of an *increase in the autonomy of scientific understanding*. In this sense, idealism is not in conflict with a reductive materialism *as a theory* that can explain the emergence of mind; instead, it should be taken as a theory of such theories. It insists that a distinction must be drawn between the nonmental out of which the mental emerges, and the nonmental to which the scientific understanding returns. For reductive theories, which reveal the elegant simplicities of nature, are possible only as a result of a corresponding advance in technical, social, and methodological complexities. And it is this fact the objective idealist finds among the most interesting he has encountered. He sees as part of his task the attempt to give an account of how this process of theorizing comes about, and, once more, it is on this basis that his metaphysics takes a transcendental turn.

Rescher seems to argue that conceptual idealism is not and ought not to be concerned with what goes on in the material realm, that is, is not a *causal* idealism; rather than being an *explanatory* theory of the emergence of mind, it is supposed to be only an *analytical* theory of the categories of conceptualization and mind-involvement.[21] Again this places him at odds with objective idealism, which *is* a form of causal idealism in that it seeks to explain, among other things, and in a general fashion, what the causal mechanisms are that make possible causal explanations. Wilfrid Sellars has attempted such an explanation in his theory of the emergence of the "scientific image" out of the "manifest image," and for this reason Sellars's own *transcendental realism* can be seen to be very much more in harmony with the overall program of the objective idealist than is conceptual idealism.[22] As long as the *a posteriori* approach confines itself to the subjective realm of mind-invocation alone, it can never break out of the circle of particular experience. This vicious circle of explaining mind by matter only after matter has been explained by mind (science) is to be broken only by the transcendental reflection that it is mind after all, in its scientific endeavor, that puts forward theories of mind-from-matter. Idealism must begin with what is given, as was indicated above, and in this case it means it must begin with the very fact of science, and not with matter or with a lifeless planet of eons before. In Rescher's idealism conceptual instruments used to understand reality are mind-made and mind-patterned, which gives them a "mentalistic" origin for him.[23] Whether the criticisms presented here are ultimately to apply to this approach, will depend on how the term *mentalistic* is understood. If it is understood in a highly subjective sense, then conceptual idealism has very little in common with objective idealism; however, if it is given a social and historical dimension, as Rescher seems to give it at times, then there is wider room for agreement.

Besides Rescher's particular accounts of "mind-invoking-ness," which, as noted, should be considered viable for contemporary idealism, deficiencies, or at least improper emphases, in his approach to the transcendental and metaphysical dimensions of idealism suggest that these traditional metaphysical issues continue to remain of central importance as well. In Muirhead's account a "theory of the absolute" was also deemed important to any idealism,[24] and it is this more than anything else that constitutes the greatest deficiency of Rescher's idealism. It remains in the province of idealism to construct explanatory models of the origins and destinies of the universe and all contained therein; indeed, it is called upon to do this if it wishes to make intelligible both what science explains and that it explains it. *What* the nature of that model will be is another question. At present, the general theory of systems is attempting to sketch out one such model, employing notions from cybernetic, information, and evolutionary theory. Here, objective idealism can be construed as another name for the meta-theory out of which the model is cast. Even the earlier distinctions come into play: to the extent that systems theory explains the processes of nature, it is a form of *Naturphilosophie,* and to the extent that it explains the processes of mind, it is a transcendental philosophy, or what is more appropriate, if contrary to current usage, a genuine *philosophy or theory of science.*

On the "Refutation of Idealism"

In the light of the above remarks concerning what is viable in idealism today, it may be worthwhile to reassess some of the earlier attempts to "refute" idealism. Generally, these refutations, which seemed to be in greatest vogue during the turn of the century, have accomplished little, except perhaps to reveal the predilections of their originators. In this section those of Kant, Moore, Perry, and Russell will be considered.

Kant. In the first edition of the *Critique* Kant gives in the

fourth Paralogism what is generally considered to be a refutation of idealism. Here idealism is taken to be the doctrine that
outer appearances are merely ideal because they are encountered
only perceptually. External things cannot be perceived insofar
as perception is a modification of inner sense, and so must be
inferred. But if they cannot be perceived it is uncertain whether
they are the causes of our perceptions. And this raises the
possibility that outer perceptions result from "a mere play of
our inner sense."[25]

Against this, Kant claims that in accordance with his own
transcendental idealism external objects are nothing but representations of which we are immediately conscious. But by
external objects he means here "the representations of matter
and of corporeal things," that is, empirical objects, and not
transcendental objects.[26] He does not deny that if external
objects in a transcendental sense are the causes of our perceptions, it could *not* be established beyond doubt that the latter
were not ideal. But this puts his own position uncomfortably
close to the paralogistic doctrine he seeks to deny, and so he
makes a further distinction *within* the realm of our outer
appearances—between their spatial form of presentation, which
is internal, and their "material or real element," which "necessarily presupposes perception."[27] And here Kant tells us significantly that this element, with its essential qualitative nature,
must be simply and immediately given in sensation since it
could not have been invented *a priori* by the imagination. This
reply is satisfactory to Kant, and should be, he suggests, even
for the "most rigid idealist."[28] But there is no reason an idealist
must confine his philosophical questioning to the limits Kant
has placed on it, that is, in terms of Kant's formulation of what
it is for something to be an outer representation. For the givenness of sensation is not incompatible with the ideality of
appearances, something Kant himself eventually concedes.[29]
Also, along with this "immediate proof" of the realistic origins
of outer appearance, Kant supplies us with a rule: *Whatever is
connected with a perception according to empirical laws, is
actual.*[30] Now he has an even more complicated task of

establishing actuality in this fashion, that is, if he is not to mean it in the sense that an idealist is inclined to sanction as well. It turns out then that Kant's critique of ideality applies only to someone who mistakenly construes appearances as things in themselves. The idealist's question of whether or not objects can be said to "underlie" outer appearances has not been met, and it is no wonder Kant found this a troublesome issue when he came to rework the *Critique* for its second edition.

In the second edition, a specifically named Refutation of Idealism appears in the Second Analogy, where now Kant thinks its proper place should be. Here he seeks to *prove* in a stronger sense, rather than merely show by presumption, that the inner depends on the outer, and so in no way could the outer be reduced to the inner. In the First Analogy Kant had argued that either of the time-relations (simultaneity and succession) implies something permanent in the stream of appearances, for if (1) time itself is not perceived, and (2) duration in time is possible, there must be something that remains unchanged during change of appearance. Now, in the Second Analogy Refutation he adds to this the claim that this substratum cannot be found in me, "for all grounds of determination of my existence which are to be met with in me are representations," which, as in the case of outer appearances, require a substratum as well.[31] And so, he concludes, both outer appearances and inner self-consciousness necessarily presuppose a permanent *thing* outside of me. In fact, he goes on, self-consciousness is at once also consciousness of outer things. To establish this crucial second premise Kant claims that in the representation "I am" there is only existence and not *knowledge,* for, strictly speaking, there is nothing to know in it. This "I," he says, contains not "the least predicate of intuition, which, as permanent, might serve as correlate for the determination of time in inner sense."[32]

Clearly, however, Kant's analysis here presupposes his theory of the self as being only the locus for fleeting representations of the Sensibility. He has not ruled out that his argument, while perhaps formally correct, could establish a substratum *within the self*. His own second thoughts, contained in footnotes, of this second-thought Refutation, reveal that he remained concerned with the question of the self and its mysterious power of imagination. At one point he calls upon the distinction between receptivity and spontaneity as relevant to a genetic account of representations, even when it may only characterize certain features of certain acts of representing, including those of inner sense.[33] And he also appeals to rules of experience to distinguish between sense and imagination, but unlike in the first-edition argument, he does not seek to establish an essentially qualitative character for outer sense.[34] Now the rules alone must supply the demarcation.

Again, Kant is working within the limitations set by transcendental idealism as he understands the phrase, his talk of "things" notwithstanding; and his Refutation of Idealism amounts to no more than the claim that experience contains both an inner and outer character. But that the inner must depend on the outer because of the particular nature of the time-relation in our experience, his argument does not establish. In fact, all of the interesting questions of the idealist remain. Even the reformulation of the Refutation by Strawson and Bennett, which tries to show in a more refined sense how Kant took the claim that the inner depends on the outer, leaves these questions aside. Strawson takes the outer to be an "objective spatial order," which Kant himself does not formally establish, while Bennett takes it to be "objective states of affairs," which are required in order to check our memories.[35] Nothing akin to objective idealism has been refuted by this, and it is even doubtful that a subjective and "problematic" idealist could not find a sense of "outer" in all this to suit his own needs.

Moore. In his *Mind* article of 1903, "The Refutation of Idealism," G. E. Moore carefully notes that it is not his intent to refute what he takes to be the overall idealistic thesis that "reality is spiritual," but rather to weaken it by overturning one of its major claims: that *esse* is *percipi.* He observes that some idealists also claim that *esse* is *percipere,* and this question involves "a vast quantity of further argument" on their part, which he leaves aside in his own argument.[36] However, he also claims that, as far as he can see, idealists have only attempted to establish the latter by means of the former claim. That such an approach was not taken by Schelling or others, evidently Moore did not know. For this reason, his approach appears to concern itself primarily with a refutation of phenomenalism. Even so, it is still largely taken to be an argument against idealism in whatever form, and thus is worth consideration.

Moore argues that if, as should be clear, *esse* is not synonymous with *percipi*, then there must be some character in the *esse* distinguishable from the fact that it is *percipi*. Now, in order to establish a synthetic link between these two different items, the idealist argues that there can be no instance of *esse*, in the fullest sense, without a subject's experience. But here, Moore notes, the idealist both fails to distinguish a *something* from the experience of it, and yet must make such a distinction at the pain of making a tautology. And so he is led into "a kind of antinomy."[37] Of course, this argument hinges on whether or not idealists *do* fail to distinguish between noetic act and noematic content, and realizing that many do not, Moore embarks on his second argument.

At this point, he proposed to investigate what it means for something to be a sensation or idea. We all know, he holds, that there is a difference between the sensation of blue and the sensation of green, and yet if they are both sensations, they must have something in common, namely, consciousness. Here then is the distinction between consciousness (noesis) and its object (noema). It is also clear that there are times when I do not have a sensation of blue, and hence it becomes plausible to ask whether, when the sensation does exist, "it is the consciousness which exists, or the blue which exists, or both."[38] Now, because all three possibilities differ, Moore holds, anyone who said that blue was the same as the consciousness of blue was plainly contradicting himself. As stated, this argument appears to be simply a reformulation of the previous one. However, Moore gives it a different interpretation. Instead of speaking of "blue" as the *object of consciousness,* he now speaks simply of *blue*. And from this he concludes: "If we are told that the assertion 'Blue exists' is *meaningless* unless we mean by it that 'The sensation of blue exists,' we are told what is certainly false and self-contradictory."[39] *All* philosophers, according to him, have failed to distinguish between *blue* and *blue-sensed,* and for this reason they have let "sensation of blue" trade for both. A notion of a *blue object* would have remedied this, he claims.

Surely, by such an "object" he cannot mean object-of-consciousness, for then *esse* would be *percipi.* Rather, Moore must mean a blue *something,* a blue object that exists independently of experience, something textual evidence seems to bear out.[40] There is no absurdity in imagining such an object, and the following situation might be used on his behalf: We might imagine that the world had been constituted in such a manner that blue and all other colors were capable, with great technological expertise, of being literally "peeled off" the objects said to manifest these colors, leaving those objects perfectly invisible; and it is further possible that, given all of the analytical instrumentation available to even the most advanced scientists, it might still be found that these delicate "blue films" would be blue *through and through,* at least as far as we can humanly tell. Here would be a sense in which we could distinguish blue as an object *simpliciter* from blue as an object of consciousness, thus factually refuting the phenomenalist. Unfortunately for Moore's distinction, however, we do not live in that kind of universe. The idealist notes that in the world in which he lives blue has only an essentially perceptual reality, and that is why previous philosophers have failed to heed Moore's distinction. He observes, for example, that it is possible to produce blue sensations with unblue objects (prisms, wave action, etc.), and therefore can only conclude that there is no blue in the absence of blue-sensed, though this does not mean that the sensing literally "creates" the blue. This now leaves Moore only with the distinction between noesis and noema.

In the remainder of the Refutation, Moore analyzes the various aspects of noesis and noema. In speaking of noematic *content,* he observes, we cannot mean that the noesis takes on the character of the noema. Rather, the two remain distinct, and the noesis is simply an *awareness* of the noema, even a transcendental one — "the moment we try to fix our attention on consciousness . . . it seems to vanish"[41] — while the relation between the two becomes one of intentionality: "I am aware *of* blue."[42] From this Moore concludes that we must distinguish between a sensation and its object, and so to have a sensation "is to know something which is as truly and really *not* a part of my experience, as anything which I can ever know."[43] Clearly, Moore has not established this; nor has he established that in his sense of *awareness* we can be aware that our object of awareness "is precisely what it would be, if we were not aware."[44] This, and the common-sense credo with which he closes his argument, is actually as unvarnished a metaphysics as there could be, particularly insofar as he claims to have established, in this Refutation, reasonable grounds for such claims. If anything, he has left the subjective idealist more secure than ever.

If, as has been argued, Moore's intentionality-argument shows idealism to be inadequate, then it must be explained how, for example, Husserl's phenomenology and his own transcendental idealism are in essential conflict.[45] Idealists do not reject intentionality; indeed, since Kant they have made it one of the touchstones of their transcendental method. Nearly the whole of Fichte's early philosophy is given over to the question of what it means for consciousness to intend an object. The same may be said for much of Hegel's analysis in the *Phänomenologie*, except that Hegel *begins* his argument where Moore leaves off. Moore himself struggled in later years with the status of sense-data, and their relation to common-sense perception, and grew less inclined to let intentionality establish a *prima facie* case for realism.

Perry. Ralph Barton Perry's "The Ego-Centric Predicament" (1910) has several points in common with Moore's argument. Like Moore, he points to the self-contradictory nature of literally identifying *esse* and *percipi,* and generally wishes to show the subjective character of what he calls "onto-logical idealism." The latter he takes to be the doctrine that all things are cognitively related to some mind, and that such a relation in some special way defines the nature of those things. How then, Perry asks, is such a relation to be established? Induction will not do to establish a principle of such broad generality, nor will the truism that everything is definable by whatever relation it can have suffice. Rather, we must establish an essential (necessary) connection between the mind and the world, one that makes the mind "peculiarly indispensable" to the world.[46]

In order to accomplish this, we must be able to discern what difference mind makes to what is known; we must discern the modification produced by mind on what is known, and to achieve this we must *compare* the object known with the object unknown. But immediately this becomes impossible — we are at once caught in an egocentric predicament. By itself, of course, this difficulty applies to any form of epistemology, even to the view that mind makes *no* difference to what is known, and Perry carefully notes this. No statement about the relation of mind to the world can be inferred from the situation in which the philosopher finds himself, and so ontological idealism cannot be established as part of this.

At this point, the idealist, or realist for that matter, might reply that the soundness of his position is not grounded on his being able to discern (cognitively) cognitive and noncognitive relations. Instead, it is based on a *theory*, transcendentally deduced in the case of the idealist, about the relation of mind and its objects, which as far as he can see is most plausible for explaining certain facts about mind and world. Perry considers three such theories: the *creative* theory, which argues that mind literally creates the world; the *formative* theory, which asserts that mind shapes the world; and the *identity* theory, which holds that mind and world are identical.

To say that "the world is my idea," Perry notes, is only to establish an *agreement* between my mind and its objects. And from this he concludes: "But the method of agreement, unless tested by the method of differences, affords no proof especially when, as in this case, there is an accidental reason for the invariability of the agreement."[47] Of course, the egocentric predicament rules out the method of difference, and so Perry's objection would not apply to a solipsisitic form of the creative theory, one implied by the expression "*my* idea." It would apply to a version, as in the case of Judeo-Christian theism, that makes the world a product of a Divine Mind. In this case, the method of difference would have to emerge in the arguments of natural theology. It is important to note, however, that while the predicament does not enable the general theory of mind-creation to be established, it does not warrant calling the mind-world relation "accidental," unless, of course, Perry has found a way to overcome it.

As Perry describes the formative theory, it comes the closest to Schelling's form of idealism. Here an investigation of the world reveals formal characters that make it highly plausible that everything "must possess the logical qualifications for membership in one universal system." Yet, he denies that this approach is in any way idealistic, noting that "for some reason, it is often regarded as equivalent to idealism."[48] The reasons for its being associated with idealism are obvious: Perry has described here the basic posture of science, which investigates nature precisely as a system manifesting formal properties, and objective idealism, reflecting on this, asks how the world comes to be seen as a system, and how the mind enters into this process. Rather than take the argument in this direction, Perry chooses instead to interpret the formative theory as a version of the creative theory. Instead of beginning with science, he begins with the idealistic philosopher, who is made to appear as someone who *gratuitously* introduces cognitive categories in place of onto-logical categories. Perry's reasons for accounting for this are even more peculiar. The idealist, it turns out, is like most modern philosophers in that he is a nominalist, and this means that he holds categories to be only modes of thought. And so, succumbing to the egocentric predicament, he unwittingly thinks that the world's categories must be modes of thought as well. There are several confusions here over what nominalism amounts to, and whether its opposite (Realism) is at odds with the view that categories are modes of thought. But Perry's intent is clear: he seeks to describe the position as *subjectively* as possible, so that he will be in a position to say:

> Since I cannot find a category without knowing it in the manner required by categories, I can find no category that is not a mode of thought. But since this clearly has to do with the circumstances conditioning my investigation, it must be discounted in my conclusions concerning the thing investigated.[49]

But, what are the *circumstances* here? The fact that I *think* the categories? If so, then investigation of any sort is subjective in this way. Again, it appears that Perry wishes us to discount what his own argument will not allow us to discount.

In the identity theory it is claimed that mind is both identical to the world and prior to it, or so Perry argues; and this he finds to be mere nonsense, particularly the claim that it is a special revelation of mind that reveals this identity. Against this he gives Moore's argument that we cannot literally mean they are identical, for then we would not be speaking of two things. But, as Schelling would reply, two things can be identical in one sense, and not in another; as *groupings* (5 + 7) and (10 + 2) are not identical, but as summed *quantities* they are. Mind is not identical experientially with its known object, but it may be internally related to the object in the light of a larger system, and in this sense said to be isomorphic, if not literally identical, with its object and with the world at large.

The only other alternative to mind and world being literally identical, according to Perry, is that they be literally distinct; that is, that they have their own "*complete* and *essential* natures," and then they are not capable of standing in a cognitive relation.[50] But this response clearly begs the point of his argument, for what their natures are supposed to be is what is at issue. Here, the idealist takes the apparent intelligibility of nature to indicate that total separation of the sort Perry has in mind is implausible.

Perry's argument, here and there, does cut into some of the claims made by some idealists; yet its cutting edge—the egocentric predicament—moves like the scythe of the Grim Reaper, cutting down idealist and realist alike, and leaving behind only those skeptics who are willing to embrace it. Perry's own "method of analysis" does not escape it, for how are we to discover what an ego is, what a thing is, and what knowledge is—as he suggests we first must do—without eventually ending up in the same predicament as the idealist?

Russell. The critique of idealism given by Russell in his *The Problems of Philosophy* (1912) is, once more, actually a critique of phenomenalism, in this case, the view that it is not reasonable to believe in the mind-independent existence of matter. Russell admits that it is not possible to *prove* the existence of external objects, particularly inasmuch as he himself begins with a sense-data epistemology, but says that in spite of this it is *reasonable* to assume such independent existence. For it is *simpler* to account for our experience within a framework of material objects, he argues, than it is from within a phenomenalist framework. If we see a hungry cat now and again, it is more plausible to assume that there is a hungry cat in the world than that there are only minds and their ideas. Simplicity, in this sense, Russell takes to be an uncontroversial notion. However, one man's simplicity is another man's can of worms. Berkeley evidently thought a Divine Mind surrounded by souls, who directly receive ideas and beliefs from such a Being, was a far simpler picture than is implied in the common-sense framework when completely spelled out. Common sense *is* simple, but only because it is a rather adumbrated form of philosophy. When elaborated it takes on as much complexity as we would wish. Russell's contrast, then, between a sophisticaed philosophical position (idealism) and common sense is unjustified. How I come to believe that the table continues to exist while I am asleep may involved a great deal more than is involved when a Divine Mind decides on the moment to give or take away that idea. Evidently, common sense seemed simpler to Russell because it was more natural, but this fact is beside the point.

As John Dewey remarked of the position of the realist:

> He wins an easy victory because he assumes a completed ideal without telling by what criterion he distinguishes between the static ideal of possessed knowledge in which meanings do not undergo change, and the active process of getting knowledge, where meanings are continuously modified by the new relations into which they enter.[51]

Here the common-sense world is Russell's "completed ideal," untroubled by questions of how we came to know it and what that knowledge involves. And it is the idealist's habit of continually changing the meaning of terms like *matter* and *mind* in the light of new relations and new explorations that can easily make it appear that his approach involves unnecessary complexities.

One final word. While these "refutations" may have failed on substantive grounds, they did as a practical matter succeed in turning the intellectual climate of their time against idealism. And in so doing they ran roughshod over distinctions idealists had been carefully making for over a century. Philosophers like Bosanquet in Great Britain, and Creighton and Urban in America, could only throw up their hands in exasperation. One result was that the idealists sought to defuse the revolt against reason by lowering their controversial profiles. In his "Two Types of Idealism," Creighton proposed that idealism be purged of its unreflective, reductionist, and subjectivist adherents, those who try to reduce everything to mind, so that the speculative idealists, who proceed from the standpoint of experience and science may not be painted with the same brush the neo-realists use against the phenomenalists.[52] Similarly, Urban adopted the strategy of going "beyond" realism and idealism as a way of reintroducing important issues and, eventually, the idealistic standpoint itself once more.[53] Needless to say, these attempts were not successful, and speculative idealism generally continues in hibernation for the time being.

Does Naturphilosophie *Have a Future?*

It has been argued, and with some degree of plausibility, that *Naturphilosophie* caused German science to lag behind that of the French and English by at least several decades.[54] Excesses, particularly in the study of medicine, no doubt occurred. The principles of *Naturphilosophie,* it turned out, did not present the royal road to error-free diagnosis and treatment as some of the early enthusiasts, such as Kieser and Schelling himself, had hoped. Yet, even if a Liebig was to call *Naturphilosophie* "the black death of our century" for this reason,[55] subsequent developments have justified a somewhat more balanced picture of the significance of the movement. Increasingly, the role of *Naturphilosophie* in the coming age of scientific experimentation in the nineteenth century is being recognized.[56] It is often forgotten that the tradition of speculative *Naturphilosophie* in Germany did not altogether die with the passing of Schelling and Hegel, but continued up to the present century. And certainly in this environment we cannot say that German science has fared the worse for it. To the contrary, Germany produced more than its share of "speculative physicists" in the latter part of the last century, scientists who had a large part in shaping the sciences of the present day. The connection with Schelling, as would be expected, was not always direct. Helmholtz, for example, came to *Naturphilosophie* through Goethe and Johannes Müller and, although like Oersted, Prechtl, and Faraday he was more interested in research than in speculative principles, his work unmistakably reveals its influence. As a scientist he rejected the "philosophical vapouring and consequent hysteria of the 'nature-systems' of Hegel and Schelling" and thought that metaphysics had taken too much precedence over epistemology;[57] yet his early and extremely influential paper "The Conservation of Force: A Physical Memoir" (1847) clearly adopts the view of science of the *Naturphilosophen.*[58] From Helmholtz, then, to the speculative scientists of the early twentieth century it is not difficult at all to draw connections.[59] Similar such influences can be found in the work of James Prescott Joule by way of the German physician and speculative physicist Julius Robert Mayer, a man whose profound work on energy conversion was generally regarded as too obscure for its time. In short, the spirit if not the letter of *Naturphilosophie* did not remain only with those who professed to be its advocates. It moved into the mainstream of modern science and has remained there, in its speculative wings, ever since. This would be more obvious were it not so easy to forget how fragmented and desultory eighteenth-century science was before the period of grand theory in science brought about the explosion of knowledge in the last century.

Given a more balanced picture of the movement, we can see that it was less a product of a single genius than of an entire generation of thinkers who were dissatisfied with static eighteenth-century perspectives. That Schelling specifically came to see the need for revolutions in thought and culture, given his generally conservative schooling, can be traced in part to the influence of a radical interpretation of Enlightenment ideals on him and on many of the German youth of the time. A great many of the *Naturphilosophen,* born in the 1770s and 1780s, came to maturity at a period when it became increasingly possible to believe that fresh beginnings could be and, indeed, had to be made in many different areas of human activity. Along with a desire to reform the sciences, they were the first of the modern radical social critics, even if subsequent movements—Hegelianism-of-the-left, for example, have showed them to be a generally tender-minded lot. We can see now, in their insistence that myth and art and other forms of culture be given an interpretation in terms of human values and feelings, an early attempt at the "demystification" of cultural forms. Even behind their drive for grand theory in science was a motive of bringing about a reintegration of man and nature, for before man could be seen at one with nature, nature would have to be shown to be at one with itself.

No doubt the diminishing influence of the traditional religious *Weltanschauung* was central to this transition. Not only does the theistic foundation of culture collapse as a result, but also the traditional, Cartesian-oriented epistemology. In this respect, Schiller's *Aesthetische Briefe* and Schelling's *Über Mythen* can both be seen as bold, new attempts to answer the epistemological and cultural crisis in a single stroke. Social estrangement and Kantian epistemological estrangement were both seen as the outcome of the analytic method of thought, hence in order to reestablish an earlier, more natural unity of self it was necessary to reconstruct pluralistic metaphysics into monistic metaphysics by bringing all of the increasingly fragmented human activities of culture and science within a single rational plan.

Thus, even if the motives of the *Naturphilosophen* were not purely scientific, their vision is of importance to science today — not simply in the substantive claims of the theory of the World System, but in the meta-theory behind it. In both, but particularly in the latter, a ground for dialogue between them and current science can be established. These meta-theoretical assumptions and approaches largely concern a definition of *science as a human process,* and to a great extent involve the following:

(1) the idea of a unity of all natural phenomena,
(2) a belief in the underlying unity of knower and known,
(3) the attempt to construct a theory of relations applicable to scientific research,
(4) the attempt to construct a general theory of organization,
(5) the idea that science cannot dispense with holistic or cosmological considerations.

All five points can be summed up by saying that the *Naturphilosophen* believed nature to be a *unified system.* In the history of science this notion by itself was nothing new; what was new was the serious and thoroughgoing reflection they gave to this idea. Previously, nature had been regarded usually as some sort of mechanical system, and so it afforded no place for man himself. For this reason the models of Hobbes and La Mettrie were never satisfying as interpretations of the workings of the human world, the latter being far too complicated for the mechanistic approach. *Naturphilosophie,* on the other hand, represented a far richer conceptual framework than had been attempted previously. Today we would say, with specific reference to points (3) and (4), that Schelling and his followers were attempting to substitute a *cybernetic* model of nature for the traditional mechanistic and theistic models.

Out of these assumptions emerged their theory proper: *nature as a dialectical, evolutionary process.* In this model they were satisfied that they had found a way to unify, at last, epistemology and metaphysics; the autonomy and self-identity of the traditional knowing self became *subordinate* to the World System, but a knowing self, which still had sufficient dignity to be called such, *emerged* in an evolutionary process, which involved greater differentiation and rationalization. This was a middle ground between the mechanistic approach, which destroyed all things cognitive and human, and a theological approach out of touch with current scientific knowledge and procedures.

With the possible exception of some of Herder's explorations in his *Gott* (1787), to Schelling probably must go credit for first attempting to thoroughly apply dialectical thinking to widely varying processes of nature. Recently, the assumptions of a dialectical methodology were outlined by Mario Bunge in the following manner:[60]

1. Everything has an opposite.
2. Every object is inherently contradictory, i.e., constituted by mutually opposing components and/or aspects.
3. Every change is an outcome of the tension or struggle of opposites, whether within a system or among different systems.
4. Progress is a helix every level of which contains, and at the same time negates, the previous rung.
5. Every quantitative change ends up in some qualitative change, and every new quality brings about new modes of quantitative change.

These assumptions fairly accurately embody the procedure for the study of nature set forth by Schelling in the works of

1799. Bunge singles out these propositions for criticism, and to the extent that such criticisms are sound, his remarks hold against Schelling as well. At the very heart of Schelling's dialectic, for example, is the unanswered question of how light and gravity come to act in opposition to each other in the first place, the origins of polarity being the confounding enigma, it seems, for all dialecticians. This problem, in all likelihood, was behind the confusion and vacillation over how to best characterize the Absolute we find in the course of Schelling's writings. Generally, he did not appear to want to push his thought in this more difficult direction, but instead was happier in the expanding field of science where dialectical development was well on its way, at least prior to his discovery and use of the work of Böhme. As such, his thought continues to remain prey to many of the objections raised by his contemporaries and by critics today.[61]

Yet, if *Naturphilosophie* is a series of particular failures in the various exact sciences, and if its theoretical model suffers for its terminological looseness and vague empirial links — difficulties seldom avoided by *any* broad theory in science — it is possible that it will be judged an overall success, a positive contribution, in the ongoing development of science. For one thing, an increasingly theoretical science is sooner or later bound to find sympathy with the position of the *Naturphilosophen* that science must be theoretical to the point of metaphysics; this means among other things that nature must in every account be studied as if it were a unified system, and that this study must be interdisciplinary. Characteristically, the *Naturphilosophen* often moved from one discipline to another, carried from one area to another — almost always with too much haste — by their predilection for the use of analogy. Today, analogical thinking still remains the most vital source of new theoretical insights. Advances in cybernetics, the new (synthetic) theory of evolution, the mathematization of hitherto unformalizable phenomena (communication theory, perhaps, the most spectacular among these), have all come about as a result of bold and suggestive leaps across previously unconnected areas.

Indicative of this trend is Bunge's own argument in *Method, Model and Matter* for the need to reestablish the respectability of metaphysical considerations in science once more. And while it is true that the case he makes for a new "exact metaphysics" would in most cases exclude Schelling and his school from consideration by today's standards, in his own time Schelling would have come the closest to realizing Bunge's wish. These conditions for a "scientific metaphysics" suggested by Bunge are:

1. a concern for the most general features of reality,
2. a systematic (hypothetico-deductive) structure,
3. explicit use of logic and mathematics,
4. a compatibility with contemporary science,
5. a connection with key concepts in philosophy or in the foundations of science,
6. relevance to particular scientific theories.[62]

Schelling's *Naturphilosophie* would perhaps have difficulty only in meeting conditions (3) and (4). His formal notation, as Hegel noted, is tangential to his exposition, and lacks the capacity to generate new theoretical possibilities. No attempt, for example, is made by him to tie in the dialectical "law of powers" with the exponential character of physical laws, something that might have proven both provocative and fruitful. However, it was clearly the intention of at least some of the *Naturphilosophen* to establish a tie between logic and metaphysics, even though they lacked the requisite contemporary mathematical formalisms to do this.

As regards (4), *Naturphilosophie* was largely in opposition to the science of the 1780s and 1790s, both initially because it advanced newer approaches in chemistry and physics, and later because it came to be opposed by proponents of the mechanistic outlook. However, as a theoretical approach it was not so compatible with the science of its day as was, say, the atomic theory, because Schelling's "dynamic atomistics" required more knowledge of the workings of nature, and more elaborate theoretical structures (field theory, for example) to be rendered applicable. Dalton's Atomic Theory may have helped develop and explain the Law of Definite Proportions in chemistry, but it was inadequate for the more sophisticated processes involving magnetism, electricity, thermodynamics, and organic growth, for which *Naturphilosophie* sought explanations. We are still very much in the dark about a great deal of what we observe in these areas; perhaps so much so that a day may still come when the outrageous visions of *Naturphilosophie,* which regarded nature and the cosmos as a "universal organism" building itself hierarchically, will be a more easily accepted hypothesis. Among the features such a *Naturphilosophie* of the future would require would be a detailed cosmological theory—one linking macro- and microscopic phenomena, a mathematical theory of speciation and growth, and a theory of cognitive emergence. If science does manage to open up new vistas in these areas, it is possible that even some substantial connection to the old *Naturphilosophie* will be found.

Those recent theoretical developments just mentioned may in fact be taking us in this direction. It is clear that Schelling was seeking a general theory of organization, and at times described the goal of his *Naturphilosophie* in just this way. Such a theory, which has been slowly emerging from a cross-fertilization of information theory, thermodynamics, and statistical mechanics, is even somewhat reminiscent of Schelling's approach. In the characterization of organization in terms of information and entropy, given as,

$$Organization = Information - Entropy,[63]$$

we can see illustrated Schelling's insight, that an organized system involves a balance of opposing tendencies—an active, generative (in-forming) tendency, characterized by the statistical concept of *information,* and a passive, degenerative tendency, indicative of the thermodynamic notion of *entropy.* Today these speculations amount to more than just a promise; they have helped revolutionize molecular biology, among other disciplines, and were it not for the waning of the more mechanistic approaches brought about by the earlier revolutions in physics, they would now doubtless be opposed with the same vigor as Schelling's views were opposed. The main difference, as Bunge notes, is that they can be formulated in a more mathematically precise fashion, in a way allowing us to see specific relations and their ramifications. But Schelling could hardly be faulted for not anticipating and developing what it took generations of scientists and logicians to produce since then. What he did achieve, it should now be clear, warrants him a firm place in the history of science.

Notes

A Note on Schelling's Early Works

1. Schelling's greatest recent influence has probably been on existentialist philosophy; see, for example, Martin Heidegger, *Schellings Abhandlung über das menschlichen Freiheit,* ed. Hildegard Feick (Tübingen: Max Niemeyer, 1971); Karl Jaspers, *Schelling* (Munich: R. Piper, 1955); Gabriel Marcel, *Coleridge et Schelling* (Paris: Aubier-Montaigne, 1971); Paul Tillich, *Die religionsgeschichtliche Konstruction in Schellings positiver Philosophie, ihre Voraussetzungen und Prinzipien* (Breslau: Fleischmann, 1910).

2. References to Schelling are from the *Sämmtliche Werke,* 14 vols., ed. K.F.A. Schelling (Stuttgart and Augsburg: J. G. Cotta, 1856); translation of all German texts, unless otherwise indicated, is by the author.

Introduction

1. Friedrich Schiller, "Philosophische Briefe," in *Werke,* (Weimar: Hermann Böhlaus, 1962), 20:112. In this dialogue between Julius and Raphael, Julius explains his solution to the plight of Reason in the form of a "theosophie": "The Universe is a thought of God . . . . The great structure we call the "World" remains noteworthy for me only because it manifests the manifold expressions of that Being in a symbolic manner" (pp. 115-16). Schiller's *theosophie* would eventually be modified by Schelling into a *Naturphilosophie.*

2. This attitude can also be found in Herder's inability to accept Spinoza's view that God could have an infinity of attributes and the world of human experience only two. J. G. Herder, *God, Some Conversations,* trans. Frederick H. Burkhardt (New York: Bobbs-Merrill, 1940), p. 100; see also p. 44.

3. Immanual Kant, *Critique of Pure Reason,* trans. Norman Kemp Smith (New York: St. Martin's, 1965), A298,B355; hereafter references to the *Critique* will be given with *A* and *B* pagination.

4. Kant, A462, B490.

5. Kant, A480, B508.

6. Frederick Schlegel, *The Philosophy of Life and Philosophy of Language,* trans. A. J. W. Morrison (London: Henry G. Bohn, 1847), p. 363.

7. Schlegel, p. 13.

8. Schlegel, pp. 362-67.

9. Harald Höffding, *A History of Modern Philosophy,* trans. B. E. Meyer (New York: Dover, 1955), 2:577-78.

10. Karl Marx, "Philosophy after its Completion," in *Writings of the Young Marx on Philosophy and Society,* trans. and ed. L. D. Easton and K. H. Guddat (New York: Doubleday, Anchor Books, 1967), p. 62.

11. J. G. Fichte, *The Science of Knowledge,* trans. and ed. Peter Heath and John Lachs (New York: Appleton-Century-Crofts, 1970), pp. 218-24.

12. Fichte, p. 224.

13. Fichte, pp. 229f.

14. Fichte, p. 233.

15. Fichte, p. 239.

16. *The Popular Works of Johann Gottlieb Fichte,* trans. William Smith (London: Trübner, 1889), p. 215. It was apparent to Kant in 1799 that Fichte's deduction of critical philosophy was an impossible task, and in an "open letter" to Fichte made this opinion known; see an "open letter on Fichte's *Wissenschaftslehre*" in *Kant: Philosophical Correspondence, 1759-99,* trans. and ed. Arnulf Zweig (Chicago: University of Chicago Press, 1967), pp. 253f.

17. O. F. Gruppe, *Antäus: Ein Briefwechsel über speculative Philosophie in ihrem Conflict mit Wissenschaft und Sprache* (Berlin, 1831), p. 160.

Chapter 1 The Fichtean Period

1. Schelling's exposure to academic subjects at the age of fifteen was considerable. During the 1790-91 terms his studies included Theoretical and Experimental Physics, Mathematics, Metaphysics and Logic, Natural Law, the philosophies of Epictetus and Plato, Psychology, and Aesthetics. In 1791-92 he continued with Physics, Mathematics, Psychology, Logic, the theory of natural rights, and also studied Natural Theology, Kant's *Critique,* Ancient Philosophy, and Reinhold's Critical Philosophy. Biblical studies included the Gospel according to St. John, the Book of Isaiah, and the history of the apostles. Kuno Fischer has given some background to Schelling's early career in *Schellings Leben, Werk und Lehre* (Heidelberg: Carl Winter's Universität, 1902); also see Hans Jörg Sandkühler's *Friedrich Wilhelm Joseph Schelling* (Stuttgart: J. B. Metzler, 1970), pp. 63-70.

2. Fischer also mentions Herder's *Aufsatz über den Geist der hebräischen Poesie* and Kant's *Abhandlungen über den muthmasslichen Anfang der Menschengeschichte* as sources of influence on the young Schelling (p. 15).

3. *Sämmtliche Werke,* 5:370; hereafter all references to the *Werke* will be by volume and page only.

4. 5:395.

5. 5:400ff.

6. 1:48 and 51.

7. 1:55f.

8. 1:64.

9. 1:74.

10. 5:298; also pp. 426-33.

11. 5:438.

12. 5:442.

13. 5:272f.

14. 2:13.

15. 2:16.

16. 7:23.

17. 1:90; also 5:4f. and 107.

18. 1:91f.

19. 1:93.

20. Schelling has in mind Leibniz's Principle of Noncontradiction here; 1:101.

21. 1:94.

22. 1:96f.

23. 1:162.

24. 1:177.

25. 1:179.

26. 1:186.

27. 1:193.

28. 1:195-204.

29. 1:213; Years later Schelling would characterize Spinoza's system as a "formal dogmatism," that is, a system formally correct insofar as it is monistic and based on something unconditioned, but one lacking a ground in transcendental consciousness.

30. 1:217.

31. 1:221; Schelling had briefly attempted a deduction of the Kantian categories from the fundamental principle of philosophy in his *Über die Möglichkeit einer Form der Philosophie überhaupt;* see 1:107-10.

32. 1:221.

33. 1:226f.

34. 5:255; 1:228; Later in the *System des transzendentalen Idealismus* time comes to play a crucial role in the dialectical growth of consciousness from simple awareness to the most complex comprehension of intelligence. Schelling, it appears, took over Kant's approach to time, regarding it only as a form of consciousness.

35. 1:232.

36. 1:232-34.

37. 1:239; Here Schelling characterizes the empirical self as an "appearance of absolute self," but does not consider why the absolute self must appear to itself in a finite mode.

38. 1:240.

39. 1:248.

40. This view anticipates his later theory of art worked out in the *Philosophie der Kunst* (1802).

41. 1:249.

42. 1:249. In 1806 Schelling elaborated on his earlier critique of Fichte in a short piece entitled *Darlegung des wahren Verhältnisses der Naturphilosophie zu der verbesserten fichteschen Lehre.* There he accuses Fichte of accepting a concept of nature as an "empty objectivity, a mere sense world," lacking life and dynamic interaction with the self (7:11). In the *Neue Deduction* this critique emerges for the first time.

43. 1:293.

44. 1:302.

45. 1:305.

46. This remark is attributed to Lessing in Jacobi's *Ueber die lehre des Spinoza in briefen an den Herrn Moses Mendelssohn* (Breslau: G. Lowe, 1789), p. 22.

47. Reprinted in Walter Kaufmann's *Hegel: Reinterpretation, Texts, and Commentary* (Garden City, N.Y.: Doubleday, 1965), pp. 302f.

48. 1:310.

49. 1:314.

50. 1:315f.

51. Jacobi, pp. 168-79, 200-204.

52. Jacobi, p. 268; This is probably not Schelling's first encounter with the thought of Bruno. He is mentioned in J. G. H. Feder's *Logik und Metaphysik*, which had already gone through several editions before Schelling became familiar with it.

53. Jacobi, pp. 268, 270, 283.

54. 1:363-65.

55. *"der Selbstanschauung eines Geistes,"* 1:366.

56. *"ein Sein einer geistigen Natur,"* 1:368.

57. 1:379f.

58. *"alle Handlungen des Geistes,"* 1:382.

59. Ibid.; This view clearly anticipates Schelling's later *System des transzendentalen Idealismus.*

60. 1:394f.

61. 1:401, 432, 438f.

62. 1:441.

63. 2:3f.

Chapter 2 The Theoretical Groundwork of the Philosophy of Nature

1. 2:6.

2. 2:12f.

3. 2:17f.

4. 1:373.

5. G. W. F. Hegel, *Lectures on the History of Philosophy*, trans. Elizabeth S. Haldane and Frances H. Simson (London: Hegan, Paul, Trench, Trübner, 1896), p. 456.

6. Immanuel Kant, *Sämmtliche Werke*, ed. J. H. v. Kirchmann (Heidelberg: Weiss, 1870-1891), 7:174. Hereafter references to the Kant *Werke* will be by volume and page only.

7. Kant, 7:177.

8. Ibid.

9. Kant, *Critique of Pure Reason, A382f.*

10. Kant had intended that the proposed *Metaphysics of Nature* deal with the whole realm of nature. Looking at the *Critique* as a preface to what was still to be only an empirical (dogmatic) task, it loses much of the "critical" character attributed to it in so many modern and earlier interpretations. It is often forgotten that for Kant *Naturlehre* was of a wider scope than *Korperlehre* and *Seelenlehre*, and that it was not the latter that was attacked in the *Critique*, but only *"empirische Seelenlehre."* And the *Critique* itself was an example of *Seelenlehre* in the form of *Seelenwissenschaft.*

11. Kant, 7:177.

12. Kant, 7:185.

13. *Critique of Pure Reason*, A379f; also A358.

14. Kant, 7:180.

15. Ibid.

16. Kant, 7:199.

17. Kant, 7:214.

18. Kant, 7:228.

19. *Critique of Pure Reason*, A277, B333.

20. Ibid., A285, B341.

21. Ibid., A286, B342f.

22. Ibid., A266, B321f.

23. Samuel Taylor Coleridge, *Biographia Literaria* (New York: Dutton, 1962), p. 74. After spending nine months in Germany in 1799, Coleridge returned to England imbued with the spirit of the new German Idealism. Orsini's book *Coleridge and German Idealism* traces the extent of Coleridge's involvement with the idealist movement.

24. *Critique of Pure Reason*, Axxi.

25. 1:373.

26. *"Die sich selbst ihre Sphäre gibt,"* 1:379.

27. 1:380.

28. 2:23.

29. 2:215.

30. Schelling's analysis of matter, at one point, follows that of Berkeley; 2:25f.

31. 2: 217f.

32. *"Eine ursprüngliche Tätigkeit,"* 2:218.

33. 2:219.

34. 2:222.

35. 2:30.

36. G. E. Schulze, *Anesidemus, oder Über die Fundemente der von dem Herrn Prof. Reinhold in Jena gelieferten Elementar-Philosophie* (1792), pp. 108-80.

37. 2:30f.

38. *"Bloss eine ideale Aufeinanderfolge unserer Vorstellungen,"* 2:31.

39. Ibid.

40. 2:32.

41. 2:34.

42. *Critique of Pure Reason*, A78, B103.

43. Ibid., B109.

44. Ibid., B110.

45. Ibid., B111.

46. Ibid., B110.

47. Ibid., A213, B259.

48. Ibid., B257.

49. Ibid., B258.

50. Ibid., A212, B259.

51. Ibid.

52. Ibid., A213, B260.

53. Ibid., A214, B261.

54. 3:470f.

55. Alfred North Whitehead, *Process and Reality* (New York: The Free Press, 1969), p. 34.

56. *"Handlungsweisen,"* 3:471.

57. *Critique of Pure Reason*, A201, B246f.

58. Ibid., A202, B247.

59. Ibid.

60. Ibid., A208, B253f.

61. A. C. Ewing argues this point in *A Short Commentary on Kant's Critique of Pure Reason* (Chicago: University of Chicago, 1938), p. 159.

62. 3:477f.

63. 3:481.

64. H. J. Paton remarks in his commentary on the Third Analogy that "the concept of interaction is the most fundamental concept of Science"; *Kant's Metaphysic of Experience* (London: George Allen and Unwin, 1961), pp. 324f.

65. *Critique of Pure Reason*, B219.

66. Ibid., A178, B220.

67. See, for example, ibid., A186, B229.

68. Ibid.

69. Ibid., B218.

70. Ibid., B257f.

71. Ibid., A218, B265.

72. 2:34.

73. 2:34f.

74. David Hume, *An Enquiry Concerning Human Understanding* (New York: The Liberal Arts Press, 1955), p. 56.

75. Hume, p. 22.

76. Hume, p. 57.

77. Hume, pp. 67f.

78. 2:35. Schelling does not even consider Hobbes's materialist monism as the other possibility here.

79. 2:36.

80. 2:38.

81. *"Eine Naturlehre unseres Geistes,"* 2:39.

82. 2:39.

83. Gottfried Wilhelm Leibniz, *Monadology,* par. 14.

84. 2:40f. Schelling also uses the terms *Art* and *Gattung* to describe this rational principle of organization.

85. 2:41 and 44.

86. 2:42.

87. 2:43.

88. 2:45.

89. 2:47.

90. Immanuel Kant, *Critique of Judgment,* trans. J. H. Bernard (New York: Hafner, 1951), p. 219.

91. *Critique of Judgment,* p. 221.

92. Ibid.

93. Ibid.

94. Ibid.

95. Ibid., pp. 222f.

96. Ibid., p. 228.

97. Ibid., p. 232.

98. Ibid.

99. Ibid., p. 233.

100. Ibid., p. 234.

101. Ibid.

102. Ibid.

103. Ibid., p. 235.

104. Ibid., p. 233.

105. Ibid., p. 235.

106. Ibid., p. 234.

107. A summary of such views can be found in J. D. McFarland's *Kant's Concept of Teleology* (Edinburgh: University of Edinburgh Press, 1970), pp. 120f.

108. *Critique of Judgment,* p. 236.

109. Ibid., p. 237

110. Ibid.

111. Ibid.; see also p. 271.

112. Ibid., p. 237.

113. Ibid., p. 238.

114. Ibid., p. 244.

115. Ibid., p. 245.

116. Ibid., p. 246.

117. Ibid., p. 242.

118. Ibid., p. 252.

119. Ibid., p. 254; emphasis mine.

120. Kant's rejection in the *Critique of Judgment* of "a complete spontaneity of intuition" is at odds, of course, with Schelling's advocacy of intellectual intuition (p. 254).

121. 2:526.

122. "Instinct," "desire," "inclination," are all part of what Schelling means by *Trieb;* 2:527.

123. 2:529f.

124. 2:235.

Chapter 3 The Idea of Nature

1. 2:58.

2. 5:215.

3. 5:318.

4. 2:62f. and 359.

5. *"Ewigen und unendlichen sich-selber-Wollens,"* 2:362.

6. 3:275f.

7. 3:282f.

8. 3:276.

9. Ibid.

10. Ibid.

11. 3:278f.; These principles are developed in the *Einleitung zu dem Entwurf eines Systems der Naturphilosophie* (1799), a work that has probably had the greatest effect for *Naturphilosophie*. Its translation into English in one of the early issues of the *Journal of Speculative Philosophy* is one of the reasons for Schelling influence in America.

12. 3:277.

13. 3:284.

14. 3:285.

15. 3:287.

16. 3:285.

17. 3:288.

18. Ibid.

19. Ibid.

20. 3:288f.

21. 3:290.

22. 3:291; In a footnote Schelling remarks: "A traveler in Italy makes the remark that the whole history of the world may be demonstrated on the great obelisk at Rome; so likewise, in every product of Nature. Every mineral body is a fragement of the annals of the earth. But what is the earth? Its history is interwoven with the history of the whole of nature, and so passes from the fossile through the whole of inorganic and organic nature, until it culminates in the history of the universe — one chain" (3:291). This idea of *epigenesis* probably reflects the influence of Kant, as well as of Erasmus Darwin and Steffens, on Schelling.

23. Ibid.

24. 3:292.

25. 3:296; this appears to contradict a later position.

26. 3:302.

27. 3:43.

28. 3:68.

29. 2:371.

30. 3:310 and 69ff.

31. 3:71.

32. 3:309.

33. 3:312.

34. Schelling involved himself in the debate over the nature of combustion by arguing that combustion involved the release of *Lichtwesen*, which appears to us "who are endowed with life" as light (3:318). Elsewhere he characterizes the force of *Lichtwesen* as centrifugal and that of gravity as centripetal (6:261-67).

35. 2:100f. and 107.

36. 2:107.

37. 2:383.

38. 3:390.

39. 2:395.

40. 2:371.

41. 3:313.

42. 3:314f.

43. 3:317.

44. 2:315; see especially n. 5.

45. 3:315f; see n. 1.

46. 3:317.

47. Ibid.

48. Ibid.

49. 3:318.

50. This schema is an elaboration of the one given in 3:9. "Light" is understood as *Lichtwesen,* and "creative instinct," or perhaps "generative formation," as *Bildungstrieb.*

51. 3:320.

52. 3:322 and 324.

53. 3:325f.

54. Much of the ridicule that came to *Naturphilosophie* was inspired by its presentation as an axiomatic system. The *Darstellung*, however, is no mere presentation of the previous works. After 1800 Schelling speaks of nature more as Reason and God, no doubt partly due to the perspective of the *System des transzendental Idealismus*, but also, as we shall see, partly the result of the influence of Eschenmayer. The selections from the *Darstellung* quoted here are from 4:115-211. Schelling's numbering has been retained.

55. 4:122n.

56. 4:131.

57. 4:140-42.

58. 4:151.

59. In a later work Schelling suggests the following schema, based on the analogy of the magnet, to represent the relation between total identity and the relative identities of which it is comprised:

$$X \ldots \underline{\hspace{4cm}\overset{}{\vert}\overset{}{\vert}\overset{}{\vert}\hspace{1cm}}$$
$$ e \ d \ f$$
$$A^+ = B A = A A = B$$

He then observes: "The point d represents a natural body, for example, the magnet; this body is objective relative to light—there is a plus of being in it—but to another body it is perceptive" (7:184f.). The X and the open-ended line are probably meant to represent the fact that the identities will proliferate in number and increase in complexity.

60. 4:158.

61. 4:205.

Chapter 4 The World System

1. See, for example, Ervin Laszlo, *Introduction to Systems Philosophy* (New York: Gordon and Breach, 1972); *System, Structure, and Experience* (New York: Gordon and Breach, 1969); *The Systems View of the World* (New York: Braziller, 1972), Ludwig von Bertalanffy, *General System Theory* (New York: Braziller, 1968); Paul A. Weiss, *Hierarchically Organized Systems in Theory and Practice* (New York: Hafner, 1971); Arthur Koestler, "Beyond Atomism and Holism—The Concept of the Holon," in *Beyond Reductionism*, ed. Arthur Koestler and J. R. Smythies (Boston: Beacon, 1969).

2. 1:400.

3. 2:344.

4. 1:386f.; 2:348f.; see also 2:496-507 for such a systematic treatment of the concept of life.

5. 2:348.

6. 2:349f.

7. 2:349; 3:65.

8. 2:520; 3:220.

9. 2:515f.

10. 2:520.

11. 3:14.

12. 2:183; 3:148 and 206.

13. 3:15, 61, 154, and 261.

14. von Bertalanffy, p. 149.

15. Laszlo, *Introduction to Systems Philosophy*, pp. 153f.

16. Ibid., pp. 18f.

17. Schelling uses the expression *World System* in various senses. In many cases he means by it only the natural and planetary system of bodies, in contrast to the Ideal System of mind and ideas. Yet, it is clear that once the identity theory was adopted, the material and ideal systems were united. The World System in this sense is one of the more apt expressions, besides the term *Absolute,* for this identity.

18. 3:20.

19. 2:217.

20. This scheme has been reconstructed from what are only essentially suggestive remarks in 2:225f.

21. 3:334-42, 352.

22. 3:355-57.

23. 3:369.

24. 3:372.

25. 3:395.

26. 3:396.

27. Laszlo, *System, Structure, and Experience*, p. 77.

28. 3:396f.

29. 3:397f.; Here Schelling notes that this separation is the origin of philosophy insofar as it is an activity that assumes the possibility of free conscious activity, but only so that it may be in a position to achieve necessary knowledge.

30. *"Der blosse Stoff,"* 3:400.

31. 3:403.

32. 3:432.

33. 3:458f.

34. 3:462.

35. 3:466.

36. 3:471.

37. 3:482 and 487.

38. 3:478 and 481.

39. 3:484; In *Being and Nothingness* Sartre distinguishes "thetic" or "positional" consciousness from a "nonthetic" awareness of the environment of a specific consciousness, either in the self or in the world.

40. Spinoza, *Ethics,* 2:vii and xx.

41. Ibid., 2:xxiii.

42. Ibid., 2:ix and xxv.

43. Ibid., 2:xxvi.

44. Ibid., 2:xxix.

45. 3:490; *"Der verschlungene Zug der Seele,"* 1:386.

46. Laszlo deals with perception in this manner in *Introduction to Systems Philosophy*, pp. 133f.

47. 3:491.

48. Ibid.

49. Ibid.

50. 3:492.

51. 3:493.

52. 3:493.

53. 3:494.

54. Ibid.

55. 3:495.

56. 3:497.

57. Ibid.

58. 3:498.

59. Emphasis mine.

60. 3:498.

61. *"Der Durchsichtigkeit des Organismus für den Geist,"* 3:498.

62. Ibid.

63. These terms are used in the sense Husserl gives them in his *Ideen*.

64. 3:516.

65. 3:508; the meaning of *Handlungsweise* might be better translated as "procedural methods."

66. Schelling maintained that the need to supply a *substratum* behind the action is itself the product of theoretical activity that divides subject from object, and cause from effect. Intelligence is not a *substratum* manifesting concepts, but rather an activity and disposition (3:530).

67. 7:184; see also 6:369.

68. In his *Dialektik und Einbildungskraft*, Hablützel suggests another outline, one emphasizing the identity of the real and ideal, rather than, as here, their evolutionary interplay (p. 88). In Figure 2 the *continuity* of the ideal and real is also suggested and is in line with Schelling's interpretation of this relation given in 4:368.

Chapter 5 Science and *Naturphilosophie*

1. Friedrich Ueberweg, *History of Philosophy*, trans. George S. Morris (New York: Charles Scribner's Sons, 1891), 2:217.

2. Wilhelm Windelband, *A History of Philosophy*, trans. James H. Tufts (New York: Macmillan, 1901), p. 568.

3. John Theodore Merz, *A History of European Thought in the Nineteenth Century* (London: Wm Blackwood and Sons, 1912), p. 557.

4. 5:319.

5. 5:322.

6. 5:334; This statement also aptly sums up the criticism *Naturphilosophie* itself was soon to receive.

7. 5:226.

8. Kuno Fischer mentions that Schelling had some knowledge of the work of Newton and Clarke in 1791-92; *Schellings Leben, Werke und Lehre* (Heidelberg: Carl Winters Universitätsbuchhandlung, 1902), p. 11.

9. Erasmus Darwin, *Zoonomia: or The Laws of Organic Life* (London: J. Johnson, 1796), 1:1.

10. K. F. Kielmayer's "Versuche über die sogenannte animalische Electrizität" appeared in the *Journal der Physik*, ed. F. A. C. Gren (Halle and Leipzig: T. Ambrosius Barth, 1794), 8:65-76. No doubt Schelling was familiar with the wide variety of scientific studies and reports published in the Gren volumes, including the work of Guy Lussac, Davy, Dalton, and Priestly. After Gren's death L. W. Gilbert became editor of the journal, which was renamed the *Annalen der Physik* in 1799. In the following decades the *Annalen* would become a voice for opponents of *Naturphilosophie*.

11. *Briefe und Dokumente*, ed. Horst Fuhrmans (Bonn: H. Bouvier, 1962), 1:122.

12. See, for example, 2:535f. and 541.

13. 2:566; If there is any connection between Schelling's earlier liberal political views and his *Natuphilosophie*, it may be found here in the idea of freedom within the higher organisms.

14. 2:522.

15. Haller considered the nerves "the satellites of the soul." See Albrecht von Haller, *A Dissertation on the Sensible and Irritable Parts of Animals*, trans. M. Tissot (London: J. Nourse, 1755), p. 67. In the introduction Tissot remarks that "the great discovery of the present age is *irritability* . . . " (p. iii).

16. This is argued by Margarete Hochdoerfer in *The Conflict between the Religious and the Scientific views of Albrecht von Haller*, Univ. of Nebraska Studies in Language, Literature, and Criticism, No. 12 (Lincoln, Neb.: Univ. of Nebraska Press, 1932), p. 27.

17. 5:336f.; 2:522.

18. 2:532f.

19. 2:546.

20. Franz von Baader, *Beiträge zur Elementar-Physiologie* in *Sämmtliche Werke*, ed. Franz Hoffmann (Leipzig: Herrmann Bethmann, 1852), 3:213-16.

21. J. R. Partington, *A History of Chemistry* (London: Macmillan, 1962), 3:521.

22. 2:75-81.

23. 5:333.

24. 2:87, 90, 94, 104f.

25. 2:122f., 524, 555.

26. 5:231.

27. Quoted from J. P. Stern, *Lichtenberg: A Doctrine of Scattered Occasions* (Bloomington, Ind.: Indiana University Press, 1959), pp. 76, 82, 117.

28. 4:46, 59, 178.

29. Robert C. Stauffer, "Speculation and Experiment in the Background of Oersted's Discovery of Electromagnetism," *Isis* 48 (March 1957):33-50.

30. F. W. J. Schelling and G. W. F. Hegel, eds., *Kritisches Journal der Philosophie (Tübingen: J. G. Cotta, 1803), 2:51-56.*

31. Stauffer, p. 39; however, Oersted's *Der Geist in der Natur* (Munich; J.G. Cotta'schen, 1850-51), 2 vols., is not without its speculative claims about nature and science. The influence of *Naturphilosophie* on nineteenth-century science, including Oersted, is developed in Trevor H. Levere's *Affinity and Matter: Elements of Chemical Philosophy, 1800-1865* (Oxford: Claredon, 1971).

32. Thomas S. Kuhn, "Energy Conservation as an Example of Simultaneous Discovery," in *Critical Problems in the History of Science,* ed. Marshall Clagett (Madison, Wisc.: Univ. of Wisconsin Press, 1959), pp. 338f.; Justus von Liebig, "The Connection and Equivalence of Forces," in *The Correlation and Conservation of Forces,* ed. Edward L. Youmans (New York: Appleton, 1865), pp. 387-97.

33. Heinrich Steffens, *German University Life: The Story of My Career,* trans. William L. Gage (Philadelphia: J.B. Lippincott, 1874), p. 37.

34. Steffens, pp. 32 and 36.

35. *Briefe und Dokumente,* 1: 177 and 194f.

36. 2:512

37. F.W.J. Schelling, ed., *Zeitschrift für spekulative Physik* (Jena and Leipzig: Christian Ernst Gabler, 1800), 1:142.

38. *Beyträge zur innern Naturgeschichte der Erde* (Freiberg: Crazischen Buchhandlung, 1801), pp. 93f.

39. *Zeitschrift für spekulative Physik,* 1:139.

40. 5:329; see also 4: 154, 169, 481, 491.

41. *Grundriss der Natur-Philosophie* (Tübingen: Heinrich Laupp, 1832), p. x.

42. *Zeitschrift für spekulative Physik* II (1801): 1-68; it is possible that Eschenmayer may have been influenced by a similar distinction found in Schiller's *Aesthetische Briefe.*

43. 4:84 and 92.

44. 4:101-3.

45. 4:92 and 96.

46. *Die Philosophie in ihren Uebergang zur Nichtphilosophie* (Erlangen: Walterschen Kunst- und Buchhandlung, 1803), pp. 36 and 71; an interesting comparison of the systems of Eschenmayer and Schelling is given in this work (p. 94).

47. *Briefe und Dokument,* 1:320.

48. *Einleitung in Natur und Geschichte* (Erlangen: Walterschen Kunst- und Buchhandlung, 1806), pp. 14, 21, 52, 64, 156.

49. *Einleitung in Natur und Geschichte,* pp. 64ff, 96, 103.

50. During this period Eschenmayer published his*Versuch die scheinbare Magie des thierischen Magnetismus* (Stuttgart and Tübingen: J. G. Cotta'schen, 1816)

and edited along with D. G. Kieser and F. Nasse the *Archiv für den thierischen Magnetismus* (Halle: Hermmerder and Schwetschte, 1818). In his *Philosophy of Mind* Hegel claims that animal magnetism confirms the "underlying unity of soul, and of the power of its 'ideality'" (para. 379).

51. Johann Eduard Erdmann, *A History of Philosophy*, trans. Williston S. Hough (London: Swan Sonnenschein, 1892) 2:652.

52. Lorenz Oken, *Lehrbuch der Naturphilosophie* (Jena: Friedrich Frommann, 1809), p. lx.

53. Oken, p. 16.

54. C. Guttler's *Lorenz Oken und sein Verhältniss zur modernen Entwickelungslehre* (Leipzig: E. Bidder, 1884) traces the influence of Oken on nineteenth-century science (pp. 83ff.).

55. *Ahndungen einer allgemeinen Geschichte des Lebens* (Leipzig: Carl Heinrich Reclam, 1806), 1:215.

56. His *Ansichten von der Nachtseite der Naturwissenschaft* (Dresden and Leipzig: Arnoldischen, 1840) contains an elaboration of this idea.

57. *Von der Natur der Dinge* (Leipzig: Breitkopf and Härtel, 1803), p. xviii.

58. *Theodicee* (Bamberg and Würzburg: Joseph Anton Goebhardt, 1809), pp. 16f. and 23.

59. *Mathematische Philosophie* (Erlangen: Johann Jakob Palm, 1811), pp. 3-14, 25, 52.

60. Ibid., pp. 57ff., 69, 263f.

61. P. L. Adam, ed. *Erläuterungen zum Organon der menschlichen Erkenntniss* (Ulm: P. L. Adam, 1854), p. 140.

62. *Die Physik als Kunst. Ein Versuch, die Tendenz der Physik aus ihrer Geschichte zu deuten* (Munich: Joseph Lindauer, 1806), pp. 13.f, 57f., 62; The influence of Ritter on Schubert is revealed in *Briefe eines Romantischen Physikers: Johan Wilhelm Ritter an Gotthilf Heinrich Schubert und an Karl von Hardenberg* (Munich: Heinz Moos, 1966); see also Partington, 4:18 for an indication of Ritter's scientific work.

63. *Zeitschrift für Wissenschaft und Kunst* (Lanshut: Joseph Thomann, 1808), 1:10 and 16. Ast was obviously closer to the positions of Schiller and Schlegel, the latter contributing some poems to the *Zeitschrift*.

64. Klein is considered one of the most slavish of Schelling's adherents. His *Betrachtungen* presents a list of friends and enemies, the former being Daub, Dippold, Hegel, Kanne, Keiser, Krause, Marcus, Oken, C.E. Schelling, Schubert, Walter, Weber, Windischmenn, Zimmer, Görres, Steffens, and Baader; while the latter are Fries, Köppen, Link, Salat, Suskind, and Berg (pp. 182-87).

65. *Aphorismen über die Kunst als Einleitung zu Aphorismen über Organomie, Physik, Psychologie und Anthropologie* (Koblenz: Lassaultx, 1810), pp. ivf., 102f., 201f.

66. *Blicke in das Wesen des Menschen* (Aarau: H. R. Sauerländer, 1812), p. ix, 26f., 44f., 210.

67. *Naturlehre des menschlichen Erkennens, oder Metaphysic* (Aarau: H. R. Sauerländer, 1828), p. 266.

68. *Grundriss der historischen Logik* (Jena and Leipzig: Christian Ernst Gabler, 1803), pp. 3ff., 24, 130ff.

69. Still others associated with *Naturphilosophie* and Schelling to some extent or other are Carl Windischmann (1775-1839), who began with a piece in the *Zeitschrift* and whose major work is *Die Philosophie im Fortgang der Weltgeschichte* (1827-34, 4 vols.); Karl Burdach (1776-1847), the physiologist, who published a three-volume work on the brain and nervous system entitled *Vom Baue und Leben des Gehirns* (1819-1826); Karl Gustav Carus (1789-1869), the physiologist, painter, and aesthetician; and Nees von Esenbeck (1776-1858), who expanded on Goethe's morphological theories in his *Lehrbuch der Botanik.* Partly as a result of Steffens's lectures in Copenhagen in 1802-03 the influence of *Naturphilosophie* was brought to Scandinavia. The Swedish botanist and mathematician Carl Adolf Agardh (1785-1859) reflects such influence in his theory of classification; he became acquainted with Schelling's work in German and dedicated the first part of his botany handbook to him; another Swede, Israel Hwasser (1790-1860), the anatomist and physician, and Immanuel Ilmoni (1797-1844), who made zoological excursions in Egypt while accompanying Bonaparte, presented, in his morphological studies, the view that organic structures proceeded from a common form.

70. 6:28.

71. 6:40.

72. 6:47.

73. 6:65.

74. Arthur O. Lovejoy, *The Great Chain of Being* (New York: Harper and Row, 1965), p. 317.

75. 7:350.

76. 7:346.

77. 7:376.

78. 7:399.

79. 7:350 and 357.

80. 7:408.

81. 7:415.

82. 7:416.

Chapter 6 Schelling's Critics

1. G.W.F. Hegel, *Sämtliche Werk,* ed. Herman Glockner (Stuttgart-Bad Cannstatt: Friedrich Frommann, 1964), 2:20.

2. Kaufmann, p. 385.

3. 5:109.

4. Karl Leonhard Reinhold, *Beiträge zur leichtern Uebersicht des Zustandes der Philosophie* (Hamburg: Friedrich Perthes, 1802), pp. 187f., and 206.

5. *Ueber das absolute Identitäts-System und sein Verhältniss zu dem neusten (Reinholdischen) Dualismus.*

6. 5:25 and 47.

7. Wilhelm Traugott Krug, *Briefe über den neuesten Idealism* (Leipzig: Heinrich, Müller, 1801), pp. 12-28.

8. Ibid., pp. 31-33.

9. Ibid, pp. 48f., and 51f.

10. Ibid., pp. 65 and 68.

11. See Krug's *Edtwurf eines Neuen Organons der Philosphie* (Meissen and Lübben: K. F. W. Erbstein, 1801), pp. 16 and 19f.

12. *Über die verschiednen Methoden des Philosophirens und die verschiednen Systeme der Philosophie* (Meissen: Karl Friedrich Wilhelm Erbstein, 1802), p. 26.

13. Friedrich Köppen, *Schelling's Lehre, oder Das Ganze der Philosophie des absoluten Nichts* (Friedrich Perthes, 1803), p. 85.

14. Ibid., pp. 18, 45f., 64, 81.

15. Ibid., pp. 189-94.

16. Franz Berg, *Sextus, oder Uber die absolute Erkenntniss von Schelling* (Würzburg: Sebastian Sartorius, 1804), pp. 32-45.

17. Berg, p. 125.

18. H. S. Harris, *Hegel's Development: Toward the Sunlight* (Oxford: Clarendon, 1972), p. 186.

19. Johannes Hoffmeister, ed. *Briefe von und an Hegel* (Hamburg: Felix Meiner, 1952), 1:14.

20. Harris, pp. 190 and 210.

21. Harris, pp. 249f.

22. Harris, p. 510. Besides appearing in Hoffmeister's *Dokumente zu Hegels Entwicklung*, *"ein Ethik"* is also in Fuhrman, ed., *Briefe und Dokumente*, 1:69, and in *On University Studies* translated by Norbert Guterman and attributed to Schelling.

23. Kaufmann, p. 385.

24. *Lectures on the History of Philosophy*, p. 543 (hereafter referred to as *Lectures*): *Sämtliche Werk*, 9:29f.

25. *Sämtliche Werk*, 2:54.

26. *Briefe von und an Hegel*, 1:162.

27. Ibid., 1:194.

28. *Lectures*, p. 456.

29. G.W.F. Hegel, *Science of Logic*, trans. A.V. Miller (London: George Allen and Unwin, 1969), p. 180; *Sämtliche Werk*, 9:94.

30. *Lectures*, p. 512.

31. Ibid., pp. 514, 529, 535.

32. Ibid., p. 541.

33. Ibid., p. 478.

34. *Sämtliche Werk*, 1:122.

35. Ibid., 1:62, 67, 73.

36. *Lectures*, p. 521.

37. *Sämtliche Werk*, 2:10.

38. *Science of Logic*, p. 47.

39. Ibid., p. 489.

40. *Sämtliche Werk*, 2:48f.

41. *Lectures*, pp. 524f. and 542.

42. Ibid., p. 534.

43. 5:368f.

44. 5:383.

45. 5:386, 389, 407.

46. G.W.F. Hegel, *Philosophy of Mind*, trans. A.V. Miller and William Wallace (Oxford: Clarendon, 1971), par. 572.

47. *Sämtliche Werk*, 1:63—67.

48. *Lectures*, pp. 519f.

49. *Philosophy of Mind, Zusatz* to para. 449.

50. *Sämtliche Werk*, 2:51f.

51. Ibid., 2:15f., and 31; see also *Science of Logic*, p. 27.

52. *Briefe von und an Hegel*, 1:194.

53. *Science of Logic*, pp. 67 and 69.

54. Ibid., pp. 77 and 82.

55. Ibid., p. 77.

56. *Lectures*, p. 526.

57. *Sämtliche Werk*, 2:13.

58. *Lectures*, p. 527.

59. Ibid., pp. 526f.; also *Science of Logic*, p. 61n.

60. *Lectures*, p. 529; Hegel criticizes Spinoza in a similar fashion in the *Philosophy of Mind*, p. 31, and in the *Lectures*, p. 516; see also the *Zusatz* to para. 229 in *Die Logik* of the *Encyclopädie*.

61. *Sämtliche Werk*, 2:13; and *Lectures*, p. 522.

62. *Sämtliche Werk*, 2:13 and 42.

63. *Science of Logic*, p. 412.

64. *Sämtliche Werk*, 2:17.

65. Ibid., 2:15; see also *Lectures*, p. 527.

66. R. Koeber makes this point in his *Die Grundprinzipien der Schelling'schen Naturphilosophie* in *Sammlung gemeinverständlicher wissenschaftlicher Vorträge* (Berlin: Carl Habel, 1881), 16:708.

67. *Sämtliche Werk*, 2:41.

68. *Lectures*, pp. 529ff.

69. *Sämtliche Werk*, 9:629.

70. *Science of Logic*, p. 233.

71. Ibid., p. 374.

72. Ibid., p. 376.

73. Ibid.

74. *Sämtliche Werk*, 2:12f. and 41; also 9:629.

75. *Science of Logic*, pp. 214 and 253.

76. Ibid., p. 213.

77. Ibid., pp. 215 and 325.

78. *Sämtliche Werk,* 9:38.

79. Ibid., 9:182.

80. *Lectures,* p. 543, see also p. 533.

81. Ibid., p. 534.

82. *Sämtliche Werk,* 9:169; see, however, *Science of Logic,* p. 437.

83. *Sämtliche Werk,* 9:95 and 212.

84. Ibid., 9:153, 156f., and 375.

85. Ibid., 9:722 and 168.

86. Ibid., 9:290.

87. Ibid., 9:629.

Chapter 7 Schelling's Influence in Nineteenth-Century America

1. 1, no. 10 (1810), p. 232.

2. 5 (1840): 290-99; vol. 7 (1842): 308.

3. E. W. Todd, "Philosophical Ideas at Harvard College, 1817-1837," *New England Quarterly* 16 (1943):63-90; but see also René Wellek's "The Minor Transcendentalists and German Philosophy," *New England Quarterly* 15 (1942): pp. 652-80. Wellek claims that "the general lack of German books or of the knowledge of German language in America has been exaggerated." This may have been the case with respect to biblical studies, but probably less so with respect to philosophy.

4. (January 1820), no. 1, p. 1.

5. *The Harvard Lyceum,* 1, no. 11 (1810).

6. 1, no. 2 (1840):53.

7. 2 (October 5, 1839):39 and 46.

8. 10 (1844):200 and 205.

9. "Locke and the Transcendentalists," *Christian Examiner* 23 (1837): 170-94.

10. 1 (1838):86.

11. *Boston Quarterly Review* 3 (1840): 270f.

12. On April 14, 1829, Ticknor wrote to James Marsh: "German philosophy I have not now time to read or time to write; but it will please you to know that Dr. Follen of Cambridge is fully competent to excite and sustain an interest in it among us, and that it is very likely he will do so." Quoted in *Coleridge's American Disciples: The Selected Correspondence of James Marsh,* ed. John J. Duffy (Amherst, Mass.: University of Massachusetts Press, 1973), p. 85.

13. *The Harbinger* 6 (1848):110.

14. *Christian Examiner* 21 (1836):46.

15. *Aids to Reflection,* ed. H. N. Coleridge, 4th ed. (London, 1840). This edition contains Marsh's essay as well (P. 24).

16. Ibid., pp. 25, 31, and 42.

17. Joseph Torrey, ed., *The Remains of the Rev. James Marsh, D.D.* (Port Washington, N.Y.: Kennikat Press, 1971), pp. 187-210; among his sources Marsh cites

Oersted's *Identité des forces chimiques et electriques* in this essay (p. 205). Evidence of Marsh's interest in German philosophers can be found in his unpublished translations of many of them. In 1829 he was asking Ticknor to send him a copy of Schelling's *System* (Duffy, p. 93), and while Schelling may not have been the most specific or immediate influence on him, it is clear that, given the direction of his thought, it was Schelling who must be considered the most decisive influence here.

18. Duffy, p. 256; letter dated March 1, 1841, to Henry J. Raymond.

19. Quoted in George W. Cooke's *Memorabilia of the Transcendentalists in New England* (Hartford, Conn.: Transcendental Books, 1973), p. 79; letter to Caroline H. Dall, 1877.

20. 10 (1831): 305 and 307.

21. O. B. Frothingham notes the influence of this article on George Ripley in his *George Ripley* (Boston and New York: Houghton Mifflin, 1882), p. 96. It is about this time that entries on Schelling begin appearing in Emerson's Journal as well.

22. *Christian Examiner* 14 (1833): 121 and 125.

23. *The Prose Writers of Germany* (Philadelphia: Carey and Hart, 1849), p. 510.

24. *Martin Luther and Other Essays* (Boston, 1888), pp. 156f.

25. *American Quarterly Review* (1831); in the *Foreign Quarterly Review* the writer complains that Schelling's philosophy "has negatively influenced the German language with words like polarity, organism . . ., " 1, no. 2 (1827): 367; for a similar negative account of Schelling see in the same quarterly the review of Rosenkranz's *Schelling* in vol. 32 (1844); see also 24 (1840):332 for a description of Schelling's system in outline given in Figure 1 above.

26. Henry rejected the idea that the Continental philosophers could be popularized for a general audience; see his letter to Marsh (May 15, 1832) in Duffy; see also letter dated June 25, 1833, where, upon receiving Schubert's *Geschichte der Seele* from Germany, he noted: "I expect also from a brief glance, that I shall find a rich treat in Schubert."

27. *The Journals and Miscellaneous Notebooks of Ralph Waldo Emerson,* ed. W. H. Gilman and A. R. Ferguson (Cambridge, Mass.: Harvard University Press, 1963), 5:30.

28. Ibid., 9:188.

29. Ibid., 7 (1838):13; 9 (1846):359f.

30. *The Dial,* 3, no. 3:398-404; 3, no. 4:541-44. Wheeler's translation is from the *Jahrbuch der Deutschen Univeritäten.*

31. Cabot wrote the article, "Immanuel Kant," for the final number of *The Dial.* In "On the Relation of Art to Nature," written for the *Atlantic Monthly* 13 (1864): 183-99, 313,29, he notes that "the facts in Nature are not fixed, but transcendental quantities" (p. 184).

32. Elizabeth Palmer Peabody, *Reminiscences* (Boston, 1880), p. 368.

33. *Life, Letters, and Journals of George Ticknor* (Boston: James R. Osgood, 1876), 1:96; letter dated from Göttingen, June 16, 1816.

34. "Philosophy in the United States," *Mind* 4 (1879):98f. and 104.

35. *The Intuitions of the Mind Inductively Investigated* (New York, 1867), p. 75.

36. *Rational Psychology* (Auburn, N.Y.: Derby, Miller and Co., 1849), pp. 68f.

37. Ibid., p. 530.

38. Ibid., p. 554.

39. *The General Principles of the Philosophy of Nature* (Boston: Wm. Crosby and H. P. Nichols, 1848), p. 214.

40. Ibid., p. 352.

41. Ibid., pp. 15-58.

42. *The American Hegelians,* ed. William H. Goetzmann (New York: Alfred A. Knopf, 1973), p. 33.

43. *The Collected Papers of Charles Sanders Peirce* ed. C. Harshorne and P. Weiss (Cambridge, Mass.: Harvard University Press, 1931-1935), Vols. 1-6; Vols. 7-8, ed. A. Burks (Cambridge, Mass.: Harvard University Press, 1958), vol. 6, para. 102, hereafter indicated in the form 6.102.

44. 6.605, 6.102; *The Thought and Character of William James,* ed. Ralph Barton Perry (Boston: Little, Brown and Co., 1935), 2:415f.; letter dated January 28, 1894.

45. 1.341; see also unpublished manuscripts, MS 903, 905, 909; a description of these unpublished MSS contained in the Houghton Library of Harvard University has been given by Richard S. Robin in the *Annotated Catalogue of the Papers of Charles S. Peirce* (Amherst, Mass.: The University of Massachusetts Press, 1967).

46. 7.66

47. 7.190, 7.186, 8.212.

48. 2.36; also 2.38, MS 901s, MS 908.

49. 1.1.

50. Along with the numerous references in the *Collected Papers,* see also MS 871, MS 875, MS 901s, MS 942, MS 954, MS 972, L-233.

51. Josiah Royce, *Lectures on Modern Idealism* (New Haven, Conn: Yale University Press, 1964), p. 77, and in general Lectures IV and V; see also Royce's more popular *The Spirit of Modern Philosophy* (Boston: Houghton Mifflin, 1926), pp. 181-94.

52. "Self-Consciousness, Social Consciousness and Nature," in *Studies of Good and Evil* (New York: D. Appleton, 1910), pp. 206f.

Chapter 8 Idealism in Recent Times

1. Charles Hartshorne, "The Case for Idealism," *The Philosophical Forum.* 1, no. 1 (Fall 1968):8.

2. Allan Janik and Stephen Toulmin, *Wittgenstein's Vienna* (New York: Simon and Schuster, 1973), p. 132.

3. John Locke, *An Essay Concerning Human Understanding,* BK. II, chap. 1, para. 5.

4. B 128.

5. Nicolas Rescher, *Conceptual Idealism* (Oxford: Basil Blackwell, 1973), p. 23.

6. John H. Muirhead, *The Platonic Tradition in Anglo-Saxon Philosophy* (New York: Macmillan, 1931), p. 421.

7. Ibid., p. 425.

8. Ibid.

9. A. C. Ewing, *Idealism: A Critical Survey* (New York: Humanities Press, 1933), p. 57.

10. Ibid., p. 386.

11. In *Contemporary Idealism in America,* ed. Clifford Barrett (New York: Russell and Russell, 1964), pp. 41 and 33.

12. This point is argued by Muirhead, pp. 437-41.

13. Brand Blanshard, *Reason and Analysis* (La Salle: Open Court, 1962), chap. 1; J. N. Findlay, *The Discipline of the Cave* (London: George Allen and Unwin, 1966), p. 50.

14. *Conceptual Idealism,* p. 159.

15. Ibid., p. 162.

16. Ibid., pp. 115 and 163.

17. Ibid., p. 156; also pp. 34 and 177.

18. Ibid., p. 171.

19. Ibid., pp. 186-91.

20. Ibid., p. 187.

21. Ibid., pp. 191f.

22. Wilfrid Sellars, *Science and Metaphysics* (London: Routledge and Kegan Paul, 1968), and *Science, Perception, and Reality* (London: Routledge and Kegan Paul, 1963).

23. *Conceptual Idealism,* p. 193.

24. *The Platonic Tradition,* pp. 432ff.

25. A368.

26. A372.

27. A373.

28. A375.

29. A378.

30. A376.

31. Bx1, n. *a.*

32. B278.

33. B277n.

34. Bx1*i.*

35. P. F. Strawson, *The Bounds of Sense* (London: Methuen, 1966), p. 127; Jonathan Bennett, *Kant's Analytic* (Cambridge: Cambridge University Press, 1966), p. 204.

36. G. E. Moore, "The Refutation of Idealism," *Mind* 12 (1903):p. 436.

37. Ibid., p. 442.

38. Ibid., p. 444.

39. Ibid., p. 445.

40. Ibid.

41. Ibid., p. 450.

42. Ibid.

43. Ibid., p. 451.

44. Ibid., p. 453.

45. Douglas Lewis, "Moore's Realism," in *Moore and Ryle: Two Ontologists* by Laird Addis and Douglas Lewis, *Iowa Publications in Philosophy* 2 (The Hague: Martinus Nijhoff, 1965):117; also E. D. Klemke, "Did G. E. Moore Refute Idealism," in *Studies in the Philosophy of G. E. Moore*, ed. E. D. Klemke (Chicago: Quadrangle Books, 1969), pp. 3-24.

46. "The Ego-Centric Predicament," *The Journal of Philosophy* 7(1910):7.

47. Ibid., p. 9.

48. Ibid., pp. 9f.

49. Ibid., p. 10.

50. Ibid., p. 13.

51. John Dewey, "The Short-Cut to Realism Examined," *The Journal of Philosophy* 7(1910):p. 555; this reply is directed against "The Program and First Platform of Six Realists" in the same volume.

52. James Edward Creighton, "Two Types of Idealism," *Philosophical Review* 26 (1917):514-36.

53. Wilbur Marshall Urban, *Beyond Realism and Idealism* (London: George Allen and Unwin, 1949).

54. H. G. Schenk, *The Mind of the European Romantics* (Garden City, N.Y.: Doubleday, 1969), pp. 178-83; Schenk quotes Alexander von Humbolt as warning German chemists not to become involved with "chemistry in which you do not wet your hands."

55. Ibid., p. 182.

56. Barry Gower, "Speculation in Physics: The History and Practice of *Naturphilosophie*," *Studies in History and Philosophy of Science* 3 (1973):301-56.

57. *Selected Writings of Hermann von Helmholtz*, ed. Russell Kahl (Middletown, Conn.: Wesleyan University Press, 1971), p. xxiii.

58. Of the paper's reception, Helmholtz writes: "To my astonishment, however, the authorities on physics with whom I came into contact received it quite differently. They were inclined to deny the correctness of the law and, because of the heated fight in which they were engaged against Hegel's philosophy of nature, to treat my essay as a fantastic piece of speculation" (p. 471).

59. Max von Laue notes the significance of Helmholtz's nonmechanistic approach to energy in preparing the environment for Einsteinian relativity; see "Inertia and Energy," in *Albert Einstein: Philosopher-Scientist*, ed. P. A. Schilpp (Evanston, Ill.: George Banta, 1949), pp. 513ff.

60. Mario Bunge, *Method, Model and Matter* (Dordrecht-Holland: D. Reidel, 1973), p. 179.

61. Ibid., pp. 179-83.

62. Ibid., pp. 145f.

63. For an account of this notion see the author's "Remarks Toward a General

Theory of Organization," *International Journal of General Systems* 2, no. 3 (1975): 133-43.

Selected Bibliography

Adam, Max. *Schellings Jenaer-Würzburger Vorlesungen über "Philosophie der Kunst."* Dissertation Erlangen University. Leipzig: Quelle and Meyer, 1907.

Ast, Friedrich, ed. *Zeitschrift für Wissenschaft und Kunst.* Landshut: Joseph Thomann, 1808, 1810.

Atlas, Samuel H. *From Critical to Speculative Idealism.* The Hauge: Martinus Nijhoff, 1964.

Baader, Franz von. *Sämmtliche Werk.* Leipzig: Herrmann Bethmann, 1852.

Beckers, Hubert. *Ueber die bedeutung der Schelling'schen Metaphysik.* Munich: Akademie, 1861.

―――――. *Ueber die wahre und bleibende bedeutung der Naturphilosophie Schellings.* Munich: G. Franz, 1864.

Benjamin, Park. *The Intellectual Rise in Electicity.* New York: D. Appleton, 1895.

Benz, Ernst. *Schelling: Werden und Wirken Seines Denkins.* Zurich: Rein, 1955.

Berg, Franz. *Sextus, oder Über die absolute Erkenntniss von Schelling: Ein Gespräch.* Würzburg: Sebastian Sartorius, 1804.

Brandis, Joachim Dietrich. *Gedächnissrede auf F. W. J. von Schelling Abhandlungen der Königlichen Akademie der Wissenschaften zu Berlin.* 1855.

―――――. *Ueber humanes Leben.* Schleswig: Koniglichen Taubstummen—Institut, 1825.

Braun, Otto, ed. *Schelling als Persönlichkeit: Briefe, Reden, Aufsätze.* Leipzig: Fritz Eckardt, 1908.

_____. *Schellings geistige wandlungen in der jahren 1800-1810.* Leipzig: Quelle and Meyer, 1906.

Brehier, Emile. *Schelling.* Paris: Felix Alcan, 1912.

Brenner, Anton. *Schellings Verhältnis zu Leibniz.* Augsburg: Fr. Schoder, 1937.

Bruck, Reinhard. *Heinrich Steffens: Ein Beitrage zur Philosophie der Romantik.* Borna-Leipzig: Robert Noske, 1906.

Bunge, Mario. *Method, Model and Matter.* Dordrecht-Holland: D. Reidel, 1973.

Burdach, Karl Friedrich. *Blicke ins Leben.* 2 vols, Leipzig: Leopold Voss, 1842-1844.

_____. *Vom Baue und Leben des Gehirns.* 3 vols. Leipzig: Dyk'schen, 1819-1826.

Cajori, Florian. *A History of Physics.* New York: Dover, 1962.

Carus, Carl Gustav. *Organon der Erkenntniss der Natur und des Geistes.* Leipzig: F. A. Brockhaus, 1856.

Chalybäus, Heinrich Moritz. *Historische Entwickelung der Speculativen Philosophie.* Dresden and Leipzig: Arnoldische, 1848.

Choudhury, Jaganath Das. *Das Unendlichkeitsproblem in Schellings Philosophie.* Dissertation, University of Berlin: A. Collignon, 1929.

Clark, Malcolm. *Logic and System: A Study of the Transition from "Vorstellung" to Thought in the Philosophy of Hegel.* The Hague: Martinus Nijhoff, 1971.

Coleridge, Samuel Taylor. *Biographia Literaria.* New York: Dutton, 1962.

Cousin, Victor. *Über franzosische und deutsch Philosophie.* Stuttgart and Tübingen: J. G. Cotta, 1834.

Darwin, Erasmus. *Zoonomia: or The Laws of Organic Life.* 2 vols. London: J. Johnson, 1796.

Dekker, Gerbrand Jan. *Schellings Letzte Wandlung.* Munich: R. Oldenbourg, 1927.

Dewing, Arthur S. *Negation and Intuition in the Philosophy of*

Schelling. Dissertation, Harvard University, 1905.

_____. "The Significance of Schelling's Theory of Knowledge." *Philosophical Review* 19 (1910).

Donay, Franz. *Der Einheitspunkt in Schellings Philosophie*. Koblenz: Görres, 1929.

Easton, L. D. and Guddat, Kurt H., ed. and trans. *Writings of the Young Marx on Philosophy and Society*. Garden City, N.Y.: Doubleday, 1967.

Erdmann, Johann Eduard. *A History of Philosophy*. vol. 2. Translated by Williston S. Hough. London: Swan Sonnenschein, 1892.

_____. *Ueber Schelling, namentlich seine negative Philosophie*. Halle: H. W. Schmidt, 1857.

Eschenmayer, Carl August. *Einleitung in Natur und Geschichte*. Erlangen: Walterschen, 1806.

_____. *Grundriss der Natur-Philosophie*. Tübingen: Heinrich Laupp, 1832.

_____. *Die Philosophie inihren Uebergang zur Nichtphilosophie*. Erlangen: Walterschen, 1803.

_____. "Spontaneität-Weltseele, oder Das höchste Princip der Naturphilosophie." *Zeitschrift für spekulative Physik* 2 (1801): 1-68.

_____. *Versuch die scheinbare Magie des thierischen Magnetismus*. Stuttgart and Tübingen: J. G. Cotta'schen, 1816.

Eschenmayer, Carl August; Kieser, D. G., and Fr. Nasse, eds. *Archiv für thierischen Magnetismus*. Halle: Hemmerde and Schwetschte, 1818.

Ewing, A. C. *Kant's Treatment of Causality*. London: Routledge and Kegan Paul, 1924.

_____. *A Short Commentary on Kant's Critique of Pure Reason*. Chicago: University of Chicago, 1938.

Falckenberg, Richard. *History of Modern Philosophy*. Translated by A. C. Armstrong. New York: Henry Holt, 1897.

Feder, Johann Georg Heinrich. *Logik und Metaphysik*. Göttingen: J. C. Dieterich, 1786.

Ferri, Ettore de. *La filosofia dell'indentita di F. Schelling fino al*

1802 e suoi rapporti storici. Turin: G. Chiantore, 1925.

Fichte, Johann Gottlieb. *The Characteristics of the Present Age.* Translated by William Smith. London: John Chapman, 1847.

———. *The Popular Works of Johann Gottlieb Fichte.* Translated by William Smith. London: Trübner, 1889.

———. *The Science of Knowledge.* Translated and edited by Peter Heath and John Lachs. New York: Appleton-Century-Crofts, 1970.

Fick, Georg Karl. *Vergleichende darstellung der philosophischen Systeme von Kant, Fichte, und Schelling.* Heilbronn, 1825.

Fischer, Kuno. *Schelling's Leben, Werke und Lehre.* Heidelberg: Carl Winters Universität, 1902.

Ford, Lewis S. "The Controversy between Schelling and Jacobi." *Journal of the History of Philosophy* 3 (1965):75-89.

Fries, Jakob Friedrich. *Reinhold, Fichte und Schelling.* Leipzig: A. L. Reinicke, 1803.

———. *Von deutscher Philosophie, Art und Kunst: Ein Votum für Friedrich Heinrich Jacobi gegen F. W. J. Schelling.* Heidelberg: Mohr and Zimmer, 1812.

Friess, H. L. "Note on German Idealism." *Columbia Studies in the History of Ideas.* vol. 1. New York, 1918.

Geiger, Johann Philipp. *Schellings Gottesauffassung von 1795-1809.* Frankfurt: Carl Bornkessel, 1936.

Gilbert, Ludwig Wilhelm, ed. *Annalen der Physik.* Halle: Rengerschen, 1799-1824.

Glaser, Johann Karl. *Differenz der Schelling'schen und Hegel'schen Philosophie.* Leipzig: O. Wigand, 1824.

Goetz, Johann Kasper. *Anti-sextus, oder Über die absolute Erkenntniss von Schelling.* Heidelberg: Pfaehlerische, 1807.

Görres, Joseph von. *Aphorismen über die Kunst als Einleitung zu Aphorismen über Organomie, Physik, Psycologie und Anthropologie.* Koblenz: Lassaulx, 1810.

———. *Die christliche Mystik.* 4 vols. Regensburg and Landshut: G. Joseph Manz, 1836-1842.

Gray-Smith, Rowland. *God in the Philosophy of Schelling.* Philadelphia, 1933.

Gren, F. A. C., ed. *Journal der Physik.* 12 vols. Halle and Leipzig: T. Ambrosius Barth, 1790-1797.

Gruppe, Otto Friedrich. *Antäus: Ein Briefwechsel über speculative Philosophie in ihrem Conflict mit Wissenschaft und Sprach.* Berlin, 1831.

_____. *Wendepunkt der Philosophie im neunzehnten Jahrhundert.* Berling: G. Reimer, 1834.

Güttler, C. *Lorenz Oken und sein Verhältniss zur modernen Entwickelungslehre.* Leipzig: E. Bidder, 1884.

Habel, Reinhard. *Joseph Görres: Studien über den zusammenhang von Natur, Geschichte und Mythos in seinen Schriften.* Wiesbaden: Franz Steiner, 1960.

Habermas, Jürgen. *Das Absolute und die Geschichte: von der Zwiespältigkeit in Schellings Denken.* Bonn: H. Bouvier, 1954.

Hablützel, Rudolf. *Dialektik und Einbildungskraft: F. W. J. Schellings Lehre von der menschlichen Erkenntnis.* Basil: Recht and Gesellschaft, 1954.

Haller, Albrecht von. *A Dissertation on the Sensible and Irritable Parts of Animals.* Translated by M. Tissot. London: J. Nourse, 1755.

Harris, H. S. *Hegel's Development: Toward the Sunlight 1770-1801.* Oxford: Clarendon, 1972.

Hartkopf, Werner. *Studien zur Entwicklung der Modernen Dialektik: Die Dialektik in Schellings Ansätzen zu einer Naturphilosophie.* Meisenheim am Glan: Anton Hain, 1972.

Hartmann, Eduard von. *Geschichte der Metaphysik.* 2 vols. Leipzig: H. Haacke, 1899-1900.

_____. *Schellings philosophisches System.* Leipzig: Hermann Haacke, 1897.

_____. *Schellings Positive Philosophie als einheit von Hegel und Schopenhauer.* Berlin: O. Loewenstein, 1869.

Hartmann, Nicolai. *Die Philosophie des deutschen Idealismus.* Berlin and Leipzig: W. de Grüter, 1923.

Hayner, Paul Collins. *Reason and Existence: Schelling's Philosophy of History.* Leiden: E. J. Brill, 1967.

Hegel, G. W. F. *Encyclopädie der philosophischen Wissenschaften im Grundrisse.* Heidelberg: C. F. Winter, 1830.

————. *Lectures on the History of Philosophy.* Translated by Elizabeth S. Haldane and Frances H. Simson. London: Kegan Paul, Trench, Trübner, 1896.

————. *The Phenomenology of Mind.* Translated by J. B. Baillie. London: George Allen and Unwin, 1964.

————. *Philosophy of Mind.* Translated by William Wallace and A. V. Miller. Oxford: Clarendon, 1971.

————. *Philosophy of Nature.* Translated by A. V. Miller. Oxford: Clarendon, 1970.

————. *Sämtliche Werk.* Edited by Hermann Glockner. Stuttgart-Bad Cannstatt: Friedrich Frommann, 1964.

————. *Science of Logic.* Translated by A. V. Miller. London: George Allen and Unwin, 1969.

Heidegger, Martin. *Schellings Abhandlung über das Wesen der menschlichen Freiheit.* Edited by Hildegard Feick. Tübingen: Max Niemeyer, 1971.

Hennemann, Gerhard. *Naturphilosophie im 19. Jahrhundert.* Munich and Freiburg: Karl Alber, 1959.

Herder, J. G. *God, Some Conversations.* Translated by Frederick H. Burkhardt. New York: Bobbs-Merrill, 1940.

————. *Outline of a Philosophy of the History of Man.* Translated by M. Churchill. London, 1803.

Hirsch, Eric Donald. *Wordsworth and Schelling, a Typological Study of Romanticism,* New Haven, Conn.: Yale University, 1960.

Hochdoerfer, Margarete. *The Conflict between the Religious and the Scientific Views of Albrecht von Haller.* University of Nebraska Studies in Language, Literature, and Criticism, No. 12. Lincoln, Neb.: University of Nebraska, 1932.

Höffding, Harald. *A History of Modern Philosophy.* vol. 2. Translated by B. E. Meyer. New York: Dover, 1955.

Hoffmeister, Johannes. ed. *Briefe von und an Hegel.* vol. 1. Hamburg: Felix Meiner, 1952.

————, ed. *Dokumente zu Hegels Entwicklung.* Stuttgart: Fr. Frommanns, 1936.

Hohlfeld, Paul. *Die Krause'sche Philosophie.* Jena: Hermann Costenoble, 1879.

Holz, Harald. *Spekulation und Faktizität.* Bonn: H. Bouvier, 1970.

Horn, Friedemann, *Schelling and Swedenborg.* Zürich: Swedenborg, 1954.

Hörz, Herbert; Lother, Rolf; Wollgast, Siegfried. *Naturphilosophie: von der Spekulation zur Wissenschaft.* Berlin: Akademie, 1969.

Hume, David. *An Enquiry Concerning Human Understanding.* New York: Liberal Arts Press, 1955.

Ihmels, Carl. *Die Entstehung der organischen Natur nach Schelling, Darwin, und Wundt.* Naumburg: G. Pŕz'sche, 1916.

Jacobi, Friedrich Heinrich. *Ueber die Lehre des Spinoza in briefen an den Herrn Moses Mendelssohn.* Breslau: G. Lowe, 1789.

————. *Woldemar.* Stuttgart: J. B. Metzler, 1969.

Jaspers, Karl. *Schelling.* Munich: R. Piper, 1955.

Jenny, Heinrich Ernst. *Haller als Philosoph.* Basel: Basler, 1902.

Jost, Johannes. *Die Bedeutung der Weltseele in der Schelling'schen Philosophie im Vergleich mit der platonischen Lehre.* Bonn: L. Neuendorf, 1929.

Kahn-Wallerstein, Carmen, *Schellings Frauen: Caroline und Pauline.* Bern: Francke, 1959.

Kant, Immanuel. *Critique of Judgment.* Translated by J. H. Bernard. New York: Hafner, 1951.

————. *Critique of Pure Reason.* Translated by Norman Kemp Smith. New York: St. Martins, 1965.

————. *Sämmtliche Werke.* Edited by J. H. v. Kirchmann. Heidelberg: Weiss, 1870-1891.

Kaufmann, Walter. *Hegel: Reinterpretation, Texts, and Commentary.* Garden City, N.Y.: Doubleday, 1965.

Kein, Otto. *Schellings Kategorienlehre.* Berlin: Junker and Dünnhaupt, 1939.

————. *Die Universalität des Geistes im Lebenswerk Goethes und Schellings.* Berlin: Junker and Dünnhaupt, 1934.

Kelly, George Armstrong. *Idealism, Politics and History: Sources of*

Hegelian Thought. Cambridge: Cambridge University, 1969.

Kerler, Dietrich Heinrich. *Die Fichte-Schelling'sche Wissenschaftslehre.* Ulm: H. Kerler, 1917.

Kielmayer, K. F. "Versuche über die sogenannte animalische Electrizität." *Journal der Physik* 8 (1794):65-76.

Klaiber, Julius. *Hölderlin, Hegel und Schelling in ihren schwäbischen Jugendjahren.* Stuttgart: J. G. Cotta, 1877.

Klein, Georg M. *Betrachtungen über den gegenwärtigen Zustand der Philosophie in Deutschland überhaupt und über die Schellingische Philosophie im Besonderen.* Nürnberg: Leonhard Schrag, 1813.

Klemm, Friedrich., and Hermann, Armin., eds. *Briefe eines Romantischen Physikers: Johann Wilhelm Ritter an Gotthilf Heinrich Schubert und an Karl von Hardenberg.* Munich: Heinz Moos, 1966.

Klemmt, Alfred. *Karl Leonhard Reinholds Elementarphilosophie: Eine Studie über Ursprung des spekulativen deutschen Idealismus.* Hamburg: Felix Meiner, 1958.

Knittermeyer, Hinrich. *Schelling und die romantische Schule.* Munich: E. Reinhardt, 1929.

Koeber, R. "Die Grundprinzipien der Schelling'schen Naturphilosophie." In vol. 16 of *Sammlung gemeinverständlicher wissenschaftlicher Vorträge.* Berlin: Carl Habel, 1881.

Köppen, Friedrich. *Schelling's Lehre, oder Das Ganze der Philosophie des absoluten Nichts.* Friedrich Perthes, 1803.

Krause, Karl Christian Friedrich. *Abriss der Aesthetik.* Edited by J. Leutbecher. Göttingen: Dieterich'schen, 1837.

_____. *Abriss des Systemes der Philosophie.* Göttingen, 1825.

_____. *Der Briefwechsel.* Edited by Paul Hohlfeld and August Wünsche. Leipzig: Dieterichsche, 1903.

_____. *Grundriss der historischen Logik.* Jena and Leipzig: Christian Ernst Gabler, 1803.

_____. *Versuch einer wissenschaftlichen Begründung der Sittenlehre.* Leipzig: C. H. Reclam, 1810.

_____. *Vorlesungen über das System der Philosophie.* Göttingen: Dieterich'schen, 1828.

Kroner, Richard. *Von Kant bis Hegel.* Tübingen: J. C. B. Mohr, 1921.

Krug, Wilhelm Traugott. *Briefe über den neuesten Idealism.* Leipzig: Heinrich Müller, 1801.

_____. *Entwurf eines Neuen Organon's der Philosophie.* Meissen and Lübben: K. F. W. Erbstein, 1801.

_____. *Schelling und Hegel, oder Die neueste Philosophie im vernichtungskriege mit sich selbst begriffen.* Leipzig: C. E. Kollmann, 1835.

_____. *Über die verschiednen Methoden des Philosophirens und die verschiednen Systeme der Philosophie.* Meissen: K. F. W. Erbstein, 1802.

Kübner, Georg Wilhelm. *Okens Naturphilosophie.* Borna-Leipzig: Robert Noske, 1909.

Kuhn, Thomas S. "Energy Conservation as an Example of Simultaneous Discovery." *Critical Problems in the History of Science.* Edited by Marshall Clagett. Madison, Wis.: University of Wisconsin, 1959.

Leitzmann, Albert. ed. *Lichtenbergs Briefe an Johann Friedrich Blumenbach.* Leipzig: Dieterich'sche, 1921.

Levere, Trevor H. *Affinity and Matter: Elements of Chemical Philosophy, 1800-1865.* Oxford: Clarendon, 1971.

Liebig, Justus von. "The Connection and Equivalence of Forces." *The Correlation and Conservation of Forces,* edited by Edward L. Youmans. New York: D. Appleton, 1865.

Lisco, Heinrich. *Geschichtsphilosophie Schellings, 1792-1809.* Jena: J. Hossfeld, 1884.

MacCauley, Clay. *Karl Christian Friederich Krause: Heroic Pioneer for Thought and Life.* Berkeley, Calif.: Gazette, 1925.

McFarland, J. D. *Kant's Concept of Teleology.* Edinburgh: University of Edinburgh, 1970.

Mann, Gustav. *Das Verhältnis der Schleiermacher'schen Dialektik zur Schelling'schen Philosophie.* Stuttgart: Stuttgarter--Vereins, 1914.

Marcel, Gabriel. *Coleridge et Schelling.* Paris: Aubier-Montaigne, 1971.

Marquet, Jean-François. *Liberté et Existence: Étude sur la formation de la philosophie de Schelling*. Paris: Gallimard, 1973.

Martin, Gottfried. *Kant's Metaphysics and Theory of Science*. Translated by P. G. Lucas. Manchester: Manchester University, 1961.

Mehlis, Georg. *Schellings Geschichtsphilosophie in den Jahren 1799-1804*. Heidelberg: K. Rössler, 1906.

Melnick, Arthur. *Kant's Analogies of Experience*. Chicago: University of Chicago, 1973.

Merz, John Theodore. *A History of European Thought in the Nineteenth Century*. London: Wm. Blackwood and Sons, 1912.

Michelet, Carl L. *Schelling und Hegel*. Berlin: F. Dümmler, 1839.

Munk, Franz. *Einheir und Duplizität im Aufbau von Schellings System des transzendentalen Idealismus*. Mainz: Schneider, 1910.

Nauen, Franz Gabriel. *Revolution, Idealism and Human Freedom: Schelling, Hölderlin and Hegel and the Crisis of Early German Idealism*. The Hague: Martinus Nijhoff, 1971.

Nicolai, Friedrich. *Leben und meinungen Sempronius Gundibert's, eines deutschen Philosophen*. Berlin: F. Nicolai, 1798.

Nordenskiöld, Erik. *A History of Biology*. Translated by Leonard Bucknall Eyre. New York: Tudor, 1949.

Oersted, Hans Christian. *Der Geist in der Natur*. 2 vols. Munich: J. G. Cotta'schen, 1850-51.

Oeser, Erhard. *Begriff und Systematik der Abstraktion*. Vienna and Munich: Oldenberg, 1696.

Oken, Lorenz. *Allgemeine Naturgeschichte für alle Stande*. 13 vols. Stuttgart: Hoffmann, 1833-1841.

————. *Erste Ideen zur Theorie des Lichte*. Jena: Fr. Frommann, 1808.

————. *Lehrbuch der Naturphilosophie*. Jena: Fr. Frommann, 1809.

Orsini, G. N. G. *Coleridge and German Idealism*. Carbondale and Edwardsville, Ill.: Southern Illinois University, 1969.

Osthus, Gustav. *G. H. Schuberts philosophische Anfänge, unter besonderer Berücksichtigung von Schellings Einfluss*. Borna-Leipzig: R. Noske, 1929.

Partington, J. R. *A History of Chemistry*. vols. 3 and 4. London:

Macmillan, 1962, 1964.

Paton, H. J. *Kant's Metaphysic of Experience*. London: George Allen and Unwin, 1961.

Platenius, Otto. *Schellings Fortführung der Lehre Kants vom Bösen*. Hilchenbach: Adolf Wesener, 1928.

Pollock, F. *Spinoza*. London, 1912.

Portmann, Stephen. *Das Böse, die Ohnmacht der Vernunft: das Böse und die Erlösung als Grundproblem in Schellings philosophischer Entwicklung*. Meisenhein am Glan: Hain, 1966.

Reinhold, Karl Leonhard. *Beiträge zur leichtern Uebersicht des Zustandes der Philosophie*. Hamburg: Friedrich Perthes, 1802.

_____. *Ueber die Paradoxien der neuesten Philosophie*. Hamburg: Friedrich Perthes, 1799.

Reisse, Roman. *Die weltanschauliche Entwicklung des jugen Joseph Goerres, 1776-1806*. Breslau: Müller and Seiffert, 1926.

Ritter, Johann Wilhelm. "Einige Beobachtungen über den Galvanismus in anorgischen Natur." *Annalen der Physik* 2 (1799):80-86.

_____. *Die Physik als Kunst. Ein Versuch, die Tendenz der Physik aus ihrer Geschichte zu deuten*. Munich: Joseph Lindauer, 1806.

Ritterbush, Philip C. *Overtures to Biology: The Speculation of Eighteenth-Century Naturalists*. New Haven, Conn.: Yale University, 1964.

Rosenkranz, Karl. *Ueber Schelling und Hegel: Ein Sendschreiben an Pierre Leroux*, Königsberg: Gebräer Bornträger, 1843.

Royce, Josiah. *Lectures on Modern Idealism*. New Haven, Conn.: Yale University, 1934.

_____. *The Spirit of Modern Philosophy*. Cambridge, Mass.: Harvard University, 1931.

Rümelin, Frank. *Schellings Naturphilosophie in ihrer Wirkung auf die liberale Staatslehre*. Dissertation, University of Giessen, 1925.

Salat, Jakob. *Erläuterung einiger Hauptpunkte der Philosophie: mit Zugaben über den neuesten Widerstreit zwischen Jacobi, Schelling und Fr. Schlegel*. Landshut: J. Thomann, 1812.

_____. *Ueber den Geist der Philosophie*. Munich: Joseph Lentner, 1803.

Samhaber, Ernst. *Schellings Naturphilosophie: Eine Untersuchung der irrationalistischen Method.* Dissertation, University of Munich, 1922.

Sandkühler, Hans Jörg. *Friedrich Wilhelm Joseph Schelling.* Stuttgart: J. B. Metzlersche, 1970.

Sauter, Eugene. *Herder und Buffon.* Rixheim, 1910.

Schelling, Friedrich Wilhelm Joseph von. *The Ages of the World.* Translated by Frederick de Wolfe Bolman, Jr. New York: Columbia University, 1942.

———. *Anthologie aus Schellings Werken.* Berlin: W. Hermes, 1844.

———. *Aus Schellings Leben: in Briefen.* Leipzig: S. Hirzel, 1869-1870.

———. *Briefe und Dokumente.* Edited by Horst Fuhrmans. Bonn: H. Bouvier, 1962, 1973.

———. *Schelling und Cotta: Briefwechsel, 1803-1849.* Stuttgart: Ernst Klett, 1965.

———. *Gedichte und poetische Übersetzungen.*

———. *The Nightwatches of Bonaventura.* Translated by Gerald Gillespie. Austin, Tex.: University of Texas, 1971.

———, ed. *Neue Zeitschrift für speculative Physik.* Tübingen: J. G. Cotta, 1802.

———. *Of Human Freedom.* Translated by James Gutmann. Chicago: Open Court, 1936.

———. *On University Studies.* Translated by E. S. Morgan. Edited by Norbert Guterman. Athens, Ohio: Ohio University, 1966.

———. *Sämmtliche Werke.* Edited by K. F. A. Schelling. Stuttgart and Augsburg: J. G. Cotta, 1856.

———, ed. *Zeitschrift für spekulative Physik.* Jena and Leipzig: Christian Ernst Gables, 1800-1801.

Schelling, F. W. J., and Hegel, G. W. F., eds. *Kritisches Journal der Philosophie.* Tübingen: J. G. Cotta, 1802-1803.

Schenk, H. G. *The Mind of the European Romantics.* Garden City, N.Y.: Doubleday, 1969.

Schiller, Friedrich. *Werke.* Weimar: Herman Böhlaus, 1962.

Schilling, Kurt. *Natur und Wahrheit: Untersuchung über Entstehung und Entwicklung des Schellingschen Systems bis 1800.* Munich: Ernst Reinhardt, 1934.

Schlanger, Judith E. *Schelling et la Réalité finie, Essai sur la Philosophie de la Natur et de l'Identité.* Paris: Universtaires, 1966.

Schlegel, Frederick von. *The Philosophy of Life, and Philosophy of Language.* Translated by A. J. W. Morrison. London: Henry G. Bohn, 1847.

Schleiden, Matthias Jakob. *Schelling's und Hegel's Verhältniss zur Naturwissenschaft.* Leipzig: W. Engelmann, 1844.

Schmidt, Friedrich W. *Zum Begriff der Nagativität bei Schelling und Hegel.* Stuttgart: J. B. Metzlersche, 1971.

Schmitz-Dumont, O. *Naturphilosophie als Exakte Wissenschaft.* Leipzig: Duncker and Humblot, 1895.

Schneider, Robert. *Schellings und Hegels schwäbische Geistesahnen.* Würzburg-Aumühle: K. Triltsch, 1938.

Schneiter, Rudolf. *Schellings Gesetz der Polarität.* Hans Schellenberg Winterthur, 1968.

Schröter, Manfred. *Der Ausgangspunkt der Metaphysik Schellings.* Dissertation, University of Munich, 1908.

———. *Kritische Studien: Über Schelling u. z. Kulturphilosophie.* Munich: Oldenbourg, 1971.

Schubert, Gotthilf H. *Ahndungen einer allgemeinen Geschichte des Lebens.* Leipzig: Carl Heinrich Reclam, 1806, 1807, 1821.

———. *Ansichten von der Nachseite der Naturwissenschaft.* Dresden and Leipzig: Arnoldischen, 1840.

———. *Die Geschichte der Seele.* Stuttgart and Tübingen: J. G. Cotta'scher, 1833.

———. *Die Krankheiten und Störungen der menschlichen Seele.* Stuttgart and Tübingen: J. G. Cotta'scher, 1845.

———. *Die Symbolik des Traumes.* Leipzig: F. A. Brockhaus, 1840.

Schultz, Franz. *Charakteristiken und Kritiken von Joseph Görres aus den Jahren 1804 und 1805.* Cologne: J. P. Bachem, 1900.

———. *Der Verfasser der Nachtwachen von Bonaventura: Untersuchungen zur deutschen Romantik.* Berlin: Weidmannsche, 1909.

Schulz, Walter. *Fichte-Schelling Briefwechsel*. Frankfurt/Main: Suhrkamp, 1968.

Schulze, G. E. *Anesidemus, oder Über die Fundamente der von dem Herrn Prof. Reinhold in Jena gelieferten Elementar-Philosophie*. 1792.

_____. *Kritik der theoretischen Philosophie*. 2 vols. Hamburg: Carl Ernst Bohn, 1801.

Schütz, Christian Gottfried. "Vertheidigung gegen Hn. Prof. Schelling." Nos. 57 and 62, *Intelligenzblatt der allgem. Literatur-Zeitung*. Jena, 1800.

Schwarz, J. L. *Schellings alte und neue Philosophie*. Berlin: Carl Heymann, 1844.

Seth, Andrew. *The Development from Kant to Hegel*. London: Williams and Norgate, 1882.

Setschkareff, Wsewolod. *Schellings Einfluss in der russischen Literatur der 20er und 30er Jahre des XIX. Jahrhunderts*. Leipzig: O. Harrassowitz, 1939.

Spiess, Emil. *Ignaz Paul Vital Troxler*. Bern and Munich: Francke, 1967.

Stallo, J. B. *General Principles of the Philosophy of Nature*. Boston: Wm. Crosby and H. P. Nichols, 1848.

Stauffer, Robert C. "Speculation and Experiment in the Background of Oersted's Discovery of Electromagnetism." *Isis* 48 (1957): 33-50.

Stefansky, Georg. *Das hellenisch-deutsche Weltbild: Einleitung in Lebensgeschichte Schellings*. Bonn: F. Cohen, 1925.

Steffens, Henrich. *Anthropologie*. Breslau: Josef Max, 1822.

_____. *Beyträge zur innern Naturgeschichte der Erde*. Freiberg: Crazischen, 1801.

_____. *German University Life: The Story of My Career*. Translated by William L. Gage. Philadelphia: J. B. Lippincott, 1874.

_____. "Ueber den Oxydations- und Desoxydations Process der Erde." *Zeitschrift für spekulative Physik* 1 (1800):137-268.

Stern, J. P. *Lichtenberg: A Doctrine of Scattered Occasions*. Bloomington, Ind.: Indiana University, 1959.

Thanner, Ignaz. *Der Transcendental-Idealism in seiner dreyfachen*

Steigerung, oder Kants, Fichtes, Schellings philosophische Ansichten. Munich: J. Lindauer, 1805.

Tillich, Paul. *Die Religionsgeschichtliche Konstruktion in Schellings positiver Philosophie, ihre Voraussetzungen und Prinzipien.* Breslau: Fleischmann, 1910.

Trahndorff, Karl Friedrich Eusebius. *Schelling und Hegel, oder Das System Hegels als letztes Resultat des Grundirrthums in allem bisherigen Philosophiren.* Berlin: C. Grobe, 1842.

Troxler, Ignaz Paul Vital. *Blicke in das Wesen des Menschen.* Aarau: H. R. Sauerländer, 1812.

―――. *Naturlehre des menschlichen Erkennens, oder Metaphysik.* Aarau: H. R. Sauerländer, 1828.

―――. *Philosophische Enzyklopädie und Methodologie der Wissenschaften.* Beromünster, 1953.

―――. *Vorlesungen über Philosophie.* Bern: C. Fischer, 1835.

Ueberweg, Friedrich. *History of Philosophy.* vol. 2. Translated by George S. Morris. New York: Charles Scribner's, 1891.

Vogel, Emil Ferdinand. *Schelling oder Hegel, oder Keiner von Beyden?* Leipzig: K. Heubel, 1843.

Wagner, Johann Jakob. *Erläuterungen zum Organon der menschlichen Erkenntniss.* Edited by P. L. Adam. Ulm: P. L. Adams, 1854.

―――. *Ideen zu einer allgemeinen Mytholgie der alter Welt.* Frankfurt am Main: Andreäischen, 1808.

―――. *Mathematische Philosophie.* Erlangen: Johann Jakob Palm, 1811.

―――. *Religion, Wissenschaft, Kunst und Staat.* Erlangen: Palm'schen, 1819.

―――. *System der Idealphilosophie.* Leipzig: Breitkopf and Härtel. 1804.

―――. *Theodicee.* Bamberg and Würzburg: Joseph Anton Goebhardt, 1809.

―――. *Von der Natur der Dinge.* Leipzig: Breitkopf anf Härtel, 1803.

Wäsche, Erwin. *Carl Gustav Carus und die romantische Weltanschauung.* Düsseldorf: G. H. Nolte, 1933.

Watson, John. *Schelling's Transcendental Idealism*. Chicago: S. C. Griggs, 1892.

Weiller, Kajetan. *Der Geist der allerneuesten Philosophie der Herrn. Schelling, Hegel, and Kompagnie*. 2 vols. Munich: J. Lentner, 1803, 1805.

Weischedel, Wilhelm. *Jacobi und Schelling: Eine philosophische-theologische Kontroverse*. Darmstadt: Wissenschaftliche, 1969.

Wendell, Johann Andreas. *Grundzüge und Kritik der philosophien Kants, Fichtes und Schellings*. Coburg, 1824.

Werner, Arthur. *Schellings Verhältnis zur Medizin und Biologie*. Paderborn: Ferdinand Schöningh, 1909.

Whitehead, Alfred North. *Process and Reality*. New York: The Free Press, 1969.

Wiener, P. P., ed. *Leibniz Selections*. New York: Scribners, 1951.

Wilde, Norman. *Friedrich Heinrich Jacobi: A Study in the Origin of German Idealism*. Columbia University Contributions to Philosophy, Psychology and Education, 1 no. 1. New York: Columbia College, 1894.

Williams, L. Pearce. *Michael Faraday*. New York: Basic Books, 1964.

Windelband, Wilhelm. *A History of Philosophy*. Translated by James H. Tufts. New York: Macmillan, 1901.

Windischmann, Carl Joseph Hieronymus. *Die Philosophie im Fortgang der Weltgeschichte*. 4 vols. Bonn: Adolph Marcus, 1827-1834.

Zeltner, Hermann. *Schelling*. Stuttgart: Fr. Frommann, 1954.

———. *Schellins philosophische Idee und das Identitätssystem*. Beiträge zur Philosophie, vol. 20. Heidelberg: C. Winter, 1931.

Zimmermann, Robert. *Schellings Philosophie der Kunst. Ein Nachtrag zu meiner Geschichte der Aesthetik*. Vienna: K. Gerold's, 1875.

Zöckler, Karl. "Der Entwicklungsgedanke in Schelling Naturphilosophie." *Archiv für Geschichte der Philosophie* 28 (1915):257-96.

Schelling Bibliographies

Jost, Johannes. *F. W. J. von Schelling: Bibliographie der Schriften von ihm und über ihn.* Bonn: Friedrich Cohen, 1927.

Schneeberger, Guido. *Friedrich Wilhelm Joseph von Schelling. Eine Bibliographie.* Bern: Francke, 1954.

Index

287